African American Children and Families in Child Welfare

Ramona W. Denby and
Carla M. Curtis

African American Children and Families in Child Welfare

Cultural Adaptation of Services

COLUMBIA UNIVERSITY PRESS  NEW YORK

Columbia University Press
Publishers Since 1893
New York   Chichester, West Sussex
cup.columbia.edu

Library of Congress Cataloging-in-Publication Data
Denby, Ramona W.
   African American children and families in child welfare : cultural adaptation of services /
Ramona W. Denby and Carla M. Curtis.
      pages cm
   Includes bibliographical references and index.
   ISBN 978-0-231-13184-1 (cloth : alk. paper)
   ISBN 978-0-231-13185-8 (pbk. : alk. paper)
   ISBN 978-0-231-53620-2 (e-book)
   1. Social work with African American children.   2. Social work with African Americans.
3. Child welfare—United States.   I. Curtis, Carla M.   II. Title.
   HV3181.D46 2013
   362.7'7896073—dc23
                                                                                                2013013777

♾

Columbia University Press books are printed on permanent and durable acid-free paper.
This book is printed on paper with recycled content.
Printed in the United States of America
c 10 9 8 7 6 5 4 3 2 1
p 10 9 8 7 6 5 4 3 2 1

COVER IMAGE: Romare Bearden, *Sunday After Sermon* (1969). Museo Thyssen-Bornemisza/Scala/
Art Resource, NY. © Romare Bearden Foundation/Licensed by VAGA, New York, NY

COVER DESIGN: Milenda Nan Ok Lee

References to Web sites (URLs) were accurate at the time of writing. Neither the authors nor
Columbia University Press is responsible for URLs that may have expired or changed since the
manuscript was prepared.

Contents

Preface

The purpose of this book is to inform an approach to child welfare service delivery to African American children and families that is based on cultural adaptation as the mediating construct with the existing system of care. This approach requires identification of the current system's limitations in meeting the needs of African American children and their families, and then using the needs and conditions of families to propose policy and program responses that make requisite cultural adaptations targeted to this population. The disparate experience of African American children and youths in the out-of-home child welfare system provides the primary rationale for considering an alternative approach to the study of child welfare.

The primary objective is to describe how cultural adaptations can be used in the delivery of child welfare services to African American children and families. To accomplish the objective, the book entails a review and evaluation of the three major child welfare goals: (1) *protection*; (2) *permanency*; and (3) *well-being*. Specifically, we explore the effect of these three goals on African American children and families. An important feature of the book is the recommendations for policy, practice, and research that can guide intervention with this population.

USING THE BOOK

The book is intended for use by people who have a basic knowledge of systems of care, human behavior theories, and social work practice skills. The practitioners who use it may be enrolled in a graduate program in social work or a graduate course of study, or be a participant in training directed to government bureaucrats, administrators, or program managers concerned with improving the child welfare service delivery system. Emphasis is placed on knowledge building, policy analysis, and research to improve the strategies and skill sets used when working with African American children and families.

The book will be useful for child welfare professionals (practitioners and administrators), students, grassroots organizers and policy advocates, researchers, and instructors. With its hallmark feature, the cultural adaptation approach, it provides readers with an explication of basic skills, steps, and strategies that are useful in the delivery of child welfare services to African American children and families. The book integrates practice, policy, and research and includes study tools and resources (a glossary, discussion questions, and activities for ongoing learning); thus it can be easily incorporated into such courses as child welfare, family practice, social work and the law, social work practice, cultural diversity, policy, child welfare integrative seminar, and special topic electives. Following are recommendations for how readers can make best use of the book.

Students

We recommend that students begin by reading each chapter thoroughly. Some students might find it helpful to use the glossary as an outline to structure their note taking. The glossary contains some of the most vital concepts and content covered in the chapters. Additionally, students might want to use one or more of the chapters as a topic area or theme for a term paper. For example, a student considering child well-being as a topic for a course paper will want to pay special attention to chapter 6 and can use the components contained in that chapter as headings and subheadings to structure the paper. Students may also consider using the book as a study tool to prepare for graduate comprehensive or qualifying examinations, given the fact that it includes detailed discussion of the three major child welfare components: protection, permanency, and well-being.

Child Welfare Professionals

Chapters 4, 5, and 6, respectively, include discussions of how existing and traditional child protection, permanency, and well-being strategies can be culturally adapted so that they are more effective with African American children and families. After reading these chapters in particular, some child welfare professionals may be prompted to engage in a critical analysis of the approaches that are currently being used in their local child welfare systems. Some may find that they can use the recommended approaches in their day-to-day interactions with clients.

Grassroots Organizers and Policy Advocates

Advocates will find the conceptual framework (chapter 1), historical review (chapter 2), and policy analysis (chapter 3) compelling and useful for data mining as they prepare arguments for system reform. Several empirical studies, national analyses, and government reports have been synthesized and are presented throughout the book, especially in the first three chapters. Policy advocates will find a plethora of facts and figures they can use to educate and inform decision makers.

Researchers

A research direction and several research ideas are presented in chapter 7. Using the cultural adaptation framework, researchers are presented with a strategy for evaluating the adequacy of evidence-based interventions. Additionally, researchers can incorporate some of the suggested advocacy-based research strategies into their own work. Finally, some may be motivated to develop pilot studies or seek funding for demonstration sites that test the proposed performance-based research approach.

Instructors

Instructors can use this book in multiple ways: First, as required reading for undergraduate and graduate students, instructors can use the chapters and the related discussion questions as lecture topics or in group or class discussions. Second, instructors can use the recommended projects and assignments as tools to increase students' comprehension of class and book content. Third, although the entire book is useful for all students, instructors will find that the first three chapters are especially valuable for bringing undergraduate and early-stage graduate students up to speed on the history and nature of the child welfare system. The remaining chapters and especially chapter 8 provide excellent food for thought for advanced students as they prepare major papers.

In short, whatever the status of the reader, this book is best used as a tool for challenging one's critical thinking skills and expanding ideas about the possibilities for reforming a child welfare system that remains inadequate to address the needs of African American children and families. The book can be used as both an academic textbook and a professional training tool.

OVERVIEW OF CHAPTERS

Each chapter is formatted so that readers can make easy reference to research citations. A glossary of terms is provided at the end of the book to facilitate the use of the book as a practical tool in the workplace or the classroom.

In chapter 1 we share our philosophy in writing the book and the critical need for an examination of the child welfare system in the United States relative to African American children and families. Using the cultural adaptation framework, we suggest strategies for more responsive interventions and policy reforms based on African American cultural tenets.

Chapter 2 discusses major historical, cultural, and political influences that shape both the condition of African American families today and the child welfare system of care as it has evolved over time. Chapter 3 provides a comprehensive list of the primary laws that inform the child welfare out-of-home care system in this country. These major laws are discussed in the context of a legal framework for child welfare, emphasizing both the legal intent and limitations associated with implementation at the state and local levels. Specifically, we discuss laws that inform the process of child protection, permanency planning, and the delivery of family support services and family reunification services. Implications of other recent statutes are also addressed, including the Keeping Children and Families Safe Act (PL 108-36), the Child and Family Services Improvement Act (PL 109-288), and the Fostering Connections to Success and Increasing Adoptions Act (PL 110-35). We propose cultural adaptations to existing policies and the creation of new approaches to child welfare policy aimed at improving overall effectiveness and strengthening service delivery, particularly relative to the most vulnerable within this system of care.

Chapters 4 and 5 explore core statutory-mandated services once considered polar opposites on a services continuum—child protection and permanency planning. With passage of PL 105-89, the Adoption and Safe Families Act, concurrent planning for all children in child protective service (CPS) is mandated. Policy implications of this statutory requirement for African American families are discussed along with consideration of how the application of policy and implementation strategies may affect outcomes.

Chapter 6 addresses child well-being and considers the effect of the social environment on family life. Emotional and physical health, education, and exposure to the criminal justice system are addressed as factors that may affect quality-of-life experiences for family members. Caregiver needs are also addressed as the quality of parenting is affected by personal challenges and obstacles that when addressed will strengthen families.

Chapter 7 articulates the critical importance of social science research to inform the practice of those who work with and on behalf of children and their families. Research outcomes in child welfare may have limited generalizability for defining evidence-based practices, based on the populations on which research is conducted. This chapter discusses the limitations of some approaches to research and offers recommendations to enhance the capacity of research to reveal critical information about African American children and families. Additionally, three essential elements pertaining to child welfare research are discussed: (1) evidence-based intervention; (2) advocacy-based research; and (3) performance-based research. The chapter proposes a specific research agenda as it pertains to African American children, based on consideration of the cultural adaptation conceptual framework and the interests of children and families served by the child welfare system.

The concluding chapter provides an integrative perspective in which conditions in the child welfare system as well as the families' social environment are discussed, with an emphasis placed on opportunities for meaningful change. Strategies are proposed for practitioners and child advocates to promote the interests and well-being of African American children in the child welfare system while also improving our system of care for all children.

A WORD ABOUT THE AUTHORS

Together we have more than thirty years of professional experience working with and on behalf of children and families. Our combined mix of experience creates a unique perspective enabling us to draw on our experiences in working directly with families in child protection; advocating for children and families at the federal, state, and local levels; and engaging in policy formulation at all levels of government. Our pooled experiences include extensive conduct of program evaluation and outcomes-focused research. Because of our shared professional experiences and the unique strengths we each bring to this effort, we shared equally the conceptualization, research, and writing, as well as our passion for the well-being of all children and their families.

Acknowledgments

I would like to thank my loving husband, Jesse, for his enduring support and insight, and for always reminding me to assume that there are "good intentions" in all aspects of life. A huge debt of gratitude is extended to my dear friend Keith Alford for his listening ear and his commitment to children and families, especially those who face vulnerabilities and challenges, which inspired my work throughout this project. I dedicate this book to social workers, students, caseworkers, legal advocates, caregivers, providers, and all who are champions of children and families and whose hard work and dedication often go unnoticed.

> And let us not grow weary of doing good, for in due season we will reap, if we do not give up. (Galatians 6:9)

Ramona W. Denby

After years of working in child welfare and advocating on behalf of children and families, I developed a keen awareness of the inequities experienced by African American children in the child welfare system, the mental health system, and the juvenile justice system. Inequities have resulted in disparate experiences among African American and other children of color served by these systems nationwide. My early contributions to social research literature were typically focused on public policy–related research and advocacy-directed practice. While sharing my experiences as social worker and social work educator, several friends and my former dean, Tony Tripodi, encouraged me to share my thoughts about what might improve our national system of child welfare, from my viewpoint. Dean Tripodi offered great advice, which I did not always follow, but it was important for me to have his counsel along the journey associated with the completion of this book. To Dr. Tripodi, Reverend Nawanna Miller, Curtis Jewel, Dr. Kevin Dixon, and others, I appreciate your spoken faith in me, which allowed me to act on faith and personal dedication and determination to bring to paper, along with my co-author, the concerns, ideals, and suggestions for improving a system of care that affects the lives of many children and their family members daily. To the late John Michel of Columbia University Press, who first received and supported the concept of this book, and to Jennifer Perillo and Stephen Wesley, also of Columbia University Press, who have also supported the idea and provided invaluable input and support along the way, I am very grateful. The technical support and assistance from Irene Pavitt and Pat Perrier was timely and consistent—thank you. I am also grateful to Maya Porter for reading through early versions of the manuscript and providing critical feedback. For family and friends who have been patient with me and loved me through it all—you are appreciated.

I dedicate this book to my family:

Two phenomenal women—my mom, Caroletta Marie, a consummate professional, my mentor and first teacher; and Candace Michelle, my "baby girl" now grown, whose loving support is an unwavering source of inspiration.

And in loving memory of my dad, Jack Leroy Curtis (1925–1998), who believed that I can do anything he put his mind to, and to my little brother, Jack Jr.

Carla M. Curtis

African American Children and Families in Child Welfare

Introduction

To those who ask, "Why do we need a book devoted specifically to African American families?" we reply that after over sixty years of nationalizing child welfare and instituting reforms aimed at improving conditions for all children in care, African American children hold a unique and uncontested disproportional position in the out-of-home care system. National reports from the federal government document a significant number of active cases among African Americans resulting from referrals to child protective service (CPS) agencies (U.S. Department of Health and Human Services, 2008). Studies have also documented the fact that African American children are not the target for family preservation services, even though they continue to represent a "special needs" population due in large part to their disproportionate numbers in out-of-home care (Denby & Curtis, 2003).

These facts result in complex questions that are difficult to answer, such as why disproportionality continues after years of policy and program reform and intervention. Ultimately, finding answers requires a change in the historical approach to examining the social conditions in which children are raised and the cultural context in which they are served and should result in a different response. Political pundits and child welfare experts alike will differ about the most appropriate response to the "why" queries, but our knowledge of history confirms one certainty—the experience of African Americans in this country is political, and the experience of children and families in the child welfare system is also political.

From the introduction of African Americans to this country through the slave trade system, to subjugation both socially and politically during slavery and its aftermath, the experience of African Americans in systems intended to educate, inform, and provide services has been fraught with discrimination and differential treatment. The child welfare system has historically been exclusionary and/or ineffective when confronted with the child welfare needs of the African American family in this country. From adoption practices in place after passage of the Social Security Act of 1935, which in effect ignored the existence of the African American family or deemed it too "pathological" and therefore too complex to "correct," to the implementation of policies aimed at correcting past failures of the out-of-home care system by reducing the number of children referred to child protective service agencies, African American children and families are not typically the focus of instructional references.

Thirty-four years ago the National Urban League published *The Strengths of Black Families*, by Robert Hill. The book documented social research findings that challenged popular assertions by some sociologists at the time, that the "black family" is " 'matriarchal,' it is unstable, it does not prepare black people for productive lives, and it is the prime source of black economic weakness" (Hill, 1972:ix). Hill's work had a tremendous impact on future conceptualizations of social policies regarding the structure and function of the black family. However, child welfare professionals continue to compare the experiences of African American families with those of whites and others and insist that the effect of policies for one segment of the population is the same for all; they approach intervention with families in like form with little consideration of cultural differences.

This book provides a focused examination of research and analyses of policies that directly affect the institutional care provided to African American children and their families. Analyses of practices, programs, policies, research, and recommendations for corrective action are based on recognition of cultural competence as an ethical tenet for the social work profession; cultural adaptation is introduced as a means of achieving needed change within the overall service system and infrastructure as it relates to African American children and families.

Policy formulation may have different effects on various segments of the population. For example, policy formulated with the goal of permanency for children may not take into account the life experiences of all families coming into contact with the CPS system. Some families in the CPS system may be negatively affected by the criminal justice system, but not all incarcerated parents are incapable of or uninterested in parenting. Policies that impose time limits or restrictions around permanent placement decisions without consideration of time incarcerated can prevent the reunification of potentially viable family units. This is a particular concern in the African American community, as statistics show that 75 percent of incarcerated women are African American (Karger & Stoesz, 2009).

One of the challenges to the profession of social work is to demonstrate the importance of and need for practitioners to assume more visible and active roles not only in offering quality services but also in advocating and formulating effective child welfare policy. Until social workers do more to inform the policy-making process that affects our practice with children, we limit our influence to reform the system of care for all children. When engaged in training professionals for child welfare service, instructors must emphasize strong analytical skills. Objective interpretation of policies and research findings may result in subjectively crafted programs aimed at addressing the specific needs of the underserved.

For example, practitioners must consider the effect of policies aimed at promoting health and safety for children, but which may in fact limit or prevent opportunities for parents to be empowered to reform behaviors and resume parenting responsibilities. Not all parents who have health-related problems with alcohol or other drugs or who may be incarcerated are incapable of resuming some of their parenting responsibility. Policies and practice methods must consider differences between stumbling blocks that may be overcome and willful behaviors that the parent has no interest in changing or treating. With a growing number of parents having their parental rights terminated, is it unreasonable to suggest a supportive role for some parents in the life of their child following incarceration and successful completion of a drug or alcohol treatment program?

Finally, we argue that an evidence-based practice approach to child welfare service delivery with African American families incorporates the cultural adaptation of practices, policies, and research goals. Such adaptations aimed at the most vulnerable children within the CPS system nationwide will benefit the entire child welfare system. This book will have immediate utility for professional practitioners, students, advocates, and policy makers because it integrates practice, policy, and research to determine the best outcomes for children.

REFERENCES

Denby, R., & C. M. Curtis. 2003. Why Children of Color Are Not the Target of Family Preservation Services: A Case for Program Reform. *Journal of Sociology and Social Welfare* 30 (2): 149–73.

Hill, R. B. 1972. *Strengths of Black Families.* Lanham, Md.: University Press of America.

Karger, H., & D. Stoesz. 2009. *American Social Welfare Policy: A Pluralist Approach.* 6th ed. Boston: Pearson Education.

U.S. Department of Health and Human Services, Administration for Children and Families, Administration on Children, Youth and Families, Children's Bureau. 2008. *Preliminary Estimates for FY 2006 as of January 2008.* http://www.acf.hhs.gov/programs/cb.

1

Cultural Adaptation in Effective Child Welfare Practice with African Americans

A CULTURAL ADAPTATION FRAMEWORK

Many authors have called for a critical examination of the United States child welfare system as it relates to African American children and families (Curtis & Denby, 2004; Denby & Curtis, 2003; Dixon, 2008; Hill, 2006; McRoy, 2008; Roberts, 2002, 2008; Testa, 2005; U.S. GAO, 2007). Examiners of the U.S. child welfare system have based their critiques on historical, cultural, political, and service reviews. Most recently, some child welfare scholars have challenged researchers to develop new theories that build on historical traditions and establish evidence-based practices and policies. Traditionally, proponents of evidence-based practices search for appropriate frameworks and practice effectiveness by questioning, searching, analyzing, and then applying and evaluating their conclusions (Cournoyer, 2004). However, the child welfare system reforms that are needed go far beyond the implementation of evidence-based models. What is required instead is a system transformation that takes into account cultural adaptations of policies, research, and practice so that the system is more responsive to the particular needs of African American children and families.

In this text we call for an analytical framework that guides policy, research, and practice interventions for African American families in the child welfare system. However, we believe that the traditional critique of the child welfare system is shortsighted in that its parameters usually extend to a mere mention of historical, cultural, and political influences. While these components are essential to advancing a sound analytical framework, we examine what cultural adaptations are needed to the overall service system and infrastructure as it relates to African Americans in the child welfare system.

The call for cultural competence as it relates to child welfare is not new. Several scholars have provided direction for cultural competency at both the individual and organizational levels, and although the literature is voluminous, several seminal pieces address the topic as it specifically pertains to African American children and families (Barber & Jager, 2007–2008; Gavazzi, Alford, & McKenry, 1996; Waites, 2009; Wells, Merritt, & Briggs, 2009).

We have chosen the framework of cultural adaptation to illustrate how child welfare reform efforts can be implemented to better address the service delivery needs of African American children and families. Given the aim of this book, which is to advance multiple-level approaches (policy, practice, and research) for child welfare intervention with African Americans, we frame the issues from a perspective of both what has caused the crisis and what potentially are some of the viable solutions for overcoming the current problems. We chose cultural adaptation as the guiding framework for four reasons:

1. For decades African Americans' plight in the child welfare system has been characterized as dire, yet the system lacks a framework that allows us to move our actions, services, and approaches into a system characterized by reform efforts.
2. Cultural adaptation is about being culturally competent, and cultural competence is an ethical and professional imperative.
3. Given the reality of underresourced child welfare systems, there is a need to advance approaches that are both practical and viable and do not place unrealistic financial burdens on systems that are already overburdened.
4. Given the child welfare system mandate of child safety/protection, well-being, and permanency, we must advance approaches that make both clients and professionals more accountable for the realization of these mandates.

Definitions of Culture

In 1949 Douglas Haring posed the question: "Is culture definable?" Implied in this question is the difficulty that many face as they search for clear, simple, and agreed upon definitions of the term *culture*. Others have suggested that defining culture is a way of drawing lines of demarcation between groups, including some while excluding others (Ortner, 1998; Park, 2005). As further evidence of the complexities associated with defining culture, Allén (1996) argues that culture is not discovered, it is constructed. The field of social work has entered the discourse, with some raising questions concerning whether culture may in fact be a marker for "difference" and arguing that it is at times used to replace race and ethnicity in categorizing minority status (Park, 2005).

The term has multiple meanings. As it has been most commonly used in social and human services professions, culture is defined as follows:

- The "collective programming of the mind which distinguishes the members of one category of people from another" (Hofstede, 1984:51).
- "Learned and shared human patterns or models for living; day-to-day living patterns. These patterns and models pervade all aspects of human social interaction. Culture is mankind's primary adaptive mechanism" (Damen, 1987:367).
- The manner in which members of a group interpret and perceive artifacts, tools, and other cultural elements. The cultural groups are distinguished by their values, interpretations, meanings, and symbols. People within defined cultural groups usually interpret phenomena in the same manner (Banks, Banks, & McGee, 1989).
- "The shared knowledge and schemes created by a set of people for perceiving, interpreting, expressing, and responding to the social realities around them" (Lederach, 1995:9).
- "A configuration of learned behaviors and results of behavior whose component elements are shared and transmitted by the members of a particular society" (Linton, 1945:32).
- "Learned and shared behavior of a community of interacting human beings" (Useem & Useem, 1963:169).

Despite the controversy concerning how and why culture is defined, social work and other human services, like many professions, have studied culture and cultural phenomena through the lens of modern anthropology. Such anthropological coding as "hereditary customs and action" or "sharing understandings" have been used to frame definitions of culture (O'Hagan, 1999). Anthropological definitions of culture also remind us that societies have multiple cultures that are often stratified and distinguished by language, attributes, and other classifications. O'Hagan has put forth a definition of culture that can be specifically applied to child and family social work:

> Culture is the distinctive way of life of the group, race, class, community, or nation to which the individual belongs. It is the product of the values, ideas, perceptions, and meanings which have evolved over time. These values, ideas, perceptions, and meanings constitute the individual's knowledge and understanding of the world in which he or she lives, and they derive from, and are embodied in, the physical environment of birth and upbringing, in language, institutions, family and social relationships, child rearing, education, systems of belief, religion, mores and customs, dress and diet, and in particular uses of objects and material life. Culture embraces all of these, and the individual may regard each of them, or any number of them, as culturally significant. (273)

The manner in which people organize and classify their collective experiences is critical, and it is a starting point in the examination of the African American family's engagement with the child welfare system. We will examine how child welfare experiences that African Americans encounter are arguably best understood within a cultural context. In doing so, in subsequent chapters we consider the possibility that cultural classifications can be used to pathologize behaviors observed in individuals, families, and communities, which may account for some of the adverse conditions that African American children and families face while in the child welfare system. Nonetheless, we consider culture to be a strength, and we use the meanings that African American communities may associate with their culture to propose a set of strategies to adapt policies, practices and research to better address the needs of African American children and families.

Definitions of Adaptation

Webster's dictionary uses such words as *modify, revise, adjust,* and *alter* to define *adapt.* Like culture, the meaning of adapt or adaptation varies, depending on the area of study or context in which it is used. Biologists and anthropologists think of adaptation as evolutionary or generational processes whereby species or populations better match or conform to their new environments. In human services disciplines, notions of adaptation again derive from anthropological meanings but have been largely framed from research in psychology whereby, simply put, adaptation can be thought of as adjustment, alteration, or change that is motivated by or prompted by voluntary or involuntary new experiences, encounters, or information. Today adaptation is most often defined as Whaley (2003) discusses it: the ability to change one's behavior and attitudes in order to fit within one's environment.

Cultural adaptation has long occurred in the context of human service delivery systems. However, the traditional form of cultural adaptation has been one-sided, whereby we have asked clients (individuals, families, groups, and communities) to adapt their behaviors, culture, and environments to fit into available services, program structures, and models of intervention. Traditional cultural adaptation closely adheres to anthropological perspectives of cultural evolution. Barger (2009:17) defines anthropological cultural adaptation as "changes made by a group of people to develop a more viable interaction between the conditions of their environment and their total behavioral patterns." Implicit in this definition is the belief that adaptation is a positive condition and a group process as opposed to an individual one.

THE NEW ADAPTATION PERSPECTIVE

The adaptation perspective maintains that effective models and programs have sometimes not been planned with respect to the needs of special populations. This is a problem given that some special populations have service needs that are difficult to address. In fact, ethnic minority groups are seldom represented in any significant numbers in studies of evidence-based treatment (Whaley & Davis, 2007). The aim of cultural adaptation is to ensure that interventions are relevant and responsive to the needs of special populations. Therefore, if service models and interventions are targeted to the needs of special populations, the observed outcomes are truly effective. Use of the adaptation perspective has also been referred to as *hybrid interventions* or *adjusted interventions* (Holleran Steiker et al., 2008). These interventions explore those aspects of the original program model or intervention approach that are not specific to or have less relevance for the intended cultural group or special population and then make necessary adjustments. The following are examples of how cultural adaptation has been defined in the professional literature:

> [A]ny modification to an evidence-based treatment that involves changes in the approach to service delivery, in the nature of the therapeutic relationship, or in components of the treatment itself to accommodate the cultural beliefs, attitudes, and behaviors of the target population. (Whaley & Davis, 2007:570–71)

> [T]he process of adjusting the delivery of mental health services to be consistent with the client's culture. The provision of services is adapted to the culture. Simply put, cultural adaptation is the process of modifying mental health service delivery to make it culturally competent. Just as cultural competence must be addressed at the administrative, service delivery, and clinician level, so must cultural adaptations be developed at all three levels. (Hogg Foundation for Mental Health, 2010:4)

Relevant cultural adaptations can be made in any aspect of an intervention. Cultural adaptations can start with the very premise or principles on which the program is based and end with how program outcomes are measured and tracked. Employing individuals whom Holleran Steiker et al. (2008) refer to as "culturally matched implementers" (individuals who understand class and cultural differences) to deliver services is another way to apply the cultural adaption perspective, as is involving indigenous groups in the design and testing of culturally adapted programs.

Several challenges have been noted to the adaptation perspective. First, Holleran Steiker et al. (2008) report that some believe that adapting to efficacious models threatens fidelity. They argue that if an intervention or program has been shown to be effective, alterations run the risk of diminishing the effect, and therefore the model should be delivered as it was designed. Second, cost has been identified as an issue in trying to produce culturally adapted approaches. Kazdin (1993) considers the practicality of the cost of adjusting evidence-based models to fit various ethnic groups and also suggests that there is a lack of scientific proof that community-specific adaptations of programs work. Joining Kazdin's argument, Elliot and Mihalic (2004) assert that culturally modified approaches may run the risk of jeopardizing the efficacy of evidence-based programs. Third, some have argued whether cultural adaptations should occur at all (Holleran Steiker et al.). Arguably, models, programs, and interventions need not be adapted if they were designed from the outset to address the needs of a particular group or population, but frequently interventions are not intentionally designed for or normed across unique client populations.

The literature documenting the effectiveness of cultural adaptations to prevailing intervention approaches is building (Castro, Barrer, & Martinez, 2004; Catalano et al., 1993; Gorman & Balter, 1997; Harachi, Catalano, & Hawkins, 1997; Martinez & Eddy, 2005). Kumpfer, Alvarado, Smith, and Bellamy (2002) found that by making cultural adaptations to the Strengthening Families Program (SFP) for African American, Hispanic/Latino, Pacific Islander/Asian, and Native American groups, recruitment and retention rates improved by 40 percent over the use of the traditional approach (i.e., the nonculturally adapted approach). Coard, Foy-Watson, Zimmer, and Wallace (2007) found that a culturally adapted approach was effective in shoring up parenting styles and increasing parents' abilities to intervene in their children's conduct problems. Another example of the effectiveness of culturally adapted approaches is found in the results observed by Kumpfer et al. (2002) and the U.S. Department of Health and Human Services (2001) in their studies of risk and resilience in African American families. Moreover, Holleran Steiker et al. (2008) found that when evidence-based interventions are culturally adapted, attitudes and behaviors concerning drug and alcohol use are shifted.

Now that we have established the definition of cultural adaptation as it is used in this book, we move ahead with a discussion of the aspects of the child welfare system that should be adapted to better support the needs of African American children. To explore cultural adaption in child welfare practices, it is necessary to explore three main system aspects: policy, practice, and research.

REFORMING CHILD WELFARE THROUGH CULTURAL ADAPTATION

Figure 1.1 depicts the key components of a cultural adaptation framework for examining child welfare programming with African Americans. The

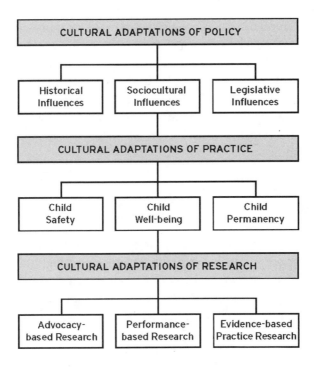

Figure 1.1 An analytical framework for examining child welfare practice with African Americans.

framework comprises three essential components of cultural adaptation: policy, practice, and research. This guiding framework embodies the philosophical premise on which this book is constructed.

First, as noted in figure 1.1, the policy component of the analytical framework recognizes the importance of summarizing salient historical, cultural, and legislative influences that have affected African American children and families who experience the child welfare system. The adaptations to legislation and policy that are advanced in this book emerged from a critical review of legislative initiatives and policy barriers that impede effective work with African American children. Second, cultural adaptation in practice involves examining three aspects of the child welfare experience as it relates to African Americans: safety, permanency, and well-being. Also, the practice chapters (chapters 4, 5, and 6) include an analysis of necessary adaptations that must occur within administrative and supervisory approaches and structures. They comprise a discussion of requisite cultural adaptations needed in training approaches and the work of providers. The practice chapters also involve a judicial component that consists of suggestions and a direction for more responsive involvement of courts and judges. Third, guided by the proposed analytical framework, we explore how cultural adaptation in research will promote advocacy-based approaches, performance-based approaches, and responsive evidence-based interventions for African American children and families.

CULTURAL ADAPTATION AND POLICY

An analytical framework for examining child welfare practice with African Americans would be incomplete without posing and answering questions about the historical service inequities that exist in the system. In fact, African American children's vulnerable status in the child welfare system has been well documented (Ards et al., 2003; Billingsley & Giovannoni, 1972; Close, 1983; Finch & Fanshel, 1985; Fluke et al., 2003; Gray & Nybell, 1990; Hill, 2006; Hogan & Siu, 1988; McRoy, 2008; Mech, 1983; Pinderhughes, 1991; Roberts, 2002; Seaburg & Tolley, 1986; Stehno, 1982, 1990). In this book we explore several critical service questions, including what service inequities exist in the child welfare system, and what services are needed by African American children and families who experience the child welfare system.

Families and children considered to be special populations are said to be the groups most needing services directed at reducing their out-of-home placements. The idea of "special populations" evolved from the experiences of groups of children for whom permanent placements were difficult to finalize. Forward-thinking advocates and policy makers forged this phenomenon of targeting services to special populations as an approach to service delivery that was first articulated in the child welfare reform legislation of 1980, the Adoption Assistance and Child Welfare Act. Researchers have documented the overrepresentation of such special populations as African American children in the foster care system (Hill, 2006; McRoy, 2008; Roberts, 2002). Preventative services are not offered to special populations as readily as they are to nonspecial population groups. Arguably, since African American children disproportionately occupy the foster care rolls, a significant effect can be made by reducing their rate of placement. In this book we consider the reasons that African

American children and families are not targeted for preventative service delivery despite the intent of federal legislation.

Significant policies, legislation, and federal initiatives have been enacted to address the conditions of children and families involved in the child welfare system. However, some policy analysts and observers of the system believe that the policies, services, and administrative restructuring have been woefully inadequate and are resulting in a breakdown of the system (Allen, 1993; Schorr, 2000; Sconyers et al., 1996; Tolchin, 1991; Williams, 1993). In this book we ask how key child welfare legislation has affected African American children and families, what services and interventions have resulted from child welfare legislation, and what effect these services have had on African Americans.

CULTURAL ADAPTATION AND PRACTICE

The child welfare system carries as its primary mandates the responsibility for protecting children (ensuring safety), safeguarding their well-being, and achieving permanency in the most expeditious manner possible. These mandates are carried out with a high regard for strengthening families and supporting parents so that they are better equipped to provide for the needs of their children. The evidence shows that African American children experience unfavorable outcomes along most points of service related to the three mandates.

Child Protection

Child protection is a government-mandated action of safeguarding children (i.e., protecting them from harm or preventing harm to them) who may be currently experiencing or are at risk of experiencing the effects of harmful conditions. Although many child welfare services are locally run, the primary responsibility for child welfare services resides with the states. State authorities safeguard vulnerable children by implementing the provisions of such federal laws as the Child Abuse Prevention and Treatment Act (CAPTA) of 1974, which requires states to establish child protection processes and structures and implement appropriate child welfare services. A cultural adaptation process driven by a reform approach directs attention to five main components concerning the issues of safety and protection: child abuse and neglect, child protection services and investigation procedures, assessment, child welfare court process and court involvement, and foster care.

Federal and state statutes define child abuse and neglect (or child maltreatment, as it is also called). As directed by CAPTA, child abuse and neglect is defined as any recent act or failure on the part of a parent or caretaker that results in death, serious physical or emotional harm, or sexual abuse or exploitation, or an act or failure to act that presents an imminent risk of serious harm. Categories of child abuse and neglect can include neglect, physical abuse, sexual abuse, emotional/psychological maltreatment, abandonment, or drug exposure. In 2008 child welfare authorities nationally received approximately 3.3 million referrals of alleged child abuse and neglect affecting 6 million children. Of these 6 million cases of children who are reported annually as abused and/or neglected, approximately 63 percent are actually investigated or assessed. About 24 percent of the investigations result in a determination that a

Child Abuse and Neglect Rates Among African American Children

The third National Incidence Study (NIS-3), sponsored by the federal government, examined incidents of child maltreatment nationally and found that African American children's rate of maltreatment is the same as that of other ethnic groups. However, cycle 4 of the NIS does note racial differences in abuse and neglect: African American children's incidences of maltreatment in every reporting category are greater than those of all other ethnic groups. Drake et al. (2011) concur, finding that racial bias in reporting may not be the driving force in the disparities observed in child welfare profiles. Still, others have surmised that the disproportionality of African American children in the child welfare system is not the result of these children being abused at higher rates than other groups.

The issue of disproportionality along each point in the child welfare service continuum (e.g., investigation, removal, reunification) is well established (Chibnall et al., 2003; U.S. GAO, 2007). Disproportionality (a phenomenon whereby African American children are represented in the child welfare system at a rate that far exceeds their population totals) is believed to be the result of larger, societally based, social structural issues (poverty), system bias (e.g., worker subjectivity), and the interplay between structural and system issues (Chibnall et al., 2003).

Divergent Points of View: Establishing Patterns of Maltreatment Among African American Children

Studies that examine the issue of racial patterns and child abuse and neglect report inconsistent findings. For example, Sedlak and Schultz (2001) found that although race does not predict whether a family will be investigated for abuse and neglect, it does have an effect if the allegation of abuse is emotional maltreatment, physical neglect, drug exposure, or fatal or serious injury. Also, Eckenrode et al. (1988) report that African American children are more likely than European American children to be substantiated in cases involving physical abuse. However, other studies have discovered no racial differences in substantiation rates (Ards, Chung, & Myers, 1999).

child is a victim of abuse (U.S. Department of Health and Human Services [USDHHS], 2010b).

Child protective services is typically thought of as an entity within an overarching county- or state-administered child welfare system. Divisions of child protective services units generally receive child abuse and neglect reports, investigate those reports, and provide crisis services and follow-up referral information. The process of investigation involves the search for and examination of facts after a child welfare agency has received a report of abuse or neglect (USDHHS, 2010d).

Assessment is the collection of information that enables a child welfare official to make decisions concerning children and their families (USDHHS, 2010d). Most often the types of assessments that are done in the course of a child welfare investigation involve risk and safety. Risk assessments as defined by the Child Welfare Information Gateway (CWIG) involve the collection and analysis of data or information to predict the presence of key factors that are considered to increase the likelihood of future maltreatment.

In most states, following the receipt of an abuse or neglect allegation, a juvenile, family, tribal, or general trial court presides over a child's progression through the child welfare system. Although there is great variance from state to state, most child welfare systems have eight processes or steps: (1) rendering of a petition; (2) custody or protective hearing; (3) pretrial conference; (4) adjudicatory hearing; (5) disposition; (6) periodic review; (7) termination of parental rights; and (8) appeals.

The Effect of Racial Bias: Establishing Maltreatment Rates Among African American Children

Morton (1999) warns about structural issues in his analysis of the racial-bias effect that operates in child welfare proceedings. He claims that such an effect is created by the manner in which (1) cases are substantiated, (2) risk assessments are used, and (3) workers' claims of abuse and neglect substantiation typically undergo no adversarial challenge. He further explains that once cases are opened and service decisions begin, the racial-bias effect becomes compounded, and such action over just four decisions could double the representation of a group of children.

Other studies of risk assessment and caseworker decision making have also led to discoveries of potential race bias. Rolock and Testa (2005) found that European American caseworkers (more than African American workers) tend to substantiate a larger portion of their substance-exposed infant cases when the children are African Americans.

Finally, according to the 2007 USDHHS GAO report, child welfare directors in twenty-one states indicated that worker bias, cultural misunderstanding, and inadequate training of staff are factors that contribute to African American children's entry into the child welfare system.

When Termination of Parental Rights Does Not Lead to Permanency: The Plight of African American Children

The Adoption and Safe Families Act (ASFA) of 1997 allows states to initiate termination of parental rights proceedings for parents whose children have been in care for fifteen of the past twenty-two months. According to Morton (1999), the child that is most likely to have been in care for fifteen of the past twenty-two months is African American. To remain eligible for federal reimbursements, states must adhere to ASFA's guidelines on the termination of parental rights. However, for African American children the expediency of termination of parental rights does not correlate with the acquisition of permanency. The likelihood of achieving permanency after parental rights have been terminated is lower for African American children compared to their counterparts (Kemp & Bodonyi, 2002).

Foster care, intended as a temporary service, is a planned, goal-directed service provision designed for children who cannot live with their birth family (Child Welfare League of America, 2008). The most common types of foster care are family, therapeutic, and kinship (relative) care. Family foster care is a service provided by child welfare agencies whereby children under their care live with nonrelatives who have been specifically trained, certified, and monitored to provide such care. Nearly half the children in the child welfare system reside in a nonrelative family foster home (USDHHS, 2010d). Therapeutic/treatment foster care is designed for placement of children who have specific types of medical or mental health needs. Therapeutic/treatment foster parents typically receive more training and monitoring and higher stipends than do providers of regular family foster care, and they often are limited in the number of children that can reside in their homes (usually a lower number than regular family foster care) (USDHHS, 2010d). Kinship foster care is a formal arrangement whereby a relative (usually a grandparent, aunt, or uncle) provides day-to-day care for a relative's child who is under the supervision of the child welfare system. Kinship foster parents can be licensed by their local child welfare agency to provide care for their relatives' children and can receive financial reimbursement. At other times a kinship foster parent may not be licensed to provide care

Racial Inequities, Disparities, and Disproportionality

African American children enter and remain in foster care in higher proportions than other groups. According to the U.S. DHHS Government Accounting Office (U.S. GAO, 2007), African American children are about 15 percent of the national child population yet are about 34 percent of the child welfare population. Although African American children are disproportionately represented in the foster care system, they are more likely to receive regular foster care as opposed to the more therapeutic option of treatment foster care (Larson, 2010).

African American children tend to be placed with relatives more often than European American children. For African American children, kinship care is thought to have positive benefits: less stress to the child, preservation of family ties, fewer foster care moves, and lower reentry rates. However, it is also believed to have negative effects: longer lengths of stay and unenforced court orders prohibiting parental contact (U.S. GAO, 2007).

and may not receive any formal financial support from the child welfare authority but is recognized as the caregiver of record because the agency has approved the placement. In these instances, the title of kinship foster parent is often replaced with the notion of *relative placement*, which may more accurately portray the caregiving arrangement that is in place.

Well-Being

Many of the children who are involved in the child welfare system experience a myriad of risk factors and high needs prior to their entry into the system. These conditions and factors can become even more pronounced while they are in the custody of the child welfare system. Some of the risks factors that affect children's well-being include poverty, poor prenatal care, educational gaps, poor school performance, and unstable environments. Federal entitlements are in place to enhance well-being, and some are directed particularly at the needs of young children and children with developmental challenges. For example, the Keeping Children and Families Safe Act of 2003 (PL 108-36), which amended the Child Abuse and Prevention Treatment Act (PL 93-247), mandates early intervention service provisions for child welfare system-involved children under the age of 3 and directs funding under part C of the Individuals with Disabilities Education Act (IDEA) (PL 108-446). Through Early Step services and public school programming, children with developmental delays can be given necessary early intervention support. More recently, the Child and Family Services Improvement and Innovation Act of 2011 (PL 112-34), the reauthorization of the Stephanie Tubbs Jones Child Welfare Services Program, and the Promoting Safe and Stable Families (PSSF) Act require child welfare agencies to produce more positive outcomes by focusing on child well-being (Stoltzfus, 2011). States are required to make a number of changes, including appropriate use of psychotropic medications, specific planning for meeting the needs of very young children, implementation of response models to address emotional trauma, provisions for educational stability planning (e.g., enrolling children in a timely manner into appropriate school settings), and responsive caseworker visitation models. These federal efforts have been enacted to promote some of the core components of child well-being, some of which are discussed below.

The core components of well-being are often not present in foster youth. These core components include healthy development, protective mechanisms, resilience, relational competency, and protective factors. As shown in table 1.1, some of the threats and risks to achievement by a young person of the core components of well-being include lack of education, unemployment or underemployment, housing instability, legal system involvement, and the presence of mental health and substance-abuse disorders (National Research Council and Institute of Medicine, 2009).

TABLE 1.1
Threats/Risks to the Core Components of Well-Being

	Youth in the General Population	Youth in Foster Care
Education	Approximately 8% of American youths drop out of high school.	Approximately 50% of foster youths do not graduate from high school (2005).
Employment	The unemployment rate for youths and young adults (16–24) in general is 18.9 %.	The unemployment rate for foster youth who exit care is 52%.
Housing	Some 5–7 % of American youths become homeless in any given year.	Almost 30% of former foster youth experience homelessness at least one time by age 23 or 24.
Legal System	Less than 0.1% of youths in general are involved in the juvenile/criminal justice system.	Some 25% of foster youth who age out of the system are involved in the juvenile/criminal justice system.
Mental Health	About 20% of the youth population in general experience mental disorders.	About 38% of foster youth who age out of the system experience mental disorders.

Sources: Cook (1991); Courtney et al. (2005); Davis et al. (2008); Dworsky & Courtney (2010); Edwards & Hertel-Fernandez (2011); Merikangas et al. (2010); National Coalition for the Homeless (2008); U.S. Department of Education, National Center for Education Statistics (2010); Wagner & Wonacott (2008); Wolanin (2005).

Research has shown that what produces some of the core components of well-being for youth are relationships with supportive, caring adults and peers and their family of origin (Ahrens et al., 2008; Collins, Spencer, & Ward, 2010; Gowen, 2011; Greeson & Bowen, 2008). Many foster youth lack the protective barrier that comes from connections with family, friends, and other significant individuals. Most serious among these risk factors, particularly as it relates to the experiences of African American children, are the outcomes experienced in the categories of mental health, health, education, and delinquency and juvenile justice involvement.

Children who present to the child welfare system with psychological or physical challenges have high service needs and often require inordinate amounts of the case workers' and foster parents' time and attention (Kortenkamp & Ehrle, 2002). Using a nationally representative study, Kortenkamp and Ehrle discovered that children in foster care tend to have more emotional and behavioral problems than do children who do not live in foster care or those who live with a low-income single parent. Such challenges can include school suspension or expulsion; truancy; placement in special education programs; a confirmed physical, learning, or mental health condition; and fair to poor health.

Also, Kortenkamp and Ehrle discovered that 17 percent of child welfare system–involved children are cared for by caregivers who report symptoms of poor mental health, and child welfare youths are more likely than their counterparts to have a caregiver with aggravated conditions (i.e., a caregiver self-report of being bothered by the child, anger toward the child, and a sense of having to give up too much of one's life to care for a child who the caregiver perceives as being more difficult to care for than most children). In considering the issue of child well-being, we explore five areas: mental health, physical health, education, delinquency, and caregiver risk factors.

In some states more than one-third of the children under the supervision of the child welfare system suffer diagnosable mental health conditions, and nationally about half of the children in foster care have adaptive functioning scores that are in the problematic range (National Child Welfare Resource Center for Family-Centered Practice, 2003). Severe emotional disturbances (SED) classification means that children meet criteria for a psychiatric disorder and experience significant impairment in academic, social, or emotional functioning.

Disparities in Child Well-Being

The well-being of African American children involved in the child welfare system is even more problematic than for the general child welfare population (Beckett & Lee, 2004). African American children are thought to be more likely to have emotional, behavioral, and developmental challenges (Kortenkamp & Ehrle, 2002). Despite their need, African American children are less likely than European American children to receive mental health services, and even when such variables as insurance use, severity of condition, or maltreatment status are controlled, the services that African American children receive are of poorer quality than their European American counterparts (Garland et al., 2000; Garland, Landsverk, & Lau, 2003; Leslie et al., 2004; McMillen et al., 2004).

In response to a congressional mandate, the Administration for Children and Families (ACF) launched the first-ever National Survey of Child and Adolescent Well-Being (NSCAW) study, which was a multiwave (1999–2007) study of more than 6,200 children who had been abused or neglected. Among several highlights of the NSCAW study, it was discovered that many abused and neglected children suffer chronic health conditions that warrant extensive health and social service intervention (USDHHS, 2010e). The NSCAW found that about half of the children have a special health need, with asthma being the most

Unmet Needs: American Children's Health Care Status

According to the U.S. GAO (2007), African American children in foster care are slightly more likely than their European American counterparts to be diagnosed with medical conditions and other disabilities. Research indicates that children in kinship foster care when compared to those in regular foster care are more likely to lack health insurance and equally likely to experience poor health status (Berman & Carpenter, 2004). Given African American children's concentration in kinship care, such health care findings raise questions about whether the children receive health care services commensurate with their needs.

commonly reported health condition and learning disabilities being the most commonly reported special need.

Children in foster care are at a high risk of experiencing school failure (Altschuler, 1997; Cohen, 1991; Jackson, 1994; Stein, 1994). Child welfare system–involved youth have poor educational outcomes that have been attributed to developmental delays (Courtney et al., 2001; Wertheimer, 2002), poverty (Barth, Wildfire, & Green, 2006), and multiple school moves (Heinlein & Shinn, 2000; Mantzicopoulos & Knutson, 2000). Additionally, there is a high probability of the need for special education services for children involved in the child welfare system, as the NSCAW discovered that 7 percent of the children have cognitive problems, 16 percent exhibit behavioral problems, and more than 30 percent need special education services.

Juvenile justice system involvement is highly prevalent among child welfare system youth. The NSCAW study reported that nearly 20 percent of child welfare system–involved youth have some involvement (e.g., unruliness, skipping school) in the juvenile justice system. The NSCAW

African American Children's Educational Outcomes

While involved in the child welfare system, African American children are more likely to experience lower educational achievement (Yancey, 1998). Only 51 percent of African American children graduate from high school (Casey Family Program, 2004). African American children are disproportionately represented in special education and vocational tracks in the school system (Gordon, 1998).

The Tale of Two Systems

The connection between the child welfare and the juvenile justice system is demonstrated in the Child Welfare League of America's (1997) study that discovered that abused and neglected children are sixty-seven times more likely to be arrested. This finding, taken with the fact that African American youth are disproportionately represented in the juvenile justice system, leads experts to assert that dire consequences await African American youths involved in the child welfare system (McRoy, 2005).

African American Children in Kinship Care

African American children are more likely than their ethnic counterparts to be cared for by relative caregivers. Although kinship care is considered a positive placement option (Denby, 2011; U.S. GAO, 2007), many relative caregivers face tremendous risk factors and challenges that may affect the children in their care (Denby, 2012). Caregivers tend not to have completed high school and to be female, poor, unemployed, and struggling with health issues (Hairston, 2007), and they have high rates of mental health issues (Fuller-Thomsen & Minkler, 2000; Minkler et al., 1997).

examined the arrest rate of young adults who were adolescents at the beginning of the study and discovered that it was four times the national rate.

Caregiver well-being is an important consideration when assessing the well-being of children involved in the child welfare system. The NSCAW recorded significant caregiver risk factors, including disproportionate rates of domestic violence, criminal activity, and depression histories.

Permanency

The permanency process involves planning and working to achieve an end goal where children are placed in a loving, nurturing, healthy, and enduring environment with caregivers or family members who are expected to provide for their care. African American children experience great difficulty achieving permanency once they become involved in the child welfare system.

Family reunification is both a process used in the child welfare system and a desired outcome of the system. Reunification involves placing a child back into the care of his or her family of origin once the child has been removed and placed in out-of-home care following an investigation of child abuse and neglect (USDHHS, 2010d). Most of the children who are removed from their parents and placed in out-of-home care are reunited with their parents.

Such supportive services as group therapy, drug and alcohol counseling, parenting classes, housing services, and crisis intervention are

The African American Child's Foster Care Experience

African American children are less likely to be reunited with their parents (Noonan & Burke, 2005), are slower to be reunited (Courtney, 1994; Testa, 1997; Wells & Guo, 1999), or generally exit foster care more slowly than other children (Smith, 2003). Research shows that African American children are in foster care significantly longer than children of other races (CWLA, 2008).

Underutilization of Supportive Services

African American children and families receive and use fewer supportive services than do European Americans during their involvement in the child welfare system (Benedict et al., 1989; Courtney et al., 1996; Hill, 2006; Libby et al., 2006; Rodenburg, 2004; U.S. GAO, 2007)

typically offered to children and parents during their involvement in the child welfare system. Service use is highly encouraged given the fact that rates of service use are predictive of successful reunification and the eradication of problems that cause children and families' involvement in the child welfare system (Bellamy, 2008; Carlson et al., 2006; Lau et al., 2003).

Typically administered as intensive family preservation services (IFPS), service provisions exist for families who are in crisis and who face the potential imminent removal of their child as a result of child maltreatment or a parent's inability to effectively care for the child. IFPS can also be given to families after a child has already been removed from the home. The focus of services involves both birth and adoptive families. The delivery of IFPS is usually premised on a set of core values and beliefs. Some of these values are that the highest priority is placed on child safety, the family is the focus of services, children are better off with their own families whenever their safety can be relatively ensured, troubled families can change, families and IFPS staff should operate as partners, the system should respect a family's beliefs and values and instill hope, crisis is

Preserving African American Families

The Family Preservation and Support Services Act of 1993 directed states to use funding "as a catalyst for establishing a continuum of . . . culturally relevant services for children and families" (USDHHS, 1994:2). Family preservation services, designed to reduce placement rates, should target those children most at risk for placement. However, research demonstrates that African American children are not the target of family preservation services (Denby & Curtis, 2003; Denby, Alford, & Curtis, 2003).

an opportunity to bring about change, and inappropriate interventions are harmful. IFPS are typically characterized as immediate, accessible, specialized, tailored to families' needs, intensive, goal-directed, and focused (National Family Preservation Network, 2010).

Guardianship is a legal way for an adult other than a child's parent to assume responsibility and authority for the child (McCarthy et al., 2003). Although guardianship is intended to be a permanent arrangement, parental rights do not have to be terminated in order for guardianship to be established. When adoption is not a viable permanency outcome for children, child welfare systems look at the possibility of securing guardianship for children who have been removed from their parents' care. Approximately 7 percent of the children who were in foster care on September 30, 2009, exited the system via guardianship (USDHHS, 2010a). Subsidized guardianship can be provided for children who have special needs. It is used to support children's departure from the system, and some states use it to promote permanent homes for children with their relatives before involvement in the child welfare system.

In the context of child welfare, adoption typically refers to foster care adoption when a state or county child welfare agency (or a private agency that may be contracted by the local public child welfare authority) establishes legal and permanent parents for children whose biological parents' rights have been terminated by a court of law or whose parents have voluntarily relinquished their rights. The majority of the children adopted from the child welfare system are adopted by their foster parents (54 percent); the rest are adopted by relatives (30 percent) or by an adult not related to them (16 percent) (USDHHS, 2010c).

The Preferred Path to Permanency

Subsidized guardianship has been shown to substantially decrease racial disparities in foster care placement rates and length of stay (Chibnall et al., 2003). Research demonstrates that African American caregivers prefer the permanency option of guardianship over adoption (U.S. GAO, 2007) because it does not require termination of parental rights (Denby, 2012). But the guardianship option does not provide the same level of financial safeguard as adoption. According to the GAO report, state officials believed that the difficulty in finding permanent homes for African American children was partly due to the fact that there was no federal reimbursement to states for subsidies to guardians. However, there is hope that the new federal Guardianship Assistance Program (GAP) created under the Fostering Connections to Success and Increasing Adoptions Act will encourage more permanence through the use of subsidized guardianships.

Awaiting Adoption

African American children constitute half of the children legally free and awaiting adoption from the child welfare system, yet they wait a significantly longer time than other ethnic groups. African American children were 30 percent of the national foster care population in 2009 but constituted only 25 percent of the children who were adopted from the system that same year. Comparatively, European American children were 40 percent of the foster care population in 2009 but were 44 percent of the adoptive population that year. According to the GAO (2007), some of the factors that challenge states to find permanent homes for African American children in a more expeditious manner include insufficient numbers of adoptive homes and the belief that African American children are more likely to have special needs. Finally, the likelihood of achieving legal permanency after termination of parental rights is lower for African American children (Kemp & Bodonyi, 2002).

CULTURAL ADAPTATION AND RESEARCH

The call for the use of evidence-based practices in social work and child welfare is gaining momentum. Consumer groups, professional organizations, and social work scholars are among those advocating for the use of evidence-based practice. According to Cournoyer (2004) there is a difference between evidence-based and empirical-based practice. Empirical-based practice, which has had a long history in many professions, emphasizes ways of knowing that are derived from scientific research. Evidence-based practice involves a broader purview than empirical-based practice. Evidence-based practice can involve phenomena that are both observed and unobserved,.or intuited. In offering a definition of evidence-based practice, Cournoyer reminds us that social work has yet to reach consensus about what constitutes sound evidence. Based on this assertion, it is reasonable to conclude that what constitutes the basis for effective practice may depend on what one views as legitimate evidence. Moreover, in the absence of practice models specific to the needs of African American children and families, how are child welfare professionals to determine the basis for effective intervention? In fact it is the lack of evidence-based models that has resulted in child welfare professionals using their instinct, intuition, or judgment to conclude which practice approaches are best. Of course, subjective assessments are riddled with bias and prejudices that not only negatively affect client outcomes but also result in clients being unduly judged and mismatched with services.

Marshall (1998) defines advocacy research as a type of descriptive policy research done with the purpose of heightening public awareness of social problems so that action can be taken to ameliorate the problems. The cultural adaptation framework that we present in this book espouses an advocacy approach to research that includes data convening/participation, data gathering, and data diffusion. Data convening involves the participation of professionals and people indigenous to the child welfare experience. Child welfare research on behalf of African American children and families should operate along the lines of what is referred to as *engaged research* in which the target population and other stakeholders are incorporated into research designs, decision making, and data collection. The cultural adaptation to research presented here advances data-gathering strategies for using child welfare informatics that help to set policy directions to change African American's experiences in the child welfare system. As cultural adaptations are made to policies and services, accurate and timely data will be vital; thus the rationale for an African American child welfare informatics system. Finally, the data diffusion strategies presented serve to accomplish four major purposes: (1) raising awareness, (2) promoting desired change, (3) solidifying workforce preparation, and (4) developing organizational commitment to embrace new practices (Chadwick Center on Children and Families, 2004).

The cultural adaptation to research called for in this book involves the use of performance-based service authority as one strategy for promoting more accountability for the outcomes experienced by African American children in the child welfare system. The cultural adaptation to research framework involves multiple strategies for increasing system accountability. For example, local child welfare system performance would be defined collectively by a broad stakeholder base. Also, research demonstration sites would be established to evaluate the effectiveness of performance-based allocation of federal funding to local private entities or public-private partnerships that prevent and reduce out-of-home child placement rates. Chapter 7 presents a discussion of the strategies, challenges, and possible benefits of implementing and researching performance-based service authority models.

SUMMARY AND CONCLUSION

African American children are not abused or neglected more often than any other ethnic group of children. Yet under states' mandates to provide child protection, African American children are removed from their homes in disproportionate numbers. Statistical patterns suggest race-based bias, and we must therefore institute reform in investigation, assessment, court procedures, and foster care. We must reform the well-being aspect of child welfare services. Purportedly, African American children are removed from their homes to protect them from abusive and neglectful parents, but the system does not correct the physical and mental health, education, and legal difficulties that the children experience, and in some instances it actually exacerbates them.

Like child safety, achieving permanency for children involved in the child welfare system is an important objective. Although African American children are removed from their parents at rates disproportionately higher than those of any other ethnic group, the system does not provide equitable access to such services as counseling, support, reunification, and family preservation. Also, the pattern of disproportionality that African American children experience throughout every service point ends when it comes to adoption. Although removed at higher rates, African American children are not adopted at higher rates than those of their ethnic counterparts. It is clear that reform is needed in the provision of permanency services.

In this introductory chapter we have presented the case for why change to the child welfare system is needed on behalf of African American children. We defined the concept of cultural adaptation and addressed the risks and benefits of its use. The chapters that follow provide direction for how a cultural adaption to policy, practice, and research can be used in the child welfare system to improve the outcomes experienced by African American children.

DISCUSSION QUESTIONS

1. Discuss three practical things that a child welfare worker can do on a daily basis to illustrate that he or she is making cultural adaptations appropriate to fit the needs of his or her African American client family.

2. It has been suggested that cultural adaptations of existing programming amount to a debate concerning "fit vs. fidelity." Discuss whether it is more important that models, strategies, and interventions be implemented exactly as designed or that models be adjusted so that they are culturally appropriate and responsive to the needs of diverse client populations.

ACTIVITIES FOR ONGOING LEARNING

1. Work as a group of three. One person should contact a local child welfare worker. Another person should contact a local child welfare administrator. The third person should contact a child welfare supervisor. Conduct a brief interview during which you ask the assigned official to pinpoint strategies and approaches that have been used to make necessary cultural adaptations to better serve the African American children and families cared for by the person's agency/system.

2. Rates of child abuse and neglect do not differ by ethnic groups. Develop an issue brief (three to five pages) that discusses the reasons for African American children's disproportionate representation in the child welfare system.

REFERENCES

Ahrens, K. R., D. L. DuBois, L. P. Richardson, M. Y. Fan, & P. Lozano. 2008. "Youth in Foster Care with Adult Mentors During Adolescence Have Improved Adult Outcomes." *Pediatrics* 121 (2): e246–52.

Allen, D. G. 1996. "Knowledge, Politics, Culture and Gender: A Discourse Perspective. *Canadian Journal of Nursing Research* 28 (1): 95–102.

Allen, M. 1993. *Making a Difference for Families: Family-Based Services in the 1990s. The Prevention Report.* National Resource Center for Family Centered Practice. Iowa City: University of Iowa School of Social Work.

Altschuler, S. 1997. "Reveille for School Social Workers: Children in Foster Care Need Our Help." *Social Work in Education* 19:121–27.

Ards, S., C. Chung, & S. Myers. 1999. "Letter to the Editor." *Child Abuse and Neglect* 23:244.

Ards, S. D., S. L. Myers, A. Malkis, E. Sugrue, & L. Zhou. 2003. "Racial Disproportionality in Reported and Substantiated Child Abuse and Neglect: An Examination of Systematic Bias." *Children and Youth Services Review* 25 (5/6): 375–92.

Banks, J. A., C. A. Banks, & C. A. McGee. 1989. *Multicultural Education.* Needham Heights, Mass.: Allyn & Bacon.

Barber, A., & K. Jager. 2007–2008. "Collaborative and Empowering Practices with African American Families in Child Welfare." *Michigan Child Welfare Law Journal* 11 (2): 3–10.

Barger, W. K. 2009. "Cultural Adaptation: A Model from the Canadian North." *Anthropology and Humanism Quarterly* 7 (2–3): 17–21.

Barth, R., J. Wildfire, & R. Green. 2006. "Placement into Foster Care and the Interplay of Urbanicity, Child Behavior Problems, and Poverty." *American Journal of Orthopsychiatry* 76 (3): 358–66.

Beckett, J. O., & N. L. Lee. 2004. "Informing the Future of Child Welfare Practices with African American Families." In *Child Welfare Revisited: An Africentric Perspective.* Edited by J. Everett, S. Stukes Chipungu, & B. Leashore. Piscataway, N.J.: Rutgers University Press.

Bellamy, J. L. 2008. "Behavioral Problems Following Reunification of Children in Long-Term Foster Care." *Children and Youth Services Review* 30 (2): 216–28.

Benedict, M., R. White, R. Stallings, & D. Corneley. (1989). "Racial Differences in Health Care Utilization among Children in Foster Care." *Children and Youth Services Review* 11:285–97.

Berman, S., & S. Carpenter. 2004. *Children in Foster and Kinship Care at Risk for Inadequate Health Care Coverage and Access.* http://www.hcfo.org/pdf/findings0704.pdf.

Billingsley, A., & J. M. Giovannoni. 1972. *Children of the Storm.* New York: Harcourt Brace Jovanovich.

Carlson, B., H. Matto, C. Smith, & M. Eversman. 2006. "A Pilot Study of Re-unification Following Drug Abuse Treatment: Recovering the Mother Role." *Journal of Drug Issues* 22:878–902.

Casey Family Program. 2004. A *Road Map to Learning: Improving Educational Outcomes in Foster Care*. Seattle: Casey Family Program.

Castro, F. G., M. Barrera, & C. R. Martinez. 2004. "The Cultural Adaptation of Prevention Interventions: Resolving Tensions Between Fidelity and Fit." *Prevention Science* 5 (1): 41–45.

Catalano, R. P., J. D. Hawkins, C. Krenz, M. Gillmore, D. Morrison, E. Wells, et al. 1993. "Using Research to Guide Culturally Appropriate Drug Abuse Prevention." *Journal of Consulting and Clinical Psychology* 61:804–11.

Chadwick Center on Children and Families. 2004. *Closing the Quality Chasm in Child Abuse Treatment: Identifying And Disseminating Best Practices*. San Diego: Chadwick Center on Children and Families.

Chibnall, S., N. M. Dutch, B. Jones-Harden, A. Brown, R. Gourdine, J. Smith, A. Boone, & S. Snyder. 2003. *Children of Color in the Child Welfare System: Perspectives from the Child Welfare Community*. Washington, D.C.: U.S. Department of Health and Human Services, Children's Bureau.

Child Welfare League of America. 1997. *Sacramento County Community Intervention Program: Findings from a Comprehensive Study by Community Partners in Child Welfare, Law Enforcement, Juvenile Justice, and the Child Welfare League of America*. Washington, D.C.: Child Welfare League of America.

———. 2008. CWLA Testimony to the House Subcommittee on Income Security and Family Support for the Hearing on Racial Disproportionality in Foster Care. http://www.cwla.org/advocacy/fostercare080731.htm.

Close, M. M. 1983. "Child Welfare and People of Color: Denial of Equal Access." *Social Work Research and Abstracts* 19 (4): 13–20.

Coard, S., S. Foy-Watson, C. Zimmer, & A. Wallace. 2007. "Considering Culturally Relevant Parenting Practices in Intervention Development and Adaptation: A Randomized Control Trial of the Black Parenting Strengths and Strategies (BPSS) Program." *Counseling Psychologist* 35:797–820.

Cohen, D. L. 1991. "Foster Youths Said to Get Little Help with Educational Deficits." *Education Week on the Web*. http://www.edweek.org/login.html?source= http://www.edweek.org/ew/articles/1991/06/12/10320025.h10.html&destination=http://www.edweek.org/ew/articles/1991/06/12/10320025.h10.html&levelId=2100.

Collins, M. E., R. Spencer, & R. Ward. 2010. "Supporting Youth in the Transition From Foster Care: Formal and Informal Connections." *Child Welfare* 89 (1): 125–43.

Cook, R. 1991. *A National Evaluation of Title IV-E Foster Care Independent Living Programs for Youth*. Rockville, Md.: Westat.

Cournoyer, B. R. 2004. *The Evidence-Based Social Work Skills Book*. Boston: Pearson.

Courtney, M. E. 1994. "Factors Associated with the Reunification of Foster Children with Their Families." *Social Service Review* 68 (1):81–108.

Courtney, M. E., R. P. Barth, J. D. Berrick, D. Brooks, B. Needell, & L. Park. 1996. "Race and Child Welfare Services: Past Research and Future Directions." *Child Welfare* 75:99–135.

Courtney, M., A. Dworsky, G. Ruth, T. Keller, J. Havlicek, & N. Bost. 2005. *Midwest Evaluation of the Adult Functioning of Former Foster Youth: Outcomes at Age 19.* Chicago: Chapin Hall Center for Children at the University of Chicago.

Courtney, M. E., I. Piliavin, A. Grogan-Kaylor, & A. Neesmith. 2001. "Foster Youth Transitions to Adulthood: A Longitudinal View of Youth Leaving Care." *Child Welfare* 80 (6): 685–717.

Curtis, C. M., & R. Denby. 2004. "Impact of ASFA (1997) on Families of Color: Workers Share Their Thoughts." *Families in Society: Journal of Contemporary Human Services* 85 (1): 71–79.

Damen, L. 1987. *Culture Learning: The Fifth Dimension in the Language Classroom.* Reading, Mass.: Addison-Wesley.

Davis, A., C. Tsukida, S. Marchionna, & B. Krisberg. 2008. *The Declining Number of Youth in Custody in the Juvenile Justice System.* Oakland: National Council on Crime and Delinquency.

Denby, R. W. 2011. "Predicting Permanency Intentions Among Kinship Caregivers." *Child and Adolescent Social Work Journal* 28 (2): 113–31.

———. 2012. "Parental Incarceration and Kinship Care: Caregiver Experiences, Child Well-Being and Permanency Intentions." *Social Work in Public Health* 27 (1/2): 104–28.

Denby, R., K. Alford, & C. Curtis 2003. "Targeting Special Populations for Family Preservation: The Influence of Worker Competence and Organizational Culture." *Family Preservation Journal* 7:19–41.

Denby, R., & C. M. Curtis. 2003. "Why Children of Color Are Not the Target of Family Preservation Services: A Case for Program Reform." *Journal of Sociology and Social Welfare* 30 (2): 149–73.

Dixon, J. 2008. "The African American Child Welfare Act: A legal Redress for African American Disproportionality in Child Protection Cases." *Berkeley Journal of African-American Law and Policy,* 109–45.

Drake, B., J. M. Jolley, P. Lanier, J. Fluke, R. P. Barth, & M. Jonson-Reid. 2011. "Racial Bias in Child Protection? A Comparison of Competing Explanations Using National Data." *Pediatrics* 127 (3): 471–78.

Dworsky, A., & M. E. Courtney. 2010. "The Risk of Teenage Pregnancy Among Transitioning Foster Care Youth: Implications for Extending State Care Beyond Age 18." *Children and Youth Services Review* 32 (10): 1351–56.

Eckenrode, J., J. Powers, J. Doris, J. Munsch, & N. Bolger. 1988. "Substantiation of Child Abuse and Neglect Reports." *Journal of Consulting and Clinical Psychology* 56:9–16.

Edwards, K., & A. Hertel-Fernandez. 2011. *The Kids Aren't Alright: A Labor Market Analysis of Young Workers.* Economic Policy Institute. http://www.epi.org/page/-/bp258/bp258.pdf?nocdn=1.

Elliott, D. S., & S. Mihalic. 2004. "Issues in Disseminating and Replicating Effective Prevention Programs." *Prevention Science* 5:47–53.

Finch, S. J., & D. Fanshel. 1985. "Testing the Equality of Discharge Patterns in Foster Care." *Social Work Research and Abstracts* 21 (3): 3–10.

Fluke J. D., Y. T. Yuan, J. Hedderson, & P. A. Curtis. 2003. "Disproportionate Representation of Race and Ethnicity in Child Maltreatment: Investigation and Victimization." *Children and Youth Services Review* 25 (5/6): 359–73.

Fuller-Thomsen, E., & M. Minkler. 2000. "The Mental and Physical Health of Grandmothers Who Are Raising Their Grandchildren." *Journal of Mental Health and Aging* 6 (4): 311–23.

Garland, A. F., R. L. Hough, J. A. Landsverk, K. M. McCabe, M. Yeh, W. C. Ganger, & B. J. Reynolds. 2000. "Racial and Ethnic Variations in Mental Health Care Utilization Among Children in Foster Care." *Children's Services* 3 (3): 133–46.

Garland, A. F., J. A. Landsverk, & A. S. Lau. 2003. "Racial/Ethnic Disparities in Mental Health Service Use Among Children in Foster Care." *Children and Youth Services Review* 25 (5–6): 491–507.

Gavazzi, S. M., K. A. Alford, & P. C. McKenry. 1996. "Culturally Specific Programs for Foster Care Youth: The Sample Case of an African American Rites of Passage Program." *Family Relations* 45:166–74.

Gordon, R. 1998. *Education and Race.* Oakland: Applied Research Center.

Gorman, J., & L. Balter. 1997. "Culturally Sensitive Parent Education: A Critical Review of Quantitative Research." *Review of Educational Research* 67 (3): 339–69.

Gowen, L. K. 2011. "Introduction: Healthy Relationships." *Focal Point* 25:3–4.

Gray, S. S., & L. M. Nybell. 1990. "Issues in African American Family Preservation." *Child Welfare* 69 (6): 513–23.

Greeson, J. K. P., & N. K. Bowen. 2008. " 'She Holds My Hand': The Experiences of Foster Youth with Their Natural Mentors." *Children and Youth Services Review* 30 (10): 1178–88.

Hairston, C. F. 2007. *Focus on Children with Incarcerated Parents: An Overview of the Research Literature.* Report prepared for the Annie E. Casey Foundation. Baltimore: Annie E. Casey.

Harachi, T. W., R. F. Catalano, & J. D. Hawkins. 1997. "Effective Recruitment for Parenting Programs Within Ethnic Minority Communities." *Child and Adolescent Social Work Journal* 14:23–39.

Haring, D. G. 1949. "Is 'Culture' Definable?" *American Sociological Review* 14 (1): 26–32.

Harris, M. S., L. J. Jackson, K. O'Brien, & P. J. Pecora. 2009. "Disproportionality in Education and Employment Outcomes of Adult Foster Care Alumni." *Children and Youth Services Review* 31:1150–59.

Heinlein, L. M., & M. Shinn. 2000. "School Mobility and Student Achievement in an Urban Setting." *Psychology in the Schools* 37:349–57.

Hill, R. B. 2006. *A Synthesis of Research on Disproportionality in Child Welfare: An Update.* Washington, D.C.: Center for Study of Social Policy & Casey Family Programs.

Hofstede, G. 1984. "National Cultures and Corporate Cultures." In *Communication Between Cultures.* Edited by L. A. Samovar & R. E. Porter. Belmont, Calif.: Wadsworth.

Hogan, P. T., & S. F. Siu. 1988. "Minority Children and the Child Welfare System: An Historical Perspective." *Social Work* 33 (6): 493–98.

Hogg Foundation for Mental Health. 2010. *Cultural Adaptations of Evidence-Based Practices.* http://www.hogg.utexas.edu/initiatives/cultural_adaptation.html.

Holleran Steiker, L. K. 2008. "Making Drug and Alcohol Prevention Relevant: Adapting Evidence-Based Curricula to Unique Adolescent Cultures." *Family & Community Health* 31 (1S): S52–S60.

Holleran Steiker, L. K., F. G. Castro, K. Kumpfer, F. F. Marsiglia, S. Coard, & L. M. Hopson. 2008. "A Dialogue Regarding Cultural Adaptation of Interventions." *Journal of Social Work Practice in the Addictions* 8 (1): 154–62.

Jackson, S. 1994. "Educating Children in Residential and Foster Care." *Oxford Review of Education* 20 (3): 267–79.

Kazdin, A. E. 1993. "Adolescent Mental Health. Prevention and Treatment Programs." *American Psychologist* 48 (2): 127–41.

Kellam, S. 1999. *The Color of Care.* http://www.connectforkids.org/.

Kemp, S. P., & J. M. Bodonyi. 2002. "Beyond Termination: Length of Stay and Predictors of Permanency for Legally Free Children." *Child Welfare* 81 (1): 58–86.

Kortenkamp, K., & J. Ehrle. 2002. *The Well-Being of Children Involved with the Child Welfare System: A National Overview.* National Survey of America's Families Series B. No. B-43. Washington, D.C.: Urban Institute.

Kumpfer, K. L., R. Alvarado, P. Smith, & N. Bellamy. 2002. "Cultural Sensitivity and Adaptation in Family-Based Prevention Intervention." *Prevention Science* 3:241–46.

Larson, A. 2010. "Children in Treatment Foster Care: Using Agency Data to Study Cross-System Child Outcomes." *Children and Youth Services Review* 32:89–97.

Lau, A. S., A. J. Litrowik, R. R. Newton, & J. Landsverk. 2003. "Going Home: The Complex Effects of Reunification on Internalizing Problems Among Children in Foster Care." *Journal of Abnormal Child Psychology* 31:345–58.

Lederach, J. P. 1995. *Preparing for Peace: Conflict Transformation Across Cultures.* Syracuse: Syracuse University Press.

Leslie, L. K., M. S. Hurlburt, J. Landsverk, R. Barth, & D. J. Slymen. 2004. "Outpatient Mental Health Services for Children in Foster Care: A National Perspective." *Child Abuse & Neglect* 28 (6): 697–712.

Libby, A.M., H. D. Orton, R. P. Barth, M. B. Webb, B. J. Burns, P. Wood, & P. Spicer. 2006. "Alcohol, Drug, and Mental Health Specialty Treatment Services and Race/Ethnicity: A National Study of Children and Families Involved with Child Welfare." *American Journal of Public Health* 96:628–31.

Linton, R. 1945. *The Cultural Background of Personality.* New York: Appleton-Century.

Mantzicopoulos, P., & D. J. Knutson. 2000. "Head Start Children: School Mobility and Achievement in the Early Grades." *Journal of Educational Research* 93:305–11.

Marshall, G. 1998. *Advocacy Research.* http://www.encyclopedia.com/doc/1O88 -advocacyresearch.html.

Martinez, C. R., Jr., & J. M. Eddy. 2005. "Effects of Culturally Adapted Parent Management Training on Latino Youth Behavioral Health Outcomes." *Journal of Consulting and Clinical Psychology* 73:841–51.

McCarthy, J., A. Marshall, J. Collins, G. Arganza, K. Deserly, & J. Milon. 2003. *A Family's Guide to the Child Welfare System.* Washington, D.C.: U.S. Department of Health and Human Services Children's Bureau.

McMillen, J. C., L. D. Scott, B. T. Zima, M. T. Ollie, M. R. Munson, & E. Spitznagel. 2004. "Use of Mental Health Services Among Older Youths in Foster Care." *Psychiatric Services* 55 (7): 811–17.

McRoy, R. G. 2005. "Overrepresentation of Children and Youth of Color in Foster Care." In *Child Welfare for the Twenty-First Century: A Handbook of Practices, Policies, and Programs.* Edited by G. Mallon & P. Hess, 623–34. New York: Columbia University Press.

———. 2008. "Acknowledging Disproportionate Outcomes and Changing Service Delivery." Special issue. *Child Welfare* 87 (2): 205–10.

Mech, E. V. 1983. "Out-of-Home Placement Rates." *Social Service Review* 57 (4): 660–67.

Merikangas, K., et al. 2010. "Lifetime Prevalence of Mental Disorders in U.S. Adolescents: Results from the National Comorbidity Survey Replication-Adolescent Supplement (NCS-A)." *Journal of the American Academy of Child & Adolescent Psychiatry* 49 (10): 980–89.

Minkler, M., E. Fuller-Thomsen, D. Miller, & D. Driver. 1997. "Depression in Grandparents Raising Grandchildren." *Archives of Family Medicine* 6:445–52.

Morton, T. 1999. "The Increasing Colorization of America's Child Welfare System: The Overrepresentation of African American Children." *Policy and Practice* 57 (4): 23–30.

National Child Welfare Resource Center for Family-Centered Practice. 2003. *Best Practice/Next Practice.* Washington, D.C.: National Child Welfare Resource Center for Family-Centered Practice.

National Coalition for the Homeless. 2008. *Homeless Fact Sheet.* http://www .nationalhomeless.org/factsheets/.

National Family Preservation Network. 2010. *What Is Intensive Family Preservation.* http://www.nfpn.org/preservation/what-is-ifps.html.

National Research Council and Institute of Medicine. 2009. *Preventing Mental, Emotional, and Behavioral Disorders Among Young People: Progress and Possibilities.* Washington, D.C.: National Academies Press.

Noonan, K., & K. Burke. 2005. Termination of Parental Rights: Which Foster Care Children Are Affected? *Social Science Journal* 42:241–56.

O'Hagan, K. 1999. "Culture, Cultural Identity, and Cultural Sensitivity in Child and Family Social Work." *Child and Family Social Work* 4:269–81.

Ortner, S. B. 1998. "Identities: Hidden Life of Class." *Journal of Anthropological Research* 54 (1): 1–17.

Park, Y. 2005. "Culture as Deficit: A Critical Discourse Analysis of the Concept of Culture in Contemporary Social Work Discourse." *Journal of Sociology & Social Welfare* 32 (3): 11–33.

Pinderhughes, E. E. 1991. "The Delivery of Child Welfare Services to African American Clients." *American Journal of Orthopsychiatry* 61 (4): 599–605.

Roberts, D. 2002. *Shattered Bonds: The Color of Child Welfare.* New York: Basic Books.

———. 2008. "The Racial Geography of Child Welfare: Toward a New Research Paradigm." *Child Welfare* 87 (2): 125–50.

Rodenberg, D. 2004. "Services to African American Children in Poverty: Institutional Discrimination in Child Welfare?" *Journal of Poverty* 8:109–30.

Rolock, N., & M. Testa. 2005. "Indicated Child Abuse and Neglect Reports: Is the Investigation Process Racially Biased?" In *Race Matters in Child Welfare: The Overrepresentation of African American Children in the System.* Edited by D. Derezotes, J. Poertner, & M. Testa, 119–30. Washington, D.C.: Child Welfare League of America.

Romanelli, L. H., K. E. Hoagwood, S. J. Kaplan, S. P. Kemp, R. L. Hartman, C. Trupin, W. Soto, P. J. Pecora, T. L. LaBarrie, P. S. Jensen, & Child Welfare-Mental Health Best Practices Group. 2009. "Best Practices for Mental Health in Child Welfare: Parent Support and Youth Empowerment Guidelines." *Child Welfare* 88 (1): 189–212.

Schorr, A. L. 2000. "The Bleak Prospect for Public Child Welfare." *Social Service Review* (March): 124–36.

Sconyers, N., D. Langill, K. Kharod, & A. Fries. 1996. *Ready, Willing, and Able? What the Record Shows About State Investments in Children, 1990–1995.* Washington, D.C.: National Association of Child Advocates.

Seaburg, J. R., & E. S. Tolley. 1986. "Predictors of the Length of Stay in Foster Care." *Social Work Research and Abstracts* 22 (3): 11–17.

Sedlak, A., & D. Schultz. 2001. "Race Differences in Risk of Maltreatment in the General Population." Paper presented at the Race Matters Forum, Chevy Chase, Md., January 8–9.

Smith, B. D. 2003. "After Parental Rights Are Terminated: Factors Associated with Exiting Foster Care." *Children and Youth Services Review* 25 (12): 965–85.

Stehno, S. 1982. "Differential Treatment of Minority Children in Service Systems." *Social Work* 27 (1): 39–45.

————. 1990. "The Elusive Continuum of Child Welfare Services: Implications for Minority Children and Youths." *Child Welfare* 69 (6): 551–62.

Stein, M. 1994. "Leaving Care: Education and Career Trajectories." *Oxford Review of Education* 29 (3): 349–60.

Stoltzfus, E. 2011. *Child Welfare: The Child and Family Services Improvement and Innovation Act (PL 112-34).* Washington, D.C.: Congressional Research Services. http://aaicama.org/cms/federal-docs/CRS_PL_112_34.pdf.

Testa, M. 1997. "Kinship Foster Care in Illinois." In *Child Welfare Research Review.* Vol. 2. Edited by J. D. Berrick, R. Barth, & N. Gilbert, 101–29. New York: Columbia University Press.

————. 2005. "The Changing Significance of Race and Kinship for Achieving Permanency for Foster Children." In *The Overrepresentation of African American Children in the System: Race Matters in Child Welfare.* Edited by D. M. Derezotes, J. Poertner, & M. F. Testa, 231–41. Washington, D.C.: Child Welfare League of America.

Tolchin, M. 1991. "Panel Seeks Foster Care Reform." *New York Times*, February 27. http://www.nytimes.com/1991/02/27/us/panel-seeks-foster-care-reform.html.

U.S. Department of Education, National Center for Education Statistics. 2010. *The Condition of Education 2010.* NCES 2010–028, Indicator 20. http://nces.ed.gov/fastfacts/display.asp?id=16.

U.S. Department of Health and Human Services (USDHHS). 1994. *Highlights from the Family Preservation And Support Services Program Instruction.* January. Washington, D.C.: USDHHS.

————. 2001. *Mental Health: Culture, Race and Ethnicity—A Supplement to Mental Health: A Report of the Surgeon General.* Rockville, Md.: USDHHS, Substance Abuse and Mental Health Services Administration, Center for Mental Health Services.

————. 2010a. *The AFCARS Report.* http://www.acf.hhs.gov/programs/cb/stats_research/afcars/tar/report17.htm.

U.S. Department of Health and Human Services, Administration for Children and Families, Administration on Children, Youth and Families, Children's Bureau. 2010b. *Child Maltreatment 2008.* http://www.acf.hhs.gov/programs/cb/stats_research/index.htm#can.

————. 2010c. *Adopting Children Through a Public Agency (Foster Care).* http://www.childwelfare.gov/adoption/adoptive/foster_care.cfm.

————. 2010d. *Child Welfare Information Gateway. Intake, Investigation, and Assessment.* http://www.childwelfare.gov/responding/iia/.

———. Office of Planning, Research, and Evaluation. 2010e. *Research Brief, Findings from the NSCAW Study.* http://www.acf.hhs.gov/programs/opre/abuse_neglect/nscaw/reports/children_fostercare/children_fostercare.pdf.

U.S. Government Accountability Office (GAO). 2007. *African American Children in Foster Care: Additional HHS Assistance Needed to Help States Reduce the Proportion in Care.* U.S. GAO-07–816. July. http://www.gao.gov/news.items/d07816.pdf.

Useem, J., & R. Useem. 1963. "Men in the Middle of the Third Culture: The Role of American and Nonwestern People in Cross-Cultural Administration." *Human Organizations* 22 (3): 169–79.

Wagner, J., & Wonacott, M. 2008. *Youth Aging Out of Foster Care.* Learning Work Connection, Youth Work Information Brief, No. 34. http://cle.osu.edu/lwc-publications/youth-information-briefs/downloads/Youth-Aging-Out-of-Foster-Care.pdf.

Waites, C. 2009. "Building on Strengths: Intergenerational Practice with African American Families." *Social Work* 54 (3): 278–87.

Wells, K., & S. Guo. 1999. "Reunification and Reentry of Foster Children." *Children and Youth Services Review* 21 (4): 273–94.

Wells, S., L. Merritt, & H. Briggs 2009. "Bias, Racism and Evidence-Based Practice: The Case for More Focused Development of the Child Welfare Evidence Base." *Children and Youth Services Review* 31 (11): 1160–71.

Wertheimer, R. 2002. Youth Who "'Age Out' of Foster Care: Troubled Lives, Troubling Prospects." *Child Trends* 59:1–8. Washington, D.C.: Annie E. Casey Foundation: Child Trends.

Whaley, A. L. 2003. "Ethnicity/Race, Ethics, and Epidemiology." *Journal of the National Medical Association* 95 (8): 736–42.

Whaley, A. L., & K. E. Davis. 2007. "Cultural Competence and Evidence-Based Practice in Mental Health Services." *American Psychologist* 62 (6): 563–74.

Williams, C. 1993. "Red Tape Snags Poor: Improved System Sought." *Arizona Republic.* January 10, A12.

Wolanin, T. 2005. *Higher Education Opportunities for Foster Youth: A Primer for Policymakers.* Institute for Higher Education Policy. http://www.ihep.org/assets/files/publications/m-r/OpportunitiesFosterYouth.pdf.

Yancey, A. K. 1998. "Building Positive Self-Image in Adolescents in Foster Care: The Use of Role Models in an Interactive Group Approach." *Adolescence* 33: 253–67.

2

Child Welfare in Perspective

Historical Factors Influencing African American Families and Policy Formulation

SOCIOPOLITICAL FACTORS

This book primarily examines the effect of the child welfare system on African American children and families, directing special attention to those aspects of the system that work now and those that could serve families more effectively if they were culturally adapted and improved. This focus requires a thoughtful, analytical understanding of past child welfare policy or laws and a thorough consideration of the social condition of African American families today, along with the factors that affect that condition. Paradoxically, in the United States the law has been alternatively the basis for discrimination and also a means of protecting the civil rights of African Americans.

Slavery

Some legal scholars suggest that slavery in the United States was supported in the Constitution by the founding fathers to ensure a sovereign and viable economy (Azmy, 2002; see also Curtis & Denby, 2011). Whether or not one believes slavery was assumed to be essential to the economic well-being of the United States, clearly the Thirteenth Amendment to the Constitution officially ended chattel slavery in the country (Azmy, 2002). The Thirteenth Amendment states: "Neither slavery nor involuntary servitude, except as a punishment for crime whereof the party shall have been duly convicted, shall exist within the United States, or any place subject to their jurisdiction." The legacy of racism institutionalized through slavery did not disappear with the adoption of this amendment, however, and the effect of racism on the African American family continued to be disabling.

The Civil Rights Act of 1866 was enacted on the authority of the Thirteenth Amendment; both documents were expected to guarantee all persons equal fundamental rights (Azmy, 2002). Economic independence and social mobility for African Americans were expected to follow. However, the stated goal of the government after the passage of the Thirteenth Amendment and the Civil Rights Act of 1866 was not to create equality and civil rights for all; on the contrary, the period after the Civil War—the Reconstruction era—was characterized by the enactment of laws and practices that resulted in an informal system of slave labor. The involuntary servitude that characterized the Reconstruction era was institutionalized through enactment of Black Codes that tied African Americans and eventually immigrant whites to "long periods of debt bondage, known as peonage. Peonage was chattel slavery's direct descendant and generated nearly equally harsh images of convict labor and an all-black chain gang" (Azmy, 2002:4). Life for the African American family at this time was characterized by demeaning conditions, total dominion by others over their economic opportunity through the use of private coercive labor agreements, and family strife and disruption.

The African American family was seriously damaged by the period of slavery, as relationships and familial interactions were often fractured. According to one historical account of family life during this era, "One of the slaves' principal indictments of chattel slavery was its violation of the bond between parent and child" (Berlin & Rowland, 1997:193). The practice of slavery allowed many thousands of children, adolescents, and young adults to be removed from their families and sold into the slave trade across the lower South, especially to work in the cotton fields.

Enslaved parents had no legal claim to their sons and daughters, who were, like themselves, property. In theory, the property owners were responsible for the well-being and care of their wards; however, some parents found ways to influence the lives of their children in spite of their owners. "Parents directed the activities of their children, shaped the conditions of their daily lives, and guided their development under circumstances dictated by the owner, not the parents" (Berlin & Rowland, 1997:193). Enslaved African Americans saw childrearing as the work of their whole community, and they attempted to prepare the children for the dehumanizing experience life held for them.

The Reconstruction period provided even greater challenges in some regards. The introduction of the Black Codes or Jim Crow laws resulted in demeaning social conditions and economic domination. Parents expected that emancipation would give them "the opportunity to gain control over their own progeny" (Berlin & Rowland, 1997:193), but in addition to limitations that individuals experienced trying to provide for themselves and their families, legal battles are recorded of former slave owners refusing to relinquish custody of enslaved children to their parents or family members. While former owners abdicated responsibility for the care of elders who had devoted their lives to service, legal battles over children were numerous and primarily economic in nature. It has been argued that child labor was a necessary support for freed families struggling to establish economic stability, particularly in the agricultural lower South; former slaveholders sought to regain control over their property, often resulting in child labor (Berlin & Rowland, 1997; Gutman, 1976).

Status of the African American Family

One reason for reviewing the social history of the African American family here is to examine the primary link through which culture is transmitted. The social pathology of life experiences during and after slavery has arguably had lasting if not permanent effects on the culture and development of familial relationships among families of African descent (Berlin & Rowland, 1997; Frazier, 1957; Gutman, 1976).

In 1965 Daniel Patrick Moynihan generated much controversy and impassioned debate with the publication of his book *The Negro Family: The Call for National Action.* In effect, Moynihan asserted that after World War II, migration of poor southern African Americans to northern cities, coupled with high unemployment, resulted in "the deterioration of the Negro family." Strained circumstances of family life resulted in some husbands leaving their families for work so that wives were left to care for their children, while other fathers "deserted," leaving women to raise children alone, without the benefit of a husband (Moynihan, 1965).

Some criticized Moynihan's work, and others felt that it offered some explanation of the breakdown in the nuclear family in urban centers across the nation. It is true that Moynihan drew from the work of others, like noted black historian E. Franklin Frazier and Stanley M. Elkins, who analyzed the experiences of low-income African American families in urban areas after slavery and reconstruction (Gutman, 1976). This period in history—the late 1890s through the late 1920s—is referred to as the era of social reform.

During the time he studied the family, Frazier (1957) pointed out the weaknesses within the African American family unit, including the growing presence of the matriarchal prototype. Frazier asserted that the negative qualities of family life among low-income black families were tied to seventeenth- and eighteenth-century African slavery and its aftermath. Moynihan (1965) asserted that the presence of the matriarchy was pathological, and he declared that this pattern of pathology began during the slave trade era and continued into the postindustrial era and beyond (Hill, 1972).

Some people have criticized and challenged Frazier because his initial assessment of urban, low-income African American families was not balanced. Acknowledging that weaknesses and problems existed in the postslavery family, we should consider the sociopolitical and economic effects of slavery. Perhaps more important, the ability of any population to endure and survive such oppression and inhumane treatment is a testament to unparalleled strength and collective determination. Robert Hill's analysis of Frazier's complete body of work posits a "more balanced treatment of urban black families than is commonly believed" (1972:57). Hill suggests that Frazier's work was exploited by those who did not bother to test his theories or consider other data that were not available to Frazier when his work was first published but were documented later.

Despite the controversy around the publication of Moynihan's work, the report spurred others to consider and challenge postulations about the culture and socialization of the black family. In a comprehensive study of family life among African Americans prior to and after emancipation, historian Herbert G. Gutman (1976) examined census schedules in urban and rural settings. Gutman hypothesized that if the assertions of Frazier and others concerning the "weaknesses" in the black family during the period of social reform were true, and if Moynihan's assertions were correct concerning the condition of black family life during the 1950s and 1960s, similar patterns of social confusion and disintegration within the black family should be present both during slavery and immediately following emancipation.

Gutman examined the condition of ex-slave marriages and households in 1865 and 1866 based on recordings by the Freedman's Bureau. Added to these analyses were data collected from throughout the state of New York from the late nineteenth century through 1925. The conclusions offer a different view of family life for African Americans both during slavery and after emancipation. Findings reveal the capacity of families to develop and maintain meaningful domestic arrangements. Reports of intact family units both during and after slavery are documented; there are personal letters of women maintaining communication with the fathers of their children who were sent to serve in the Union army during the Civil War. After the war it was rare that families reconnected; however, women actively sought out the fathers of their children, and some women married surviving soldiers to provide a home for the children. Letters from African American soldiers who fought in the Civil War and who were distraught over the vestiges of war and the agony over the separation from their women and children are fully documented (Berlin & Rowland, 1997; Gutman, 1976).

The work of Gutman and others provides a view of family life for slave and former slave families as impassioned and deeply concerned about family members and loved ones (Berlin & Rowland, 1997). Gutman documents the efforts of fathers in the state of New York in the 1920s to connect with their children, even when economic survival was uncertain. This documentation of the social history and nature of families during difficult times demonstrates that the importance of family was shared and passed through the generations during a period of extreme chaos and demeaning conditions for African Americans. "Socialization nearly always occurs first in families, and it is through families that historically derived beliefs usually pass from generation to generation" (Gutman, 1976:xxi). This is a particularly important point in light of the social confusion and disorganization that plagued the lives of newly freed people.

As Joyce Ladner (1971), Andrew Billingsley (1968), and Robert Hill (1972) effectively demonstrate through research, the viability and legitimacy of the family, but particularly a family shrouded in the darkness of a history of forced servitude, must be considered from a balanced perspective—a strengths perspective. When considering the strengths of African American families, Vernon E. Jordan stated that "despite tremendous odds, the black family has been a bulwark of black achievement, that it has proved a flexible and adaptable instrument of black survival, and that it has been the nourishing foundation of positive aspects of the black experience" (quoted in Hill, 1972:x).

THE EFFECT OF SOCIAL AND POLITICAL FACTORS ON POLICY

The institution of slavery in this country is typically characterized by social and political historians as an economic institution. However characterized, the system of economically based servitude shrouded in a belief system that certain people of color were inherently inferior left a legacy of institutional racism and discrimination resulting in segregated systems of public accommodations and services for a major portion of our recent history. Segregation by race was institutionalized with the enactment of Black Codes and other laws that sanctioned discrimination based on race. We did not experience legal challenges to sanctioned segregation until 1948, when President Harry Truman, through executive order, called for the desegregation of facilities used by the armed forces, and later in *Brown v. Board of Education of Topeka* when the U.S. Supreme Court held that racial classification was unreasonable because it was damaging to African American children. "It was not until the early 1960's that the U.S. Supreme Court ruled as unconstitutional the last of the laws from the Jim Crow era" (Alexander, 2005:20).

The system of child welfare was racially segregated for many years. Though racial segregation is not legally sanctioned today, the child welfare system is still characterized by inequity and differential treatment (Curtis & Denby, 2004; Denby & Curtis, 2003; Roberts, 2002). The evolution of this structured system and some of the major themes that have characterized service goals and objectives are revealed through a review of the history of child welfare in the United States. A more detailed look at the policy framework for child welfare today is considered in chapter 3.

Policies that inform the child welfare system emanate from a lawmaking process within the U.S. government. Because people of African descent were viewed and treated as less than human during the era of slavery and reconstruction, laws and practices that were first put in place to ensure the health and safety of children in this country were not intended for children of African descent or for Native Americans, who first inhabited this country.

There is a legal basis for child welfare in the United States. Prior to the nineteenth century, the principal objectives for a legal system in relationship to children were related to "reinforcing social sanctions against proscribed conduct and . . . protecting private interests in property" (Rosenheim, 1976:423). English common law, and American law that followed, did not set forth blanket protections that were universally applied to children or "minor age" individuals.

Historical Beginnings of Out-of-Home Care

During the colonial period, as today, the term *parens patriae* referred to the presumption that government entities will assume responsibility for the care of children when their parents are unwilling or unable to do so. This concept involved the sovereign right of the government (the king under English common law) to assume authority and to protect children. This right was initially intended to control any income generated as a property right during the feudal period in England; in colonial America *parens patriae* was intended to address the needs of children orphaned and neglected in the New World. However, for the children of African descent who were orphaned or left without a family or parent owing to their treatment as chattel of the slave trade, any support provided was generated through the system of slavery.

Caring for children removed from their family is firmly established with the history of traditions, practices, and policies for substitute care that formally commenced during colonial times. The current practice of legally making permanent the separation of parent from child also had its origin during this period of history (Wilhelmus, 1998). Legal proceedings were rare because children were often informally removed from their homes, families, and loved ones. Severed parent-child relationships resulted in children being placed in orphanages, used as cheap labor, apprenticed out to artisans, and placed in almshouses or work houses.

Acts of severing parent-child relationships, whether informal or formal (legally determined), were established through *parens patriae*. Though rare, external to the institution of slavery, children were permanently removed from their family home if parents refused to place a child in service if directed to do so by the town authorities; parents who refused to attend religious services also had children removed from their homes (Costin, 1985). Idleness and poverty were viewed as personal weaknesses, and therefore settlers were not motivated or expected to "be their brothers' keeper"; such intervention would be contrary to Calvinist social theory and theology that placed great importance on individual effort and hard work and viewed idleness as "ungodly" (Trattner, 1989).

A system of apprenticeship, or indenture, borrowed from England permitted local authorities in charge of the poor to place a child with an artisan or workman. The workman's household provided safety and security as well as an opportunity for the child to learn a trade. History provides mixed evidence about this system: some accounts assert that children were harshly treated, while others portray a system that was successful. Indentured children fared better than children who were committed to almshouses (Costin, 1985).

Also borrowed from England, the Elizabethan Poor Laws established an obligatory tax to address the needs of the poor and residency requirements so that aid would not be provided unless residence was established. Creation of this tax-based system became a critical resource for managing a growing demand to support the poor and dependent children.

Growth in population and the onset of industrialization influenced the need for options to care for those who were unable to work, as well as for orphaned children. Outdoor relief, or public aid, and indoor aid, also called almshouses, provided support for children not cared for through indenture. Outdoor relief was provided to families and enabled children to remain in their homes. However, when families received relief, the Calvinistic orientation ensured that they would be ostracized by the community and their lives would be miserable (Costin, 1985).

Indoor relief required children to be confined to almshouses with adults, many of them criminals, mentally ill, and aged. Accounts of the treatment of children in these institutions were publicized and coincided with a growing recognition in the nineteenth century of the unique developmental needs of children, previously viewed as "little adults." Recognition of childhood as a unique period of development resulted in a growing number of institutions directed to serve only children.

Though limited to serving only children, many orphanages continued to be characterized by harsh conditions, including unsanitary conditions, poor or no educational offerings, substandard medical care, the use of corporal punishment, and sexual abuse (Wilhelmus, 1998). Orphanages existed in nearly every state, and the conditions or practices that characterized these institutions varied greatly. Many were managed by religious groups. Facilities run by profit-motivated managers were overcrowded; services and educational support were kept to a minimum. Religious-managed facilities were better maintained. Policies limiting adult contact with children were imposed, and most programs required strict religious instruction (Costin, 1985). Institutional life was generally very labor intensive and restrictive.

Social Reform's New Approaches

Efforts to improve the conditions and experiences of dependent children in orphanages did not produce major changes prior to the nineteenth century. During the nineteenth century, however, there was a major dissemination of child development theories that acknowledged the potential negative effects of long-term institutionalization—specifically, such care could limit appropriate developmental growth and the acquisition of needed life skills (Grotberg, 1977).

It was during this time that the New York Children's Aid Society adopted a practice of "placing-out" dependent children to family homes, used by some missionaries in urban centers. Reverend Charles Loring Brace believed that this practice would enable better control of "dangerous classes" of immigrant families whose children were not always well kept or were left to care for themselves and run the streets in the urban cities of the industrialized northeast (Trattner, 1989; see also Curtis & Denby, 2011). It was during this time that the first cases of physical maltreatment of children were publicly acknowledged and documented.

In the mid-1850s Brace's strategy was to relocate children from the dark, crime-ridden streets in cities to the open frontier states of the Midwest and Great Plains regions. The presumption of *parens patriae* enabled Brace to intervene in the lives of children on behalf of the government. Children were placed on trains (referred to as orphan trains) that moved them across the country, stopping at strategic points along the way. Christian homeowners would come to the train station, observe the children, and typically select younger ones to take into their homes and adopt as their own, or older ones who could offer a much-needed source of the cheap labor that was essential to developing the land and establishing a homestead in underdeveloped parts of the country (Trattner, 1989). Children of African descent and Native American children were not included in this child welfare reform effort.

As settlers moved westward, the frontier was more agrarian, unlike the Northeast and Northwest, where the introduction of the railroad enhanced industrialization. Brace was convinced that life outside the city was a better environment for raising children, and therefore the orphan trains transported children westward. Approximately 50,000 children were sent away from New York and placed in cities and communities throughout the west. Many sibling groups were separated and never heard from each other again. In total approximately 200,000 children were removed from their families and sibling groups via orphan train placements between 1854 and 1929. Decades later, some siblings in their seventies and eighties were reunited for the first time since infancy or early childhood (Warren, 1996).

The motivation behind Brace's so-called rescue movement is uncertain. It has been suggested that his dislike for poor and immigrant families prompted his actions; on the other hand, concern about increasing gang affiliation and vagrancy among minor youth and prostitution rings that preyed on the vulnerability of dependent children and youths are also believed to have motivated him. While his actions recognized, in theory, the importance of family life, the need to support poor children in their own home with their immigrant families was not a priority (Trattner, 1989).

Interestingly, the professionalization of social work began in the latter part of the nineteenth century. Two primary strategies evolved for working with children and families who migrated to the United States and struggled with language and cultural differences: social casework emphasized the importance of personal change to correct nonsocial behaviors and promote conformity with the cultural standards of the day, and settlement work stressed structural or macro changes to better accommodate the unique needs of immigrant families from different cultural backgrounds to facilitate their transition to a different way of life.

Policy Exclusion of African American Families

Many freed slaves and their families migrated to the "free North" during this same period. Looking for employment and opportunities to rebuild their families and become independent and self-sufficient, African

Americans migrated en masse north of the Mason-Dixon Line seeking the same jobs associated with developing industrialization that were also sought by emigrants from other countries seeking a new life in America.

African American families were not, however, the target of reform work among social workers. Be it a social casework or settlement house orientation, there was no cultural adaptation of existing programs or policies to address the needs of African Americans. Consequently they established their own institutions that provided needed social support and services, such as fraternal organizations that helped create networks for finding employment and health care (Karger & Stoesz, 2009). These organizations served as substitutes for the mostly white settlement houses.

Yet it was settlement house workers, and among them social workers, who recognized that the social and economic limitations of immigrant poor, unskilled parents limited their ability to parent effectively (Trattner, 1989). The notion that anyone with the desire could make it in this country was not borne out in the experience of many immigrant urban dwellers challenged by a different language, culture, education, and training. By the beginning of the twentieth century, social workers' emphasis on the total environment of the family, including unemployment, homelessness, and a family's inability to care for its children, led to the creation of new systems in support of children and their families. These service systems did not typically address the needs of African Americans. From recreational and educational supports to basic public health services, burial support, support for those temporarily without housing, the need for food, help with literacy and job-related skills development, as well as the need for parental help with a developmentally challenged child, African American families came together to create self-help networks of services and support. These services were available to the extent self-help or self-support initiatives among African American families were put in place. For extensive discussions of the strengths of African American families and their patterns of family life during and after slavery, see Franklin and Higginbotham's *From Slavery to Freedom* (2011), Hill's *Strengths of Black Families* (1972), and Gutman's *The Black Family in Slavery and Freedom* (1976).

The discontinuation of reliance on orphan trains and a focus on assisting children by providing support to their families was evidenced during the first and second White House Conferences on the Care of Dependent Children in 1909 and 1919. Out of the first conference came the creation of the Children's Bureau and the call for an "unofficial" national organization aimed at promoting the care of children—the result being the Child Welfare League of America, organized in 1915 and incorporated in 1928 in New York. Advocacy efforts aimed at reforming social conditions and the focus on national, state, and local policy to benefit vulnerable children and their families were lost as the country dealt with the economic downturn and social workers changed their focus (Grotberg, 1977; Trattner, 1989).

The social work profession was criticized by sociologists and others who challenged the scientific merit of progressive intervention strategies aimed at social reform. In response, the profession began to direct more attention to the social casework model and individual deficits. Because this model centered on the strengths and weaknesses of individuals, evidence-based research protocols could more readily generate findings to demonstrate the ability of the individual to overcome fear and poor life circumstances when inner strengths are nurtured and resources provided (Trattner, 1989).

It took many years for the child welfare system to gain public attention. In the 1950s the foster care system was growing rapidly because it was believed that foster care was an ideal placement for children not suffering from serious emotional or behavioral problems. Foster care was intended to be a form of temporary treatment for a family with child behavior problems. However, in 1959 *Children in Need of Parents* was published (Maas & Engler, 1959), shattering the notion of treatment attached to foster care; children placed in care experienced long stays, and families did not receive the services necessary to terminate placement. If children were not returned to their homes within eighteen months of placement, rarely did they return to the home before aging out of placement. Children and parents were not supported in establishing visitation; when visitation was not scheduled and supported by caseworkers, the possibility of the child returning home was reduced. Not only were parent-child visits limited, agencies had no consistent contact with parents after an out-of-home placement was made (Maas & Engler, 1959).

Simultaneously, the use of contraceptives among white women increased during the late 1950s and early 1960s. Once abortion became legalized, coupled with the use of other forms of contraception and delays in parenting, live birthrates among white couples dropped. Some African American women who were not supported or served by the voluntary child welfare system and did not typically use abortion or other contraception methods began to seek other options for the care of children they could not afford to raise. As a result of these circumstances, the first placements of African American children in white homes for adoptions were made during the 1950s through private agencies or attorneys (Curtis, 1996).

This practice of placing African Americans for adoption continued to increase during the 1960s and 1970s. Informally African Americans provided childcare support for relatives and friends when parents were unable or unwilling to care for their children. Hill (1972) documented this practice, which was not acknowledged or supported by traditional child welfare agencies. When African American children were removed from their homes and placed for adoption, the number of transracial placements—placing African American children in the homes of white families—increased. The National Association of Black Social Workers challenged the appropriateness of transracial placement because of concern for the long-term effects on the child. These objections also directed attention to long-standing discrimination practices in child welfare relative to recruiting African American families as foster or adoptive parents and approving their homes for permanent or temporary placement.

NATIONAL CHILD WELFARE REFORM MOVEMENT

By the 1970s the failures associated with the child welfare system were well documented. A coalition of social workers, juvenile judges and lawyers, legislators, and others began to promote change on a variety of levels and in different arenas. Of particular concern was the phenomenon of foster care drift, or the movement of children in and out of foster care placements without the benefit of a plan to ensure permanency for them. One outcome of the growing attention to the out-of-home care system was a focused attention on the database for the system, which limited the capacity to track the outcomes of investigations into maltreatment, placement decisions, or service options provided to families. It was argued that the lack of information resulted from failure in both case management and case planning (Whitelaw-Downs, Moore, & McFadden, 2009; Wilhelmus, 1998).

A longitudinal study by Fanshel and Shinn (1978) documented findings from case studies of outcomes for children in out-of-home placements. They found that extended time in the system was also characterized by being moved from home to home. Children were not being returned to their homes, and they were not being adopted. When children were placed in one home for a period of time, there was no certainty about the permanence of the placement; they did not know when or if they would be returned to their biological parents. Fanshel (1979) also documented the experiences of younger children: toddlers entering the out-of-home system would spend an average of seven years in foster care.

Foster care placement research began to address the long-term effect of placement on mental health and self-esteem. Research affirmed the debilitating effects that long-term placement has on a child's sense of self and feelings of being loved (Fanshel & Shinn, 1978). Mnookin (1973) asserted that the "drift" in foster care creates psychological barriers that inhibit a foster child's search for stability and consistency. Other studies on attachment theory bolstered the widely held belief that "the indeterminacy and uncertainty of the foster condition inhibits development in foster children of self-confidence, a firm sense of identity, and an ability to risk close personal relationships" (Wiltse, 1985, cited in Wilhelmus, 1998). Finally, the popular book *Best Interests of the Child* affirmed the critical role of a permanent home in promoting the welfare of a child (Goldstein, Freud, & Solnit, 1973).

Increased concern about foster care drift; lack of involvement by the birth parents once children were temporarily placed; poor planning for permanent outcomes, including addressing the issues or problems that resulted in placement; and growing concerns for the future of the fastest growing segments of children in out-of-home care—African American children, Native American children, older children, and sibling groups—contributed to reform measures that culminated in the passage of the Adoption Assistance and Child Welfare Act (AACWA) of 1980 (PL 96-272). Ironically, the AACWA was intended to address many of the concerns addressed by settlement house social workers, primarily advocating parent-child reunification when the family was supported to achieve a level of functioning thought to ensure healthy growth and development for the child.

The intent of the law was to prevent out-of-home placement, reunite a child and the biological family when safe to do so, use family foster care as the preferred out-of-home placement, and foster timely adoptions when a child should not be reunited with the biological family. These goals were tied to themes associated with child welfare reform: prevention, service delivery in the least restrictive environment, permanency planning, and reunification.

Prevention is consistent with Congress's intent of keeping a family together. The law requires that preventative services be available to the family to keep children from being unnecessarily removed from their homes and placed in foster care (Public Health and Welfare, 1997). Prevention services may include crisis care, respite care, child daycare, emergency shelters, group homes, or counseling (U.S. House of Representatives, 1974). "Least restrictive environment" promotes the idea that when it is necessary for the state to intervene in a family's affairs, it should be in a format that is least disruptive to the life of the family unit. From the nineteenth century to today, the role of government in response to the concerns of children has tended to reflect a pattern of intervening aggressively and removing the child from the home, or a pattern of deferring to parental control and responsibility for the care and protection of a child.

The legislative intent around permanency and reunification is correlated to accounts of children being removed from their homes for a long period of time with no review of their cases. It was therefore impossible to determine if the circumstances that prompted placement had been corrected. Little effort was being made to reunite children with their biological families with regard to an understanding of the social conditions of the family. The goal of permanency planning is to create a process by which children are protected from institutional indifference and to ensure that a plan is in place to create a permanent home for each child; reunification with the biological parent/s or guardian is a goal when such appears to be in the best interest of the child.

Some critics have asserted that the reforms associated with the passage of the Adoption Assistance and Child Welfare Act failed (Pecora, Whitaker, & Maluccio, 1992). Analysis of the law and legislative history, including reports from Congress, may prompt another perspective (U.S. House of Representatives, 2006). The law conveys a clear intent by lawmakers; the failure came with the regulatory language that left much discretion to states in determining when and if "reasonable efforts" had been made to prevent the removal of a child from the home. PL 96-272 was passed by Congress and signed into law by President Jimmy Carter, a supporter of the reform measures articulated in law. The regulations that provided direction to states for implementing the law were subsequently promulgated under the leadership of a different group of bureaucrats committed to the ideals of new federalism espoused by President Ronald Reagan. Consistent with policy assumptions in new federalism, many social service programs experienced draconian cuts, including funding for prevention and reunification services.

There is no national criterion to define what "reasonable efforts" must include, nor the duration of such support aimed at preventing the removal of a child from the home. There are no restrictions, for example, on providing drug rehabilitation treatment for drug-addicted parents; the likelihood of such intervention to enable family reunification is minimal at best owing to costs and increasing demand for service with dwindling resources.

The law made clear that out-of-home placements should be the last option, not the first, after services to preserve or reunify the family have been exhausted or determined inappropriate. Decisions as to what is reasonable when it comes to directing a course of action and identifying services to strengthen the family's capacity are dependent on funding, agency priorities, and worker discretion. The courts ultimately determine whether the child welfare system has made reasonable efforts to prevent the removal of a child from his or her home and reasonable efforts to rehabilitate the parent or parents and reunite children and their families.

The initial focus on prevention in the AACWA changed as poorer outcomes for children in general resulted in greater emphasis on the permanency goals of the law. Funding, as previously mentioned, played a major role involving the capacity of states to serve children in the out-of-home care system. Title IV-B of the AACWA was the primary source of funding to states for family preservation and family support services. Funding for foster care maintenance and adoption (Title IV-E) was at three times the rate of preventive and reunification services. Child welfare advocates and legislators worked together to identify alternative ways of funding preventative family support services and addressing gaps in the service delivery system (Pecora, Whittacker, & Maluccio, 1992). In 1993 President Bill Clinton signed into law the Omnibus Budget Reconciliation Act, which created the Family Preservation and Support Services Program (FPSSP), an amendment to the AACWA (Public Health and Welfare, 1997).

The FPSSP amended the Adoption Assistance and Child Welfare Act by creating a separate funding stream under Title IV-B for family preservation and support services. Family preservation services are provided to families at risk of maltreatment or already in crisis. These services include, but are not limited to, counseling, respite care, and intensive services provided in the home to prevent foster care placement. Family support services include child care, parenting services, or other community-based services aimed at strengthening family functioning. The FPSSP also provides funding "for courts to assess and improve their handling of placement proceedings, for states to initiate automated data systems, and for training of staff, foster parents and adoptive parents to assist children in the child-placement system and to support the parents who adopt and foster them" (Curtis, 1996:162).

Despite the intent of the new funding stream in Title IV-B to protect and preserve the family, problems that plagued the child welfare system continue. Reports of maltreatment have increased while children entering foster care experience a system in crisis.

The first piece of legislation that followed the creation of the FPSSP that emphasized permanence was the Multiethnic Placement Act of 1994 (MEPA) (PL 103-382), sponsored by Senator Howard Metzenbaum of Ohio. This law (Sec. 552[b]) aims to reduce the time children spend in foster care by reducing the time they wait for adoption; prevent discrimination in the placement of children based on race, color, or national origin; and enable the identification and recruitment of foster and adoptive families who can meet children's needs. While Senator Metzenbaum testified that he introduced the legislation to encourage transracial adoption when same-race placements were not available, the effect was to provide ammunition to those who argue that "giving preference to same-race adoptions and foster care placement denies thousands of minority children a permanent, loving, and stable home" (Curtis, 1996:161). In 1997 additional amendments were adopted that made the law more restrictive by prohibiting public or private agencies from receiving government funds when they delay or deny adoption because of race, color, or national origin of the child or adoptive or foster parent.

The National Association of Black Social Workers (NABSW) has provided the strongest vocal opposition to transracial placements for adoption and permanent foster care. However, the organization has worked with community-based groups to develop tools to aid the adoption process when transracial placements do occur; agencies typically provide adoptive parents with resource materials to help provide culturally specific information for adopted children of different racial or ethnic heritage. This does not, however, dismiss the system's failure to actively and effectively engage communities of color, particularly the African American community, in addressing the lack of availability of families of color for foster and adoption placements in many communities throughout the country. "It is ironic that those espousing policies that are in the best interest of children seldom address the issues of licensing more African American families or eliminating the institutional barriers that inhibit the effective recruitment and retention of African American foster and adoptive parents; even less attention is given to addressing the economic and social conditions that prevent a growing number of families, regardless of race, to care effectively for their children" (Curtis, 1996:163). While structural factors may affect the capacity for building a pool of prospective families who are able to consider foster placement or adoption, structural dimensions of education, housing, employment, and income also impact family stability and the likelihood of children living with their birth parents or guardians. Race- and ethnicity-based discrimination has limited the ability of many in the areas of education, housing, and employment. For a thorough discussion of the limitations race-based discrimination may place on opportunity for economic stability and related stable family life, see chapters 5 and 6.

Emphasis on the permanency theme in the AACWA continued through the end of the twentieth century with enactment of the Adoption and Safe Families Act of 1997. Passage of this legislation was controversial in that it brought together a mix of both liberal and conservative advocates for children, as well as legislators who agreed on the pressing need to focus attention on issues related to children in foster care. Less agreement is shared around the use of reasonable efforts directed toward keeping families together or the emphasis on termination of parental rights, particularly relative to serving the black child and family (Denby & Curtis, 2003). A detailed discussion of the ASFA and other federal policies aimed at protecting the rights of children while also addressing that which is in their best interest is provided in chapter 3.

SUMMARY AND CONCLUSION

When instructing social work students in the rudimentary foundation of child welfare policy and programs, we emphasize the importance of history as the basis for understanding and evaluating what is in place now.

As a backdrop for understanding the factors that affect the well-being of African American children today, we must review the social history that has shaped the African American experience and the history of caring for children. Social workers, child and family advocates, and others working with children and their families must understand the relationship between what occurs on a day-to-day basis with clients and the formulation of laws and policy that instruct those professional working relationships. The formulation of policy, through the enactment of laws and regulations, is grounded in social traditions and values that influence our beliefs; our beliefs in turn direct the course of laws that instruct regulatory directives to guide professional practice and intervention with clients. This interactive relationship is grounded in history.

DISCUSSION QUESTIONS

1. Central to the African American experience in the United States is the institutionalization of African- and Caribbean-based slave trade. Is the slave trade experience in the United States a factor related to the disparate conditions which exist today for African American children and families in the child welfare system?

2. What would you consider the most effective mechanism is today for mitigating the disparities in child welfare: federal legislation; class action court challenges; state initiated programs and services?

3. Is there something unique to the experience of the African American family in the United States which influences the limited use of child welfare support services within this population of children and families?

ACTIVITIES FOR ONGOING LEARNING

1. Organize into small groups. Answer the following questions, using a critical-thinking perspective: ask the question, assess the facts/information, and assert a position—the triple As of critical thinking. For each question, adopt a position and share the results of the group's thinking and research.

A. Did the experience of slavery and the social and political constraints on African Americans associated with the Reconstruction era limit opportunities for cultural transmission through the institution of the family?

B. Are the values and beliefs associated with the African American family today consistent with the values and beliefs documented in this chapter as characterizing family life during slavery and its aftermath?

2. Upon completing the first assignment, prepare a response in which each group adopts the position that is directly opposite of the position adopted in responding to question 1.

3. Prepare a position paper of no more than three pages outlining the values and belief systems associated with the current child welfare system. Defend your position with documentation that is both anecdotal and data driven or fact based.

REFERENCES

Adoption Assistance and Child Welfare Act of 1980. 1357.15(e) (2), 94 Stat. 500–535, 45.

Alexander, R. 2005. *Racism, African Americans and Social Justice.* Lanham, Md.: Rowman & Littlefield.

Azmy, B. 2002. "Unshackling the Thirteenth Amendment: Modern Slavery and a Reconstructed Civil Rights Agenda." *Fordham Law Review* 71:981.

Berlin, I., & L. S. Rowland. 1997. *Families and Freedom: A Documentary History of African American Kinship in the Civil War Era.* New York: Free Press.

Billingsley, A. 1968. *Black Families in White America.* Englewood Cliffs, N.J.: Prentice Hall.

Costin, L. B. 1985. "The Historical Context of Child Welfare." In *A Handbook of Child Welfare.* Edited by J. Laird & A. Hartman, 34–60. New York: Free Press.

Curtis, C. M. 1996. "The Adoption of African American Children by Whites: A Renewed Conflict." *Families in Society: Journal of Contemporary Human Services* 77 (3): 156–65.

Curtis, C. M., & R. Denby. 2004. "Impact of the ASFA (1997) on Families of Color: Workers Share Their Thoughts." *Families in Society: Journal of Contemporary Human Services* 85 (1): 71–79.

———. 2011. African American Children in the Child Welfare System: Requiem or Reform. *Journal of Public Child Welfare* 5 (1): 111–37.

Denby, R., & C. M. Curtis. 2003. "Why Children of Color Are Not the Target of Family Preservation Services: A Case for Program Reform." *Journal of Sociology and Social Welfare* 30 (2): 149–73.

Fanshel, D. 1979. "Preschoolers Entering Foster Care in New York City: The Need to Stress Plans for Permanency." *Child Welfare* 58:67–81.

Fanshel, D., & E. B. Shinn. 1978. *Children in Foster Care: A Longitudinal Investigation*. New York: Columbia University Press.

Franklin, J. E., & E. Higginbotham. 2010. *From Slavery to Freedom: A History of African Americans*. 9th ed. New York: McGraw-Hill.

Frazier, E. F. 1957. *Black Bourgeoisie*. Glencoe, Ill.: Free Press.

Goldstein, J., A. Freud, & A. J. Solnit. 1973. *Beyond the Best Interest of the Child*. New York: Free Press.

Grotberg, E. 1977. *200 Years of Children*. Washington, D.C.: U.S. Department of Health, Education and Welfare.

Gutman, H. G. 1976. *The Black Family in Slavery and Freedom: 1750–1925*. New York: Vintage Books.

Hill, R. B. 1972. *Strengths of Black Families*. Lanham, Md.: University Press of America.

Karger, H., & D. Stoesz. 2009. *American Social Welfare Policy: A Pluralist Approach*. 6th ed. Boston: Pearson Education.

Ladner, J. 1971. *Tomorrow's Tomorrow: The Black Woman*. New York: Doubleday.

Maas, H. S., & R. E. Engler. 1959. *Children in Need of Parents*. New York: Basic Books.

Mnookin, R. 1973. "Foster Care: In Whose Best Interest?" *Harvard Educational Review* (November): 598–638.

Moynihan, D. P. 1965. *The Negro Family: The Case for National Action*. Washington, D.C.: U.S. Department of Labor, Office of Policy.

Multiethnic Placement Act of 1994. PL 103-382, Sec. 552(6).

Pecora, P. J., J. K. Whittaker, & A. N. Maluccio. 1992. *The Child Welfare Challenge*. Hawthorne, N.Y.: Walter de Gruyter.

Public Health & Welfare 42 U.S.C. Sec. 670 & 675(5). 1997.

Roberts, D. 2002. *Shattered Bonds: The Color of Child Welfare*. New York: Basic Books.

Rosenheim, M. K. 1976. *Pursuing Justice for the Child*. Chicago: University of Chicago Press.

Trattner, W. I. (1989). *From Poor Law to Welfare State: A History of Social Welfare in America*. 4th ed. New York: Free Press.

U. S. House of Representatives. 1997. H.R. Rep. No. 136, 96th Congress, Session 1, 46–47.

———. Committee on Ways and Means. 2006. PL 109-288, The Child and Family Services Improvement Act of 2006. CIS-No: 2006-H782-31. Washington, D.C.

Warren, A. 1996. *Orphan Train Rider: One Boy's True Story*. Boston: Houghton Mifflin.

Whitelaw-Downs, S., E. Moore, & E. J. McFadden. 2009. *Child Welfare and Family Services: Policies and Practice*. 8th ed.. Boston: Pearson Education.

Wilhelmus, M. 1998. "A Content Analysis of Parent Narratives in Termination of Parental Rights Trials: Emerging Themes on the Legal Loss of Children." Ph.D. diss., Ohio State University.

3

Child Welfare Policy and the African American Family

CHILD WELFARE POLICY IN CONTEXT

The child welfare system of services that society deems necessary to support and care for children when parents are unable to do so or until self-care is appropriate exists within a context of structured programs established through federal and state policies. There are generally several levels or types of child welfare services:

- Support services, which undergird the family unit and may be targeted to a child or parents and include education, information, recreation, and counseling, as well as behavioral health treatment and prevention services
- Supplemental services, such as the Supplemental Nutrition Assistance Program (SNAP), formerly called the food stamp program; the National School Lunch Program (NSLP); the Special Supplemental Nutrition Program for Women, Infants, and Children (WIC); and Temporary Assistance for Needy Families (TANF), which aim to augment basic primary needs of the family
- Substitute care, a system of care in the spirit of *parens patriae*, which is organized by the government (see chapter 2) to ensure that a child once removed from home may experience a healthy and safe living environment until the child is returned home or until a permanent replacement is secured

All child welfare services are organized around the primacy of the family in providing for its members. Social welfare history reflects a dynamic role of the federal government relative to the level of government involvement in social and economic affairs. Political and economic ideological orientations often affect the type and amount of government resources available to families via the American welfare state. A more conservative orientation is typically associated with less government intervention and financial support for social programs, while a liberal orientation generally suggests support for a strong government role in social programs to ensure equity among states and funding at levels based on prevailing need.

In recent years the demand for all child welfare programs—nutrition, health, education—has increased as unemployment rates have reached crisis proportions and wages have not kept up with inflation, particularly among the working poor. Today millions of families rely on childcare before and after school as well as early education programs (e.g., Project Head Start) so parents may work outside of the home and be assured that children are safe and receive developmentally appropriate care. The SNAP program is a critical support for millions of low-income families, as are federal child nutrition programs such as the NSLP and the School Breakfast Program (SPB), summer and after-school food programs, and the WIC Program. Access to health-care services has increased through public insurance and public health services. Medicaid coverage for millions of low-income children and extended health care to children not otherwise eligible for Medicaid through the State Children's Health Insurance Program (SCHIP) have contributed to higher rates of immunizations and lower incidences of many childhood diseases (Children's Defense Fund, 2010).

While the focus of this book is on substitute care for children through the out-of-home system of care and ancillary services, it is important to have an operational understanding of one major form of supplemental support: the block grant to states called Temporary Assistance for Needy Families (TANF). It provides the foundation of funding to states for foster care as the program allows federally subsidized cash aid to follow an eligible child from her or his home to a foster family home. Prior to the passage of TANF, federal support for foster care was provided as an optional component of a state's Aid to Families with Dependent Children (AFDC) cash assistance program, Title IV-A of the Social Security Act. In 1968 PL 90-248 made it mandatory that states include foster care payments as part of their AFDC plan. In 1980 the Adoption Assistance and Child Welfare Act (AACWA) (PL 96-272), was introduced based on calls for reform of the foster care program and concerns that some children were needlessly removed from their homes and that, once in out-of-home care, they stayed indefinitely. The AACWA created a new Title IV-E of the Social Security Act, which established federal foster care maintenance payments to states independent of the AFDC program (currently TANF), and it established federal support for adoption assistance payments for families adopting children with special needs. When the 104th Congress enacted welfare reform (TANF) through passage of the Personal Responsibility and Work Opportunity Reconciliation Act (PRWORA) (PL 104-193), states were required to operate a foster care and adoption assistance program under Title IV-E of the Social Security Act.

The AACWA placed emphasis on case planning and review requirements for children entering foster care and required states to make reasonable efforts to prevent the placement of children out of their homes. These provisions were primarily for children who met Title IV-E eligibility requirements. However, Congress determined that all children in foster care should receive the same case planning and review protections, which resulted in the passage of Title IV-B of the Social Security Act. This new funding stream was intended to create incentives for states to provide planning-related protections for all children in foster care (U.S. House of Representatives, 2009).

Since eligibility for Title IV-E funds was historically linked to eligibility for AFDC, foster or adoptive children are now eligible for Title IV-E subsidies if their families would have been eligible for AFDC in their state, as implemented in July 1996 (U.S. House of Representatives, 2009). In most cases if a family was eligible for AFDC or would have been eligible, it would also be eligible for Title IV-E assistance. When Congress repealed AFDC and replaced it with TANF (1996) under the PRWORA, states were still required to certify that they operated a foster care and adoption assistance program under Title IV-E if they also participated in TANF. The PRWORA continued to limit federal eligibility for both foster care and adoption assistance to children who were removed from homes in which they would have been eligible for cash assistance under the AFDC program as it existed in each state up until July 1996 (U.S. House of Representatives, 2009).

Title IV-B is currently referred to as the Stephanie Tubbs Jones Child Welfare Services and Promoting Safe and Stable Families (formerly Family Preservation) Program. The program is named after the late congresswoman from Ohio who was a champion of the cause for children, particularly African American and economically disenfranchised children. Amendments to Title IV-E now include the Foster Care Subsidy Program, the Adoption Assistance Program, and the Chafee Foster Care

Independence Program, all administered by the U.S. Department of Health and Human Services. Each of these programs aims to aid states in meeting obligations related to substitute care.

CHILD WELFARE POLICY FRAMEWORK

For decades the Congress of the United States and presidents have targeted child welfare reforms for the national public agenda, proposing initiatives aimed at improving a system of service and care intended to protect child safety and ensure physical and behavioral health prevention and treatment for all children, particularly those who are poor, underserved, and disabled. For a state to be eligible for federal funds to address the needs of children who may require supportive, supplemental, or substitute care, it must comply with federal requirements and guidelines (Curtis & Denby, 2011).

At the level of the federal government, a network of laws passed by Congress have created a foundation for public policy. In child welfare these laws or statutes form the basis for rules that are promulgated to provide direction to states as to how laws are to be implemented. When there are questions or challenges in how laws are enforced or rules are implemented, the courts may be called on to interpret the intent of a rule or statute or resolve such questions. In this manner case law is established through judicial decision making and provides further explanation around how programs and services are to be delivered. Thus laws, rules, and judicial decisions create a foundation for child welfare services in the United States (Stein, 2006). To this foundation, state laws and administrative rules and special state program initiatives (e.g., risk assessment requirements, worker training certification requirements) are added that collectively provide the legal basis for child welfare services— a policy framework for child welfare (figure 3.1).

Child welfare policies inform practice, or the services provided to children and their families aimed at strengthening, enhancing, supporting, or replacing the care typically offered by a parent or caregiver. Laws and regulations—or policies—evolve over time as byproducts of the values and beliefs we embrace as a society. If one thinks of programs and services in terms of the petals of a flower, they come forth because of seeds— the foundation—that evolve through a process of growth and change and result in a useful byproduct. Like the flower image in figure 3.2,

Federal Laws and Legal Statutes

+

Promulgated Rules and Reguations

+

Relevant Judicial Decisions

+

State Laws, Rules, and
Special Initiatives

=

POLICY FRAMEWORK FOR
CHILD WELFARE

Figure 3.1 Child welfare policy framework.

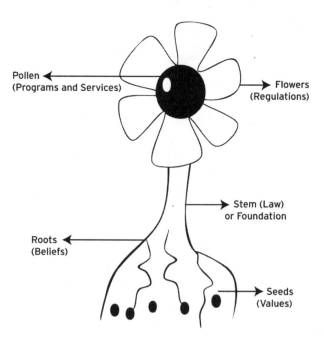

Pollen ◄
(Programs and Services)

Flowers ►
(Regulations)

Stem (Law) ►
or Foundation

Roots ◄
(Beliefs)

Seeds ►
(Values)

Figure 3.2 Elements of policy formation.

there is a relationship between what we plant and the outcome. Our values and beliefs, which change over time, influence policy that results in programs and services. Like the seeds that sprout and ultimately produce a flower, values and beliefs are the foundation through which policy—both laws and regulations—evolve. From time to time flowering plants become weak and require reseeding. Similarly, policies and the programs and services emanating from them must be evaluated for relevance and effectiveness.

To strengthen existing policies or programs, the evaluation of what has worked and what has not worked effectively should result in a change or different approach to addressing a need. Thus amendments to existing laws and rules require consideration of what is currently in place. Using the analogy of a flowering plant, when it becomes necessary or desirous to strengthen what is in place, the seeds (programs and services) from an existing plant become the basis for creating a new, stronger product.

The primary responsibility for child welfare services rests with the states, with each state maintaining legal and administrative structures for programs that address the needs of children and families. To qualify for federal funding, states must comply with specific federal requirements and guidelines associated with certain programs. The primary goal of child welfare at the state level is to reestablish a permanent home for children who enter foster care; additionally, child protection agencies develop coordinated child and family services aimed at ensuring that all children are supported in safe and caring families. Categorically, services at the state level for which federal money may be expended include (1) protecting and promoting the welfare of all children; (2) preventing the neglect, abuse, or exploitation of children; (3) supporting families who may be at risk for child maltreatment through services that allow children to remain safely with their families or return to their families in a timely manner; (4) promoting the safety, permanence, and well-being of children in foster care and adoptive families; and (5) providing training, professional development, and support to ensure a well-qualified child welfare workforce (U.S. House of Representatives, 2009:11–22).

In child welfare, federal laws that shape the delivery of child protection and other child welfare services influence state statutes and program initiatives, as the requirements for states to receive funding often necessitate legislation to implement. Having a general understanding of major federal laws enables child welfare practitioners to interpret program rules that instruct states about requirements for federal funding. It is not possible for child welfare workers and advocates to have knowledge of the legal framework for child welfare in every state, but it is imperative for those who work in child welfare to have a working knowledge of the legal foundation—specifically federal statutes and laws and a working knowledge of relevant state laws, rules, and special initiatives.

Table 3.1 provides general information on major federal child welfare laws. It is important to remember that federal program funding in child welfare is a dynamic and complex process and includes both authorization and appropriation processes. For this reason the table includes initial authorized funding versus current funding, which is often a moving target. When Congress enacts a law that requires funding for programs or services, a funding level is established or authorized based on general knowledge of related program or service needs among the states and territories. The authorization or authorized funding tied to legislation is the maximum amount of money that Congress can approve in a given fiscal year. Budget negotiations, particularly during times of federal budget deficits and concern for fiscal austerity, typically result in actual program budgets being appropriated at a level below the optimum spending level required to meet service needs at the state level. The 1974 enactment of the Child Abuse Prevention and Treatment Act (PL 93-247) signaled Congress's acknowledgment of a national crisis of child maltreatment and the need for funding and programs aimed at prevention and intervention and establishing a national database of related information.

OVERVIEW OF MAJOR CHILD WELFARE POLICY AND LAWS

When it is necessary to temporarily or permanently remove children from their homes to ensure their safety and well-being, the provisions of one or more federal laws may come into play. The particular policies discussed in this chapter are cited because of the dominant theme or priority placed on creating permanency in the life of a child. Typically these laws do not have specific provisions related to the needs of African American children.

The prevailing philosophy relative to policy formulation and adaptation is to enact laws that (presumably) will result in equitable treatment, effective service delivery, and unbiased consideration with regard to implementation. It is the responsibility of those who review and analyze policy to determine if the need for which a policy is written receives

TABLE 3.1
Major Federal Child Welfare Policy Laws

Name of Legislation	Year Enacted	Legislative Intent, Rationale, and/or Goals	Requirements and Provisions Special Provisions
Social Security Act (PL 74-271)	1935	Authorized the first federal grants for child welfare services under subpart 1 of Title IV-B. These first grants were the impetus for states to establish child welfare agencies and local programs and services.	Required states to match federal funds with state funds for child welfare services.
Aid to Families with Dependent Children (AFDC)	ADC, 1935; ADC Foster Care, 1961; AFDC, 1962; TANF, 1996	Allowed states to provide financial assistance to needy dependent children.	To assist states in complying with the 1960 Fleming Rule, ADC was amended to create a foster care component whereby states received federal matching funds to cover foster care payments for children who were removed from "unsuitable" homes.
Child Abuse and Prevention Treatment Act (CAPTA) (PL 93-247)	1974	Addressed child abuse and neglect, the first federal legislation to do so.	In exchange for funding, required states to establish child abuse reporting and investigation procedures.
Indian Child Welfare Act (ICWA) (PL 95-108)	1978	Responded to the high number of Native American children being removed from their families and placed outside the Native American community.	Gave tribes jurisdiction over child welfare decisions concerning tribal members. Established guidelines for family reunification and placement of Native American children, as well as the Indian Child Welfare Act grant program.
Adoption Assistance and Child Welfare Act (PL 96-272)	1980	Created Title IV-E of the Social Security Act, assuming ADFC-Foster Care. Created because of a significant increase in the number and length of stay of children in foster care in the 1970s. There was mounting concern that children were being removed from their homes unnecessarily. Also, reunification efforts were inadequate, and the system as a whole lacked oversight.	Established the first procedural rules for case management, permanency planning, and placements. Required states to develop plans for service delivery; defined special needs children; established reasonable efforts; created Title IV-E Adoption Assistance; and required courts to review child welfare decisions.

(*continued*)

TABLE 3.1 (*continued*)

Name of Legislation	Year Enacted	Legislative Intent, Rationale, and/or Goals	Requirements and Provisions Special Provisions
Family Preservation and Support Services Act (PL 103-66) and Promoting Safe and Stable Families (PSSF) (PL 107-133)	1993	Between 1986 and 1995 the number of children in foster care increased by 76%. PL 103-66 was established out of concern that little was being done to prevent foster care. PL 107-133 replaced PL 103-66 under the Adoption and Safe Families Act (ASFA) of 1997. In 2001 Congress reauthorized PSSF, increasing the mandatory funding level from $305 million to $505 million and encouraging postadoption and substance-abuse services. The 2001 authorization amended the Chafee law, which provided for educational and vocational training for older foster care youth exiting the system, and continued the set-aside of funding and expanded the services of the Court Improvement Program (CIP).	Provided flexible funding to prevent child abuse and neglect and to assist families whose children were at risk of removal. PSSF provided funding for time-limited family reunification services and adoption promotion and support activities. The CIP was established under PL 103-66. This was the first significant federal funding for child welfare–related court activities.
Child Welfare Waivers	1994 (part of the Social Security Amendments, PL 103-432)	The federal government issued child welfare waivers with the intent of enabling states to design and implement new approaches to delivering and financing child welfare services.	States that received waivers had to establish demonstration projects that could last no longer than five years, were cost-neutral, and were rigorously evaluated.
Multi-Ethnic Placement Act (MEPA) and Inter-Ethnic Placement Provisions (IEPP) (PL 104-188)	MEPA, 1994; IEPP, 1996	Promoted the best interests of children by ensuring a permanent, safe, and stable family. The IEPP repealed MEPA to eliminate the provision that allowed for routine consideration of race and ethnicity.	Prohibits the delay or denial of a child's placement or adoption on the basis of race; prohibits denial of any individual's opportunity to become a foster or adoptive parent on the basis of race; and requires states to diligently recruit foster and adoptive parents who reflect the racial makeup of the children in the state who need care.

Name of Legislation	Year Enacted	Legislative Intent, Rationale, and/or Goals	Requirements and Provisions Special Provisions
Personal Responsibility and Work Opportunity Reconciliation Act (PRWORA) (PL 104-193)	1996	Replaced AFDC. Provides financial assistance so that children can be cared for in their homes or in the home of a relative; promotes work, job training, and marriage; attempts to reduce out-of-wedlock births; and encourages the formation of two-parent families.	Administration of welfare benefits was altered to involve an increased role for states and local jurisdiction. Also, the role of welfare workers was redefined whereby workers were required to evaluate and facilitate clients' entry into the workforce.
Adoption and Safe Families Act (ASFA) (PL 105-89)	1997	Represents the most significant changes to federal child welfare law since 1980. Stresses that a child's health and safety must be paramount in decision making. The rationale for implementation centered around three concerns: an apparent bias toward family preservation; inadequate planning toward adoption as a permanency option; and foster care placement lengths remaining too long.	Imposed four major requirements: time limits for reunification cannot extend beyond fifteen months; termination of parental rights (TPR) can begin for a child who has been in care fifteen of the past twenty-two months; concurrent planning is required and includes case planning toward reunification and, simultaneously, planning for legal guardianship or adoption. Family Service Reviews (CFSR) must be undertaken whereby state child welfare performance is assessed.
Inter-Country Adoption Act (PL 106-279)	2000	Procedurally defines international adoption practices and in doing so ensures that the best interests of children are being met; also seeks to prevent the abduction and exploitation of children.	The Hague Convention on Inter-Country Adoption established that countries are to work only with fellow Convention countries. Also, countries are required to establish one central authority to facilitate adoptions.
Strengthening Abuse and Neglect Courts Act (PL 106-314)	2000	Enacted to help courts reduce the backlog of cases and expedite case processing by using automated and electronic procedures.	Provides small grants to child welfare courts.
Child Citizen Act (PL 106-395)	2000	Amends the Immigration and Nationality Act and in doing so confers U.S. citizenship automatically to foreign-born children adopted by U.S. citizens.	Requires that at least one of the child's parents must be an American citizen; the child must be under the age of 18; the child must be in the legal and physical custody of the American parent; and the child must be admitted as an immigrant for lawful permanent residence.

(*continued*)

TABLE 3.1 (*continued*)

Name of Legislation	Year Enacted	Legislative Intent, Rationale, and/or Goals	Requirements and Provisions Special Provisions
Safe and Timely Interstate Placement of Foster Children Act (PL 109-239)	2006	Amends Titles IV-B and IV-E of the Social Security Act. Encourages states to improve protection efforts and holds them accountable for facilitating safe and timely placements of children across state lines.	Includes several provisions: timely completion of home studies; requirement for effective use of cross-jurisdictional resources; consideration of interstate placements in permanency decisions; requirement for more frequent caseworker visits for children in out-of-state placements (from once every twelve months to once every six months); with respect to the CIPs, courts must show their effectiveness at expediting interstate placements and ensure that foster parents, preadoptive parent, and relative caregivers are notified of any proceedings held with respect to a child in care; amendment of the definition of case plan; and amendment of the definition of case review system.
Adam Walsh Child Protection and Safety Act (PL 109-248)	2006	Aims to protect children from sex offenders through the use of a nationalized sex offender registration system, prevent child abuse and child pornography, and promote Internet safety. Specific to child welfare, requires complete background checks using national crime registries for foster/adoptive parent applicants. Permits local child welfare agencies to use the national crime information database for investigating reports of abuse and neglect. Creates a national registry of substantiated cases of child abuse and neglect. Increases the penalty for any "covered professional" found guilty of failure to report child abuse (from a Class B misdemeanor to a fine and imprisonment).	Increases the capacity of governmental systems (particularly justice authorities) to share resources (e.g., registries) to identify individuals who pose a threat to children. Also provides courts with the ability to administer penalties against sexual perpetrators, and establishes funding for programs that aim to prevent crimes against children.

Name of Legislation	Year Enacted	Legislative Intent, Rationale, and/or Goals	Requirements and Provisions Special Provisions
Child and Family Services Improvement Act (CFSIA) (PL 109-288)	2006	Reauthorizes the PSSF Act for five years (FYs 2007–2011).	Enhances PSSF by allocating financing for court improvement grants, substance abuse grants, workforce development grants, and tribal improvement grants.
Fostering Connections to Success and Increasing Adoptions Act (PL 110-351)	2008	mends Titles IV-B and IV-E of the Social Security Act. Provides support to some relative caregivers, provides for tribal foster care and adoption access, and revamps incentive programs that aim to increase adoption.	Has five major provisions: to connect and support relative caregivers; to extend support for children beyond age 18; to provide health-care oversight for children in foster care; to enable Indian tribes to create their own Title IV-E program; to enhance adoption incentives; and to grant states the use of federal funds for kinship guardianship stipends.

Source: Curtis & Denby (2011).

adequate and appropriate consideration. Similarly, with rules or regulations that provide instruction as to how laws are to be implemented, program evaluators and advocates must ensure that program rules are applied equitably across all populations served.

The Social Security Act of 1935 (PL 74-271) is recognized as the foundational piece of the American welfare system. The law was designed to provide support to widows and their children who suffered from the economic collapse and beginning of the Great Depression in 1929. The act has been amended to establish funding for states to provide this support and to cover the cost of temporary foster care. The enactment of federal laws and the protections and service entitlements were not generally extended to African Americans until the U.S. Supreme Court determined under *Brown v. Board of Education of Topeka* that the use of racial classification was unreasonable.

Amendments to the Social Security Act created a funding provision for states to subsidize the costs of foster care and expanded the classification of families entitled to income support (to include families within which the father resided) to ensure the health and safety of minor children whose parents did not work or have access to regular income. In 1996 the entitlement status of Aid to Families with Dependent Children was removed and Temporary Assistance for Needy Families was enacted, imposing a limit on the number of years families may be eligible for federal income aid, unless the state determines the family to be exempt because of physical or behavioral health–related disabilities.

Research suggests there is a correlation between children living with their families and the employment status of their parents (Curtis & Alexander, 2010). Of particular note is the positive correlation between the employment status of the father or male figure in a household and the likelihood of children living with their biological family. Preliminary data on the effect of TANF on the poverty status of children suggests a relatively limited negative effect on children whose families live in states with low unemployment. Since the economic recession of 2008, limited data have been published on families who qualified for AFDC and who may or may not have received TANF. What is known, however, is that unemployment remains disproportionately high among African Americans, particularly among African American males (Curtis & Alexander, 2010). A recent report from the Children's Defense Fund (2010) states that the current economic recession has had a distinctively negative effect on poverty rates among children—the highest child poverty rate since 1959. Families living in poverty and unemployed are at greater risk for neglect and the challenges of keeping children safe and healthy.

The Child Abuse and Prevention Treatment Act first provided a framework for use by states in defining maltreatment, thus ensuring local authorities' legal sanction to intervene in the life of a child who may be at risk for abuse or neglect. In the United States, the Society for the Prevention of Cruelty to Animals was in place prior to the creation of an organization aimed at protecting children from abuse. One hundred years after the Society for the Prevention of Cruelty to Children was established in 1874, research prompted the identification of patterns of physical injuries and techniques to document or verify patterns of physical maltreatment (Crosson-Tower, 2007).

C. Henry Kempe, a pediatrician at the University of Colorado, was inspired by a colleague who reported finding multiple unexplained fractures that often healed poorly among young children. This finding and subsequent research prompted Kempe to study further this phenomenon that he would label "battered child syndrome" or the clinical condition in children who experienced severe physical abuse (Kempe et al.,

1962:17). Kempe's research received national attention and eventually led to the passage of the Child Abuse Prevention and Treatment Act. As a result of this law, states receive funding for passing laws and creating programming aimed at protecting children from maltreatment in its various forms. While some statistics suggest that a reduction in the rate of child victims of maltreatment can be attributed to CAPTA, the number of African American children entering the child welfare system nationwide has not declined precipitously.

The Indian Child Welfare Act of 1978 (PL 95-608) is unique in that it directs efforts toward a specific ethnic group to try to create permanence for children. The National Association of Black Social Workers attempted to include African American children in the law, but Congress, after holding hearings, excluded them. Dixon (2008) has argued that we cannot effectively meet the current needs of African American children within the child welfare system without a complete cultural adaptation of law and policy—the creation of legislation targeted specifically to the interests of the African American child, similar to the Indian Child Welfare Act. We believe that the interests and needs of African American children, in the absence of a policy directed to their specific interests, can and must be addressed within existing related laws and regulations. It is the practice in statutory formulation and the resultant promulgation of rules to target services. Doing so does not preclude the inclusion of others in the provision of services; it can better ensure, however, that those in greatest need are engaged with deliberate outreach to best address the needs of children for whom laws are intended.

The disproportional representation of African American children and other children of color in the out-of-home care system is operationally defined in chapter 1. This trend of children of color being disproportionately represented in foster care has existed since the 1960s (Curtis, 1996). Problems associated with child placement increased during the 1970s as more children were being removed from their homes and placed in foster care. These children would remain in care for long periods of time without being returned to their homes or parental rights being terminated so that other, permanent placement options might be considered. This phenomenon, known as "foster care drift," was the focus of congressional hearings and social science research among child welfare advocates. In 1980 Congress passed the Adoption Assistance and Child Welfare Act (PL 96-272) to effectively overhaul the system of child protection services nationwide. For the first time a law stipulated that each child in the foster care system must have a permanence plan in place to determine permanent living circumstances for the child. Permanency planning—a written plan aimed at developing a course of action to return a child to the home or facilitate relinquishment by parents or termination of parental rights so that a child can be placed in a permanent home—became a national priority. Adoption subsidies were put in place to facilitate permanency for hard-to-place or special needs children. The law identified special needs children as those in the foster care system who are older, children with medical conditions, sibling groups, and children of racial or ethnic identities.

In 1993 Congress provided permanent funding to states for a variety of services aimed at supporting children who were aging out of foster care and supporting families whose children continued in care. The Family Preservation and Support Services Act of 1993 (PL 103-66) established a new Title IV-B, subpart 2, of the Social Security Act that authorized capped or limited entitlement funding to states for provision of family preservation and family support services. The law also made certain child protections relative to assessing state compliance with federal child welfare policy mandatory for all children in foster care. Some of the creative initiatives aimed at strengthening and preserving the family unit, such as kinship care, were formally introduced as a result of this legislative support.

Child welfare workers and social service agencies were reluctant to recognize the complexities of African American family life, such as extended family networks and informal exchange systems of mutual help that were the precursors of kinship care. While kinship care is now widely recognized, the practice of "informal adoption" within the African American community, in which children were raised by relatives or close family members other than their parents, was met with intense resistance as practiced from the antebellum era through the turn of the century and throughout the 1930s, 1940s, and 1950s (Billingsley, 1968; Hill, 1972, 2001, 2006). In a national research study, social workers tended to resist targeting family preservation services—or services aimed at preventing the disruption of the family owing to maltreatment—to African American children and their families (Curtis & Denby, 2004). Some workers have argued that some problems are too great and therefore too costly to correct, such as problems associated with poverty, substance abuse, and other behavioral health disorders, and the uncertainties—such as the likelihood of probation—associated with incarceration.

The intent of the Adoption Assistance and Child Welfare Act was not fully realized because of increased demand and diminished resources. To address a trend of insufficient funding, weak regulations, and growing numbers of children being placed in the out-of-home care system while many children continued to languish in foster care, Congress enacted the Adoption and Safe Families Act (ASFA) (PL 105-89) in 1997, amending the AACWA. The problem of foster care drift for children in the out-of-home care system is particularly problematic for African Americans as compared with other races. These children are more likely to be investigated and more likely to be removed from their homes and placed into care; they are least likely to be permanently placed with adoptive families or returned to their homes in a timely manner (ACYF, 2001; AFCARS, 2008). For more information about African American children's rates of investigation, removal, and placement, see chapters 1 and 4. African American children are not typically targeted for preventive services once they are referred to child protective service agencies and remain at risk of not receiving permanent placements (Curtis & Denby, 2004).

Among the primary provisions of ASFA are incentive payments for children placed in adoptive homes or other permanent arrangements, a definition of "aggravated circumstances" that make termination of parental rights automatic, time limits for commencing parental rights termination to facilitate permanency, and a requirement for simultaneous case management for family preservation and reunification services while also planning for adoption. ASFA imposes a fifteen-month time limit for reunification; if a child has been in foster care for fifteen of the past twenty-two months, termination of parental rights can be initiated.

Based on performance standards built into ASFA, the Children's Bureau generated a performance-based evaluation in 2001 using limited data from the states. Covering the years 1998 to 2001, the *Child Welfare Outcomes Annual Report*, issued by the Administration for Children, Youth and Families (2001) does not indicate a major change in the number of children exiting foster care because of reunification, adoption, or legal guardianship subsequent to the passage of ASFA. Children in a special needs category, including those who entered the system at age 12 or older, experienced less success exiting foster care. There was more success with reunification than with adoption. Some 30 to 50 percent of children leaving the system left because of emancipation. Data from the report indicate that the most vulnerable children in the out–of-home care system, African Americans, did not experience significant success exiting foster care. Given the disproportionate number of African American children in the out-of-home care system, the goal of permanence has not been achieved for most children.

Another feature of ASFA that may have questionable effects on outcomes for African American children is the provision for termination of parental rights. Many families brought to the attention of the public child welfare system are poor. Neglect, most often associated with poverty, is the most common form of maltreatment, followed by physical abuse. Poverty, substance use and abuse, and domestic violence may become the interactive link of problems that prevent parents from providing nurturing care for their children. If problems result in incarceration or the need for long-term behavioral health care for the primary caregiver, without effective case management parents may come up·against compliance issues set forth in ASFA relative to months in foster care, which can result in termination of parental rights. Such circumstances require legal counsel that is costly but essential, particularly when kinship care is desired for the child requiring temporary placement. The evidentiary standard to terminate parental rights is relatively high and may result in lengthy legal challenges. Managing time lines and court costs can create family disruption.

ASFA includes the Promoting Safe and Stable Families Program (PSSF), which increased resources for family support and family preservation services. During congressional hearings prior to the passage of ASFA, critics argued against preservation, pointing to the increased vulnerability to unsafe outcomes among young children (Bartholet, 1999; Denby & Curtis, 2003). Members of Congress and others offering testimony relied heavily on "lurid newspaper accounts and anecdotal accounts from clinical data and individual observations to argue that efforts of family preservation had gone too far" (Stein, 2006:673). This sentiment places children of color at greater risk for having a temporary placement become permanent. Families not traditionally targeted for services will be less likely to receive more costly and time-intensive treatment services.

Every law passed by Congress is authorized to be effective for a limited number of years, after which it must be reauthorized if it is to remain law. In 2003 Congress passed the Keeping Children and Families Safe Act (PL 108-36), which amends and reauthorizes the Child Abuse Prevention and Treatment Act. In addition to maintaining the child abuse clearinghouse function for research, information, and training, this law requires the inclusion of for-profit entities as recipients of federal technical assistance. It includes a provision to collect and disseminate information on training resources for law enforcement personnel and others engaged in the delivery of anti–child abuse services (e.g., court-appointed special advocates).

Mandatory development and operations grants to assist states in improving their child protection services systems must now include interagency collaboration between the child protection system and the juvenile justice system for improved delivery of services and treatment. African American children and youth are disproportional in number in both child protection and juvenile justice systems. A report from Chapin Hall Center for Children at the University of Chicago (2008) encourages these systems to work collaboratively at all levels of government and to involve families, communities, and providers of services to address racial and ethnic disproportionality, including frank discussions about the effect of institutional racism and bias in decision making.

As a result of this legislation, states are also required to have and enforce policies and procedures to address the needs of infants born and identified as being affected by illegal substance abuse or withdrawal symptoms resulting from prenatal drug exposure (*Congressional Record*, 2003). Many women in prison for drug-related offenses are mothers, often of very young children. In the past twenty years there has been an increase in the number of women in prison; 53 percent of the women in prison are mothers. One criticism of child protective services has been resistance to making substance-abuse treatment referrals because of costs and limited community resources (Whitelaw-Downs, Moore, & McFadden, 2009). African American women are disproportionately included among incarcerated women, and if they have young children, the likelihood of their children becoming wards of the state is significant.

The Child and Family Services Improvement Act of 2006 (PL 109-288) mandates certain state plan requirements, data-reporting requirements, and funding rules under the Stephanie Tubbs Jones Child Welfare Services Program related to caseworker visits of children in foster care. Arguably, increased attention to need should result in activities and services aimed at improving the condition of families and ensuring permanence for children in foster care. Once again, however, the status of African American children in foster care remains mutable and disproportional. The intent of legislation is not always matched with efficient program implementation, professional service delivery, or adequate funding necessary to meet specific needs. This legislation requires states to ensure that the majority of children in foster care are visited by their caseworkers on a monthly basis. The majority of these visits are expected to occur in the residence of the child. A plan for how each state intends to accomplish this goal must be submitted to the U.S. Department of Health and Human Services annually.

Numerous problems may bring a child to the attention of child protective services. Domestic violence, alcohol abuse, illicit drug use, homelessness, joblessness—all of these circumstances associated with a parent or caregiver can affect adjudication and the disposition of the court concerning protective child placement decisions. Likewise, if a child or adolescent is engaged in gateway behaviors, status offenses become the order of the day. If the parent or caregiver is unable to maintain appropriate control of child behavior, family preservation or supportive services may be required to maintain family stability.

Case management for children in foster care or for those who come to the attention of child protective services is critical to promoting and stabilizing safe and healthy families. The intent of the Child and Family Services Improvement Act is to assure families and state agencies that guidelines are in place to make social workers and other child welfare workers more accountable for the outcomes for children.

One of the final acts of President George W. Bush was to sign into law the Fostering Connection to Success and Increasing Adoptions Act (PL 110-351). This legislation tries to help children and youths in foster care by promoting permanence through relative guardianship and adoption while improving education and health care for children in care (Children's Defense Fund & Center for Law and Social Policy, 2008). The law ensures that family members who assume legal guardianship will be eligible for the same payments previously made to nonrelative foster parents under Title IV-E of the Social Security Act. Family members may also obtain adoption subsidy for special needs children when a child fits the special needs category.

Prior to enactment of this law, the special needs category for which adoption assistance is available did not automatically include children eligible for the Supplemental Security Income (SSI) program, but now children are determined to be at risk based solely on medical and disability requirements. This may conceivably result in more children being designated "at risk" owing to requirements associated with the Keeping Children and Families Safe Act for documenting and reporting to child protection agencies children born with drug addictions.

We do not yet know what the long-term effect of the provisions of PL 110-351 will be for African American children. The history of African American families extending care and support to relatives during time of need has been in direct response to exclusionary practices denying access to adoption services, child care, and other family support services (Curtis, 1996). However, when the government makes financial payment incentives available to relatives who have provided temporary foster care and agree to assume permanent guardianship, the rights of parents hang in the balance (Hill, 2001). The termination of parental rights and the extent to which parents may voluntarily abdicate their rights is uncertain. The role of parents when a child is in the custody of relatives is also an unknown. If parents wish to retain permanent custody, the rules at the state level should require that documentation be filed demonstrating that all possible and reasonable efforts have been made to support the parent and to enable the parent's ability to function in a nurturing and responsible manner.

This interpretive review of major federal laws provides a foundation to understand the intent of the federal government to assist and support states in their role to ensure the healthy growth and development of children when parents are unable to fill that role. Table 3.1 provides the rationales as well as specific requirements and general provisions. This introduction to federal laws should serve as a resource and incentive for further analysis of the policy framework for child welfare, including state-level statutes that provide a blueprint for state administration and local government practice.

CULTURAL ADAPTATIONS FOR AFRICAN AMERICAN CHILDREN IN CHILD WELFARE

To ensure that African American children who are introduced to the child welfare system have the best opportunity for a healthy, developmentally appropriate childhood and receive optimal services, critical support, and professional care from competent, trained, culturally knowledgeable practitioners, the following adaptations of existing policies, or in some cases the introduction of policies and initiatives, can promote improved child well-being:

• Begin a child welfare reform movement. Such a movement will require the involvement of multiple stakeholders and the creation of partnerships. These partnerships will be critical to achieving the crucially important oversight of major federal and state child welfare laws and regulations, with the goal of reform as needed and supplanting or supplementing funding to implement reforms.

• Target employment to low-income parents whose children are more likely to experience poor physical and behavioral health outcomes. Income is also correlated with children's risky behavior that can lead to delinquent behaviors and poor academic performance, ultimately leading to dropping out of school. Ensuring that parents have steady employment can benefit overall child well-being. According to research, children who live outside of their home (away from a biological parent or guardian) in foster care are more likely to have at least one unemployed parent (Curtis & Alexander, 2010).

• Require state agencies to contract with culturally indigenous organizations that can provide safety (e.g., case management, home visiting, monitoring), permanency (e.g., adoption home studies), and well-being (e.g., behavioral health screenings and services, mentoring programs) for African American children.

• Require that all child-serving agencies that receive state or federal funding be evaluated on a performance-based model that is outcome focused.

• Implement subsidized guardianship options for prevention and permanency placements in all states and territories as a standard practice. If relatives agree to guardianship, "livable stipends" should be available blending federal funding streams—TANF and Title IV-E foster care funding. States should not limit opportunities for guardianship placements with relatives by imposing unreasonable age or income restrictions.

• Require that preventive guardianship programs be evaluated to determine what is most effective relative to implementation strategies, the current or potential effect on children's lives, and associated costs and savings to state and local governments. Up to now, preventive guardianship as a placement option has not been widely implemented or evaluated.

• Provide support for grandparents with children in their care—both for the children and for the grandparents themselves (preferably as subsidized guardians). Such support may include respite care, childcare, clothing allowances, parenting skills training, childhood immunizations, other health screenings, and transportation services.

• Strengthen and increase the availability of family support services and programs—specifically, those that enhance relationships and create processes to protect families and their members, allowing children in poverty to flourish. Consider programs that promote reading readiness and adult literacy, health education (prevention and treatment) for child and adult care, and creating and using social networks or investments in social capital formulation.

• Encourage state support of kinship coparenting initiatives for incarcerated parents. There are a growing number of mothers, a disproportionately large number of them African American, in prison. Initiatives may include training aimed at creating and maintaining effective coparenting relationships and dealing with developmental normative child challenges, such as handling noncompliance. Also important are introducing techniques to avoid blame, practicing nondefensive listening during conflict discussions, and respecting the power differential (e.g., between incarcerated parent and caregiving relative or designee).

SUMMARY AND CONCLUSION

Knowledge of many factors is required to understand the effect of laws and administrative rules on those whom a law or group of laws are intended to serve. It is critical to know the comprehensive definition or statement of the social problem that prompted the policy. The problem definition will enable practitioners to critically assess and determine if and how legislation or administrative rules correct, improve, or make worse the problem or condition in question. The federal child welfare laws discussed in this chapter exist to prevent or ameliorate the effects of poor parenting or unhealthy family life on children, and to protect children from unsafe environments or forms of maltreatment (e.g., physical abuse, sexual abuse, abandonment, and neglect).

DISCUSSION QUESTIONS

1. What makes some aspects of a policy acceptable and others not acceptable? For example, the Indian Child Welfare Act targets one underserved subpopulation of children while not targeting African American children, who statistically are overrepresented in the out-of-home child

protective service system. Do you understand the rationale for the In-dian Child Welfare Act? Should the law target only Native American children?

2. Do we continue to need the special targeted provisions associated with the Indian Child Welfare Act?

3. How do beliefs, values, ideology, customs, and traditions influence our interpretation of policies and laws?

ACTIVITIES FOR ONGOING LEARNING

1. Interview an agency director who delivers services in response to a social problem affecting children and their families. Ask the director what barriers exist that may impede or limit the agency's ability to effec-tively serve the target population. Ask what is done to ensure that policy is implemented equitably.

2. Think about the population you work with or hope to work with. What federal policies are in place to govern the services provided or pro-grams implemented? What state policies govern the same services? Are there local policies that govern the services?

3. Identify some of the challenges and opportunities you envision if you were to craft a comprehensive statute or law aimed at improving the condition of the population that you work with or hope to work with in the future.

4. Identify a social problem that you wish to address. What was the first federal policy written regarding this problem? How effective was the policy in addressing the problem?

5. Do you anticipate changes in the social dynamic or demographics associated with the problem you identified in question 4? How might such changes affect the effectiveness of existing laws or policies in ad-dressing the problem?

REFERENCES

Administration for Children Youth and Families (ACYF). 2001. *Child Welfare Outcomes 2001: Annual Report to Congress.* Washington, D.C.: ACYF.

Bartholet, E. 1999. *Nobody's Children.* Boston: Beacon Press.

Billingsley, A. 1968. *Black Families in White America*. Englewood Cliffs, N.J.: Prentice Hall.

Chapin Hall Center for Children. 2008. *Understanding Racial and Ethnic Disparity in Child Welfare and Juvenile Justice*. Chicago: Chapin Hall Center for Children at the University of Chicago.

Children's Defense Fund. 2010. *Held Captive: Child Poverty in America*. Washington, D.C.: Children's Defense Fund.

Children's Defense Fund and Center for Law and Social Policy. 2008. *Fostering Connections to Success*. Press Release. Washington, D.C.: Children's Defense Fund and Center for Law and Social Policy.

Congressional Record. 2003. A Bill to Amend the Child Abuse Prevention & Treatment Act to Make Improvements to and Reauthorize Programs Under That Act, and for Other Purposes. Report: 108-150, H5307–16. Washington, D.C.

Crosson-Tower, C. 2007. *Exploring Child Welfare: A Practice Perspective*. 4th ed. Boston: Pearson Education.

Curtis, C. M. 1996. "The Adoption of African American Children by Whites: A Renewed Conflict." *Families in Society: Journal of Contemporary Human Services* 77 (3): 156–65.

Curtis, C. M., & R. Alexander. 2010. "Correlates of African American Children in and out of Their Families." *Families in Society: Journal of Contemporary Social Services* 91 (1): 85–90.

Curtis, C. M., & R. Denby. 2004. "Impact of the ASFA (1997) on Families of Color: Workers Share Their Thoughts." *Families in Society: Journal of Contemporary Human Services* 85 (1): 71–79.

———. 2011. "African American Children in the Child Welfare System: Requiem or Reform." *Journal of Public Child Welfare* 5 (1): 111–37.

Denby, R., & C. M. Curtis. 2003. "Why Children of Color Are Not the Target of Family Preservation Services: A Case for Program Reform." *Journal of Sociology and Social Welfare* 30 (2): 149–73.

Dixon, J. 2008. "The African American Child Welfare Act: A Legal Redress for African American Disproportionality in Child Protection Cases." *Berkeley Journal of African American Law and Policy* 109:109–45.

Hill, R. B. 1972. *Strengths of Black Families*. Lanham, Md.: University Press of America.

———. 2001. "The Role of Race in Parental Reunification." Paper presented at the Race Matters Forum, Chevy Chase, Md.

———. 2006. *A Synthesis of Research on Disproportionality in Child Welfare: An Update*. Washington, D.C.: Center for Study of Social Policy & Casey Family Programs.

Kempe, C. H., F. N. Silverman, B. F. Steele, W. Droegemueller, & H. K. Silver. 1962. "The Battered Child Syndrome." *Journal of the American Medical Association* 181 (17): 17–24.

Stein, T. 2006. *Child Welfare and the Law.* 2nd ed. Washington, D.C.: Child Welfare League of America.

U.S. Department of Health and Human Services, Administration for Children and Families, Administration on Children, Youth and Families, Children's Bureau. 2008. *Preliminary Estimates for FY 2006 as of January 2008.* http://www .acf.hhs.gov/programs/cb.

U.S. House of Representatives, Committee on Ways and Means. 2009. *The Green Book.* Washington, D.C.

Whitelaw-Downs, S., E. Moore, & E. J. McFadden. 2009. *Child Welfare and Family Services: Policies and Practice.* 8th ed. Boston: Pearson Education.

Wilhelmus, M. 1998. "A Content Analysis of Parent Narratives in Termination of Parental Rights Trials: Emerging Themes on the Legal Loss of Children." Ph.D. diss., Ohio State University.

A CASE STUDY: CULTURAL ADAPTATION AND SERVICES— THE DAVIS FAMILY

We provide a case study to facilitate a thoughtful consideration of how programs and services may be culturally adapted to better meet the needs of children who are underserved or who have disproportionately poor outcomes in the child protective service (CPS) system. The case study content will be used in chapters 4, 5, and 6 on protection, permanence, and child and family well-being to illustrate opportunities the theoretical framework of cultural adaptation provides for strengthening approaches to policy formulation, program planning, and service delivery. Following is an introduction to the Davis family.

Linda Davis was the middle child of three children born to Elizabeth and Samuel Davis. From a young age this precocious African American female displayed a rare musical genius. Her talents were showcased weekly in the children's choir at church, where her parents were active members and ensured that Linda and her brother and sister, Samuel, Jr., and Sandy, also attended regularly. Linda left home after graduating from high school to attend Wilberforce University in Ohio, having earned a full-tuition scholarship. In college she was a music major. During her first year of college, Linda met Charles, a resident of the local community. Charles and Linda began to hang out and party together. Charles was a local drug dealer and introduced Linda to marijuana; eventually the drug of choice was cocaine. At age 17 Linda learned she was pregnant. Upon learning of the pregnancy Charles insisted the child could not be his and he would have nothing to do with Linda or the child. She returned home to live with her parents, initially with plans to return to her studies after the birth of her son, Dwight.

Linda's parents insisted she seek professional help for depression that she experienced throughout her pregnancy. Though a referral was made for counseling, there was no follow through. After Dwight was born Linda moved in with a friend and worked in a local restaurant. She met Michael and they began to date. When Linda became pregnant she and Michael moved in together, and together they provided care for Dwight and the baby, Jackson. Michael worked part time but supplemented his earnings by selling crack cocaine. After the birth of Jackson, Linda began to use crack to "ease her nerves" from parenting the two young children. Linda's mother, Elizabeth Davis, was not very involved with the care of her two young grandchildren at this time; she was the primary caregiver for her husband, who had been diagnosed with late-stage prostate cancer. After Mr. Davis died, Linda became more distant from her mother and siblings and more preoccupied with the use of crack cocaine.

Linda's live-in boyfriend and father of Jackson, Michael, left when Linda learned she was pregnant with a third child. Elizabeth Davis threatened to contact child protective services because she was certain Linda was still using drugs while pregnant. During the late stages of the pregnancy, Mrs. Davis did contact child protective services. CPS investigated the report but found no evidence to substantiate maltreatment of the two older children.

A second CPS referral was made when Michel was born and cocaine was detected in his system. CPS substantiated the referral and, based on Linda's agreement to participate in drug treatment services, a plan was developed for in-home services. These services continued for six months, but no ongoing case was initiated. Linda was killed in an automobile accident while she was in a car with a man she had begun to date. No one survived the accident. Mrs. Davis was contacted by the police following the accident, and an emergency placement order was initiated through juvenile court placing Dwight, age 10, Jackson, age 7, and Michel, age 15 months, in her care. At a preliminary hearing the next day, it was determined that the children would continue their stay with their maternal grandmother. After the court hearing the case was transferred to the foster care division.

Mrs. Davis is concerned whether she can adequately care for her three grandchildren by herself. In addition to the foster care payments and food stamps for the children, she receives a small pension from her recent retirement at a local manufacturing plant. Her youngest daughter, Sandy Jones, age 26, lives with Mrs. Davis along with her 5-year-old son. Sandy is divorced and has no relationship with her ex-husband, who does not pay child support. She works about thirty hours a week at a local grocery store chain while she is enrolled in college part time to complete her bachelor's degree. Because her mother allows her to live rent free and helps with the care of her son, Sandy hopes to move into her own place within another year or two.

Mrs. Davis has a son, her eldest child, who owns an insurance franchise in a neighboring community. Samuel, Jr., age 32, lives in a suburban community with his wife, who is a registered nurse, and their three children. He has been supportive of his mother and his sisters' children, but there are limits to his capacity to give money. With their three children and maintaining his business in an unstable economy, his disposable income is limited. Samuel's wife is very leery of making commitments of money that may not be sustainable. Samuel has often included Sandy's son and Linda's children—when they were accessible—on family outings.

CPS has suggested that Mrs. Davis should adopt the three children. Primarily because of her age, she is reluctant to make such a "permanent" commitment. She is also concerned that Jackson, who seemed to perform well in preschool, is now having difficulty paying attention in class, does not complete tasks assigned, and is often sent to the principal's office for fighting. The baby boy, Michel, seems "slow" and was a colicky baby. At 15 months he does not stand unassisted and is just beginning to crawl; he does not speak at all. Michel was enrolled in a program for children with developmental disabilities at age 12 months. It is not possible to determine long-term intellectual deficits at this time. Dwight, age 10, is in the 4th grade; he is an average student, getting Bs and Cs. He is a sports enthusiast and currently plays intramural basketball. Teachers describe him as pensive but likeable and helpful to other students and to teachers when asked. Teachers have observed him breaking down and crying about his mom on a number of occasions.

While the CPS agency suggested the grandmother consider adopting the minor children, some workers may question or not support relative adoptions, and some jurisdictions may prefer permanent foster care or legal guardianship over relative adoption. Responding to this case in a culturally responsive manner should begin with the social worker or caseworker exploring with the grandmother the identification of other relatives—the extended family system—such as sisters, brothers, uncles, or cousins who may be available to assist her. The involvement of the extended family to include nonrelatives who may function as blood relatives is a tradition in the African American community. Perhaps a permanency roundtable or family team meeting would be helpful to address the issues and needs of the family, bringing together collaborative partners—including CPS staff and other community providers as relevant—to coordinate services. Extended family members and agency staff can discuss a viable case plan for the children and family.

The social worker should explore with the grandmother her willingness and preparedness to assume full custody of the children. Kinship care has received increased recognition in recent years. Traditionally in the African American community many families have informally assumed responsibility for the care of relatives' children resulting from a variety of circumstances when parents cannot or choose not to parent. If the grandmother agrees to consider permanent custody and the local jurisdiction suggests permanent foster care, licensing may be a requirement for permanent placement consideration. The dynamics of change in the grandmother's life should be explored: does she have social/emotional outlets? Her need to cope with the loss of her daughter, her spouse, and the relationships with her other adult children should also be probed. The social worker should explore whether the grandmother needs to address fears or concerns about her future; she may be interested in pursuing professional counseling, for which a referral would be indicated.

The social worker might discuss with the grandmother what role community and civic memberships or affiliations play in her life and may be a source of support, such as the church, a sorority, or a mutual aid group through recreational facilities. Caregivers must be emotionally healthy and feel supported—particularly after trauma associated with the sudden and unexpected death of a child—to provide optimum nurturance and support to young children and youth.

It is critically important to assess the impact of trauma on each of the three children—for example, the sudden and tragic death of their mother and their exposure to multiple caregivers with different cultural environments and parental or disciplinary approaches. The children are at risk for having difficulty forming and maintaining relationships and behaviorally acting out as they develop and mature. It is possible that home uncertainty may result in instability—a pattern of moving or bouncing from home to home in later years if issues of safety, well-being, and permanency are not adequately addressed.

4

Safety and Protection

This chapter is the first of three that explore the services provided to children and families once contact has been made with the child welfare system. The chapter begins with a definition of child abuse and neglect and a discussion of the role of child protective services in the child welfare system. Following the review of child maltreatment categories and using the cultural adaption framework, the chapter is organized into three major sections: child investigation and protection, the child welfare court process, and out-of-home placement.

CHILD ABUSE AND NEGLECT

Categories of child abuse and neglect are typically included in the more general term *child maltreatment*, defined through both federal and state statutory and regulatory guidance. From the perspective of federal law, the Child Abuse Prevention and Treatment Act (CAPTA) defines child abuse and neglect as "any recent act or failure to act on the part of a parent or caretaker which results in death, serious physical or emotional harm, sexual abuse or exploitation; or an act or failure to act which presents an imminent risk of serious harm" (CWIG, 2008a:2). CAPTA provisions represent the minimum standards that states must use when defining child abuse and neglect. Most states provide further detail and operationalization of child abuse and neglect by establishing statutes, rules, policies, procedures, and operating manuals aligned with the parameters of local communities. State laws provide local guidance for situations that constitute maltreatment and thereby give direction for conditions that qualify for reporting, investigation, and ultimately

EXISTING TRENDS

Differentiating Child Neglect from Child Poverty

ALTERNATIVE RESPONSE: FRANKLIN COUNTY, OHIO

African American children face multiple risk factors that increase their likelihood of involvement in the child welfare system. For example, one in four African Americans lives in poverty, more than one third of all African American children live in poverty, and one in four African American households struggles to put food on the table (U.S. Department of Commerce, 2009, 2010). These conditions, along with safety and risk-assessment bias, are just two of the factors that place African American children at risk for entry into foster care, where their presence is four times that of European American children (U.S. Department of Health and Human Services, 2010).

One program, Alternative Response in Franklin County, Ohio, found a way to address the disparities in income security that place children and families at risk by frontloading services and placing children on a different response track. The Alternative Response project provides families with "a non-investigative, family-friendly assessment and a more family-driven approach" to services that has resulted in a reduction of African American foster care rates (Child Welfare Information Gateway [CWIG], 2011a). By targeting high-risk neighborhoods for services and helping referred families quickly access community-based services, the project allowed half of the families to receive an alternative response, and 93 percent of those who received an alternative response had their cases closed within forty-five days (Hawkins, 2009; Kaplan & Rohm, 2010).

substantiation. Typically, categories of child maltreatment include the following:

- *Physical abuse.* Physical abuses are harm or nonaccidental injuries to a child that are inflicted by an adult caretaker or parent.
- *Child neglect.* Child neglect is typically thought of as a parent's failure to provide the basic necessities, including food, shelter, supervision, and other concrete provisions. Neglect is also defined as a parent's failure to provide for a child's emotional, medical, and educational needs. The most common type of child maltreatment is neglect,

and it is highly correlated with poverty. For example, according to the National Incidence Studies of Child Abuse and Neglect report (NIS-4), children whose parents are unemployed experience three or more times the rate of neglect. Likewise, children from low socioeconomic status households are seven times more likely to be neglected.

- *Sexual abuse.* CAPTA defines sexual abuse as "the employment, use, persuasion, inducement, enticement, or coercion of any child to engage in or assist any other person to engage in any sexually explicit conduct or simulation of such conduct for the purpose of producing a visual depiction of such conduct, or the rape, and in cases of caretaker or inter-familial relationships, statutory rape, molestation, prostitution, or other form of sexual exploitation of children, or incest with children" (CWIG, 2008a:3).

- *Emotional abuse.* Emotional abuse may be one of the most elusive categories of abuse and neglect because child welfare authorities must be able to show evidence that a harm or mental injury has occurred. Nonetheless, emotional abuse is typically thought of as behavior or conditions that impair a child's emotional development or psychological health and growth.

- *Abandonment.* According to the Child Welfare Information Gateway (2008a), many states classify abandonment as neglect and refer to the existence of the following circumstances or conditions: the parent's identity or whereabouts are unknown, the child has been left alone and has suffered harm, or the parent has ceased contact with the child and no longer provides for the child's welfare.

- *Substance abuse.* Parents or caregivers can be charged with child abuse under the category of substance abuse when there has been prenatal exposure to illegal drugs, alcohol, and other substances; when such drugs as methamphetamines are manufactured in a child's presence; when drugs are sold or given to a child; or when the parent is impaired by drugs and alcohol to the extent that he or she can no longer provide adequate care for a child (CWIG, 2008a).

Rates and Prevalence

Child abuse and neglect prevalence rates are typically captured in statistical reports and databases that categorize state-specific findings as well as national patterns. For example, the National Child Abuse and Neglect

Data System (NCANDS) provides case-level data for all children who are involved in the child protection system. The Child Abuse Prevention and Treatment Act (CAPTA) established NCANDS, and states voluntarily submit abuse and neglect data to the system that are in turn analyzed and categorized. According to data reported for 2009, an estimated 3.3 million referrals, comprising alleged maltreatment of approximately 6 million children, were recorded (U.S. Department of Health and Human Services [USDHHS], 2009a). Nearly 62 percent of these children were screened in and responded to by the state or local child protection system. Seventy-eight percent of the 2009 maltreatment reports were incidents of neglect. Seventeen percent of maltreatment cases were physical abuse, 9 percent were sexual abuse, and about 8 percent were emotional abuse.

Another data reporting system is the National Incidence Studies of Child Abuse and Neglect (NIS), a congressionally mandated report that provides abuse and neglect estimates and also measures change in incidence from earlier time waves. According to Sedlak et al. (2010), authors of the *Fourth National Incidence Studies of Child Abuse and Neglect (NIS-4)*, three factors—parental alcohol use, drug use, and mental illness—continue to be those most frequently associated with child maltreatment. Also, trend data suggest a decline in all categories of abuse since the NIS-3 study; this decline in abuse is consistent with self-reports and the data provided by NCANDS. However, the NIS authors do caution that the declining abuse trends could be an artifact of the manner in which the data are collected.

Finally, a third major data reporting system is the Child Welfare Outcomes Report Data, published by the U.S. Department of Health and Human Services Children's Bureau. This system provides a custom report builder containing the most up-to-date data about child welfare outcomes. The annual reporting system provides state performance data in seven categories of goals: (1) reducing recurrence of child abuse and/ or neglect, (2) reducing the incidence of child abuse and/or neglect in foster care, (3) increasing permanency for children in foster care, (4) reducing time in foster care to reunification without increasing reentry, (5) reducing time in foster care to adoption, (6) increasing placement stability, and (7) reducing placement of young children in group homes or institutions (USDHHS, 2009b). The trend report that spans the years 2004 through 2007 indicates the following concerning its seven state performance markers: With respect to goal 1, reductions of recurrence of child maltreatment were noted in 56 percent of states; for goal 2, twenty-one states demonstrated improved performance. Regarding goal 3, for the most part states made significant gains in achieving permanency for the children in their care; however, they experienced less success for two categories of children: those with a diagnosed disability and those who entered care when they were over the age of 12. For goal 4, 61 percent of states showed a decline in performance in the length of foster care stay for reunified children. The length of stay for reunified children increased from 6.5 to 7.7 months. For goal 5, very few states were able to achieve timely adoptions (less than twelve months or less than twenty-four months) for the children in their care. In terms of goal 6, the report defines placement stability as a child experiencing two or fewer moves; most states were able to achieve this outcome when the child was only in care for a twelve-month period, but most states were not able to do so when the child was in care for a longer period of time. For goal 7, in about 50 percent of the states only 5.7 percent of children under the age of 12 were placed in group homes or institutions, but in twelve states 10 to 20 percent of such children were placed in group homes. Still, improvements were noted in the outcome for goal 7 in both 2006 and 2007.

Experiences of African American Children

There remains a tremendous amount of professional disagreement concerning whether African American children suffer more abuse and neglect than their ethnic counterparts or whether they are more likely to be reported as abused and neglected. For example, Drake et al. (2011) state that racial bias in reporting does not account for the disproportionate number of African American children in the child welfare system. Instead, they believe that observed racial differences are the result of the risk factors that African American families experience. These findings counter long-held beliefs that children of all ethnic backgrounds experience abuse and neglect at the same rate (see original National Incidence Study cycles—NIS reports). It is interesting to note that unlike the previous National Incidence Study cycles, NIS-4 did decipher ethnic difference in incidences of maltreatment.

In almost all reporting categories, the incidences of maltreatment for African American children were significantly higher than for white children. The observations made in this text derive from an assumption that child abuse and neglect reporting as experienced by African American children is highly complex and more than likely involves interplay among multiple factors, including larger system race bias and the reality of such risks factors as poverty, which African American children and families do experience disproportionately. A sociopolitical debate on the extent to which there is racial bias in the occurrence, reporting, and substantiation of child abuse and neglect is beyond the scope of this book. However, as we consider how we can better make cultural adaptations to practice so that we support the needs of African American children and families, it is appropriate to briefly describe here what the perceptions are concerning how African American children experience abuse and neglect and how they experience the child welfare system.

According to the NIS-4, African American children experience nearly a two-to-one rate of general maltreatment compared with white children. About 24 in 1,000 African American children are maltreated. Closer examination reveals that the maltreatment rates for African American children (as is the case with most other ethnic groups) are largely composed of incidences of neglect. Of the 24 per 1,000 children who experience maltreatment, about 10 suffer abuse, while the majority, 14, experience neglect. Trend data prepared by the NIS in which changes in maltreatment are compared between the NIS-3 and NIS-4 reports show a decrease in maltreatment for all ethnic groups but less so for African American children. For example, rates of emotional neglect decreased by 33 percent for white children but increased 30 percent for African American children. Similarly, the number of accounts in the NIS-4 rates of serious harm to children decreased substantially for white children (43 percent since the NIS-3 study) but increased by 8 percent for African American children.

For another perspective on the issue of child abuse and neglect, readers may want to consider a longitudinal database referred to as the National Survey of Child and Adolescent Well-Being (NSCAW) (USDHHS, Office of Planning, Research and Evaluation, 2011). The NSCAW studied children from 1997 to 2010 and is considered to be a primary-source database (i.e., the data are drawn from firsthand reports from children, parents, and child welfare caseworkers). The NSCAW concurs with the NIS-4 findings that child neglect is the most frequent type of maltreatment, but it departs from the findings of the NIS-4 on just about every other reporting category. According to the NSCAW, Hispanic children are those most likely to experience physical abuse but not as likely to experience neglect or parental failure to provide. African American children are the group most likely to experience parental failure to supervise, while white children and other groups are most likely to experience sexual abuse.

In short, according to NCANDS, nationally about 22 percent of the victims of child abuse and neglect are African American. This is a disproportionate representation of African American children because they constitute only about 12 percent of the U.S. population. Although African American children are reported to disproportionately experience abuse, they are less likely to receive in-home services than white children and are instead removed from parental care and placed into foster care (Roberts, 2002). Stepping aside from the often sociopolitical debate of whether African American children are abused at higher rates or just reported and substantiated more often, it becomes more difficult to explain why they continue to experience service disparities once out of the care of their parents and under the supervision of the child welfare system. For example, McRoy (2004, 2008), Courtney et al. (1996), and the Children's Defense Fund (2007) noted the extreme service disparities that African American children encounter. Once in the out-of-home care system, African American children experience poorer well-being and permanency outcomes than other groups of children. To have an influence on reducing service inequities and preventing poor outcomes for African American children once they interface with the child welfare system, we must consider what changes can take place at the initial point of engagement and throughout the service process.

CHILD WELFARE SYSTEM COMPONENTS

Although child welfare systems vary from state-to-state, most of them are structured with three basic components: (1) a child abuse investigation and protection system (typically referred to as child protection services); (2) a legal system typically organized into a family or juvenile court structure, which has the authority to make rulings about the protection and care of a child; and (3) a child placement system typically comprising a multitude of out-of-home placement or in-home supervision options, including various foster care arrangements and residential/group care placements with an often complex continuum of decision points.

Almost half of the children who exit the care of the child welfare system were in care for less than one year (USDHHS, 2009c). However, African American children experience difficulty exiting the foster care system and achieving reunification with their parents. African American children's length of stay is longer and is considered to be affected by a lack of housing, distrust of child welfare officials, and a lack of substance abuse treatment and other support services (U.S. GAO, 2007). Children can cycle through multiple decision points and court contacts, including protective, placement (or dispositional), periodic review, permanency, termination of parental rights, and adoption/guardianship hearings (for complete definitions, see the glossary). In response to the poor outcomes that children experience during their involvement with the child welfare system, different court models and protection procedures are being implemented and tested. Following is a review of protection and court procedures and the effect they have had on African American children.

Protection and Safety

The Investigation and Protection Framework

State statutes typically provide authority and guidance for child welfare officials to act locally in investigating child maltreatment allegations. Figure 4.1 depicts three interrelated components that influence the work

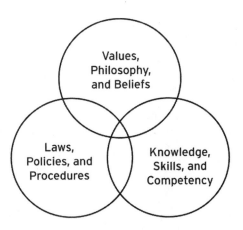

Figure 4.1 Major influences in child protection and investigation.

of child protection officials. As a "helping entity" composed largely of professionals with health and human services backgrounds, a child protection system is typically influenced by (1) guiding principles, values, and beliefs; (2) predetermined laws and bureaucratic processes and procedures; and (3) workers' knowledge, skills, and competency.

Principles, Values, and Beliefs

Traditionally, child welfare investigation procedures operate within a value system that can be characterized as having a child-protective and child-centered focus. Agencies have historically vocalized a concern for the care of children and in doing so have maintained a position whereby parents are often blamed for the lack of care and dangerous conditions that their children face. In recent decades the underlying philosophical base of child welfare investigations represents a shift toward being child protective but simultaneously demonstrating sensitivity to the notion that children are a part of families and the family's functioning must improve in order for the child's functioning to do the same. A culturally adapted child welfare investigation model that is focused on the needs of African Americans would be influenced by a belief system that stresses the importance of protecting children and their families. Professional values of client engagement emphasize respect, responsiveness, and cultural sensitivity.

As displayed in table 4.1, the culturally adapted approach extends beyond having a child- and family-centered perspective. It recognizes that given the vulnerabilities and risk factors experienced by African

TABLE 4.1
Traditional, Contemporary, and Culturally Adapted Investigation and Protection Frameworks

	Traditional	**Contemporary**	**Culturally Adapted**
Principles, Values, and Beliefs	Child protective and child centered	Child protective and family centered	Child and family protective
Laws, Processes, and Procedures	Narrowly defined and closed process	Federally directed and highly incentive driven	Culturally represented stakeholders involved in decision making
Knowledge, Skills, and Competency	Assumed and unquestioned	Emphasis on what works and evidence-based practice	Emphasis on what works culturally

American parents, there should be a professional value orientation that seeks to understand what the parent's environmental safety needs are. For example, a child welfare practitioner who encounters a child in an unsafe housing situation is concerned about securing safe housing for the child and the parent. In short, the value undergirding a culturally adapted investigation and protection framework would prioritize *cultural accountability*, expressing a belief in improving parents' capacity to care for their children.

Laws, Processes, and Procedures

Although child abuse laws are defined operationally at a local level, federal instruction is apparent within state statutes and even agencies' operating policies and procedures. Traditionally investigation and the work of child protection officials have been informed by laws and statues riddled with ambiguity and lacking specific direction. As laws began to gain more specificity, many were ineffective because of the narrow or inadequate nature of the provisions that accompanied them. Moreover, one criticism of child abuse investigation and protection laws concerns the process in which federal laws and state statues are developed. Historically stakeholders have noted the lack of involvement of key constituent groups in the formation of policies and procedures.

Contemporary approaches used to establish child abuse investigation and protection laws and policies are still federally influenced. They are responsive to reimbursement rates and other monetary incentives, but offer more flexibility in the establishment of provisions than has been the situation historically. For example, child welfare agencies have the flexibility of using Title IV-E funding to provide kinship guardianship payments, which was previously not an option for relatives. More contemporary child abuse investigation and protection procedures place an emphasis on empirically discovering effective ways to reduce African American disproportionality by altering engagement approaches. One such approach that has shown promise is the Point of Engagement (POE) model (Marts et al., 2008).

In a two-year evaluation of the POE approach, the initiative proved promising in reducing the rate of child removals, increasing timely reunifications, and increasing the acquisition of legal permanency. The POE model is more indicative of contemporary investigation and protection procedures because it involves shared decision making, cooperation with the community, and elements of alternative response. According to Marts et al., the model "provides a faster response for the provision of services and, using a team approach, actively placing an emphasis on shared decision making and comprehensive case evaluation and investigation" (343).

The core elements of the approach include informal resources, differential response, alternative response, voluntary services, intensive services workers, team decision-making/child safety conferences, and emergency response investigations. Two important features of the POE model are the *differential* and *alternative response* approaches, which are being implemented more frequently in state child welfare systems and are associated with contemporary approaches to child abuse investigation and protection. The Child Welfare Information Gateway (2008a:3) uses the work of Schene (2001) to define differential response as "a CPS practice that allows for more than one method of initial response to reports of child abuse and neglect. Also called 'dual track,' 'multiple track,' or 'alternative response,' this approach recognizes variation in the nature of reports and the value of responding differently to different types of case."

Differential response uses a two-track approach to child abuse and neglect response: investigation, involving the most severe cases of maltreatment, and assessment, which is typically reserved for the low-moderate risk cases and consists of assessing the family's strengths and needs and then implementing commensurate services. Differential response has gained momentum nationally partly as a result of child welfare officials' growing discontent with traditional ways of handling child maltreatment investigations. Thus far outcome data and research on the differential response approach suggest positive outcomes (CWIG, 2008a; Shusterman et al., 2005).

Legislative progress has yielded a few positive outcomes (e.g., increase in adoption rates), but the gains have not systematically affected the disparities experienced by African American children. Cultural adaptations to child abuse investigation policy would move the system to instituting processes that protect children and families in the least intrusive and culture-preserving manner possible. For example, although investigation authority rests with the state or county, a desire to culturally adapt procedures would usher in the frequent and serious use of citizen advisory panels that routinely review case decisions made by an agency. Such panels would be highly representative of the client population that is served. Differential or alternative response models could be culturally adapted by ensuring that the programming is community based and that it is operated by indigenous agencies with a demonstrated record of successful involvement in the African American community.

Knowledge, Skills, and Competency

Traditional frameworks of investigation and protection were thought to be highly subjective, involving a great deal of assumed or presumed knowledge and skill on the part of investigators. Investigators relied heavily on practice wisdom centered on repeated and sustained involvement or intervention in child maltreatment matters. In many respects it was the legal authority that led to unquestioned knowledge and competency. One area of child maltreatment investigation that has evolved and is illustrative of the changing nature of the field is that of safety and risk assessments. The next section considers the nature of assessment, assessment bias, and necessary cultural adaptations.

Safety and Risk Assessment

Assessment involves "the collection of information to inform decision-making about a child, youth, or family. It is always conducted as a means to an end—to identify issues the family is facing, design a plan, and provide services that will assist in resolving the issues identified" (CWIG, 2011b:1). Comprehensive assessment in the field of child welfare is usually done to determine a child's safety and risk of maltreatment, the child's ability to achieve permanency, and the progress of the child and family toward health and well-being (CWIG, 2011b). The processes of risk and safety assessments are distinguished from each other. The issue of safety is typically conceptualized as two responses (safe or unsafe), whereas risk can be multilevel, involving a low-high continuum (American Public Human Services Association, 2009). As assessment has evolved, many child welfare entities recognize the benefits of using formalized and structured tools as one of many data points in their work to understand the needs and strengths of families. However, safety and risk assessments are considered more effective and useful when used in connection with other family engagement, case monitoring, and service planning processes (CWIG, 2011b). Today the field emphasizes a concern for quality in service delivery, and there is ever-increasing attention given to evidence-based practice. Approaches to risk and safety assessment promote the need for outcomes that are effective and involve minimal bias. According to the American Public Health Association (2009:18), effective assessment processes involve the following critical questions:

1. Is there serious harm to a child?
2. Is there an immediate threat of serious harm?
3. Is there a vulnerable child?
4. Are protective capacities within the family adequate to mitigate any threats of immediate serious harm?
5. Is there a need for an immediate safety intervention or action?

These five questions are answered using the following activities:

1. Review and evaluate all available information (e.g., family history; criminal history; cultural, racial, and economic demographics).
2. Consider alternative explanations of the causes of the reported maltreatment.
3. Observe and interview all the children in the household.
4. Observe and interview all the caregivers in the household.
5. Interview other individuals who might have relevant information about the family's circumstances and case situations.
6. Develop partnerships with the family and children and conduct interviews using family engagement strategies.
7. Observe interactions among caregivers, children, and other family members.
8. Identify the factors that may cause or be associated with the maltreatment in order to control safety.
9. Analyze information objectively and consider what other information is needed to arrive at a conclusion about the family's protective capacity and the vulnerabilities a child faces. This information should be assessed from the vantage point of considering what the mitigating factors may be as the investigator draws close to a decision (American Public Health Association, 2009).

Cultural Adaptations in Safety and Risk Assessment
Increasingly, child welfare officials are using structured safety and risk assessment tools to minimize the amount of subjectivity and bias that is inherent in the process. Child welfare agencies reportedly use assessment tools as a way to systematically assess the level of risk in keeping children in their homes (U.S. GAO, 2007). Research has shown that safety and

risk assessment tools are race neutral and decrease worker subjectivity that can lead to unnecessary child removal (Johnson, 2004; Loman & Siegel, 2004). Two concerns are noted about the use of structured safety and risk assessment tools: The focus on social conditions such as poverty may increase the representation of children of color in the removal process, and a number of child welfare systems that use assessment tools have not designed them to reduce or address the disproportionate representation of African American children in the system (U.S. GAO, 2007). Cultural adaptations to the assessment process would expand the list of critical questions above in one simple step by encouraging investigators to consider the extent to which conclusions are derived from an informed perspective of the child and family's cultural background. Assessment processes would follow the principles of family engagement (CWIG, 2010) and be highly interactive between workers, clients, and family advocates. Moreover, the process could be adapted to support cultural needs and promote understanding by the following activities:

1. Use investigation activities that support assessment decisions that consider the use of cultural informants.
2. Consider the extent to which the investigation context, setting, or place is culturally compatible with the clients' needs.
3. Consider the extent to which the assessment tool has high levels of cultural fidelity.
4. Include a process that allows for a determination of the extent to which case dynamics involve true indicators of neglect as opposed to signs and symptoms of poverty.
5. Determine whether there are immediate service or safety provisions that could be supported by the clients' cultural environment.

Child Welfare System and Court Involvement

In most states child maltreatment cases are typically managed by juvenile or family courts. It can also be the case that a tribal or general court has jurisdiction over matters of child abuse and neglect. Whatever the structure, the court process is a significant determinant of how children and families experience the child welfare system. For example, according to Badeau (2004), it is the court process that may well determine children's timelines and movement throughout the child welfare system. The pace

THE DAVIS FAMILY

In a cultural adaptation model specific to the needs of Mrs. Davis and her grandchildren, it would first be a worthwhile consideration for all involved professionals and service entities to maintain a *value* stance that recognizes that both the children and the grandmother have safety needs that are equally important. A professional interventionist would view both the children and the grandmother as the client and would equally regard their unique needs. The children have need for a safe, stable, and consistent caregiver. Mrs. Davis has the need to maintain herself economically above poverty; she cannot afford to provide care for the children if doing so would catapult her into a financial crisis and compromise her living standards. All subsequent planning and intervention with the Davis family should be developed around the belief that protective factors must be enhanced for both the children and Mrs. Davis. Additionally, *agency policies, procedures, and practices* would need to be in place, incorporating the use of cultural agents or indigenous stakeholders and/or advocates, thus supporting the work that might be traditionally done by a caseworker. For example, Mrs. Davis could be offered and paired with a kinship liaison (Denby, 2011) who could serve as a mentor, supportive assistant, and guide as she prepares for the caregiving roles. It would be important for the kinship liaison to be appropriately matched from a cultural standpoint so that he or she conveys an understanding of the experiences that Mrs. Davis will soon encounter. Finally, in intervening with the Davis family, professionals will need to be adept and possess *knowledge* about why Mrs. Davis might be hesitant about adopting her grandchildren. It would be important to know from a cultural standpoint what Mrs. Davis is experiencing in relation to loss and grief issues and how such issues affect her decision to move forward with adopting Dwight, Jackson, and Michel. An important question for the interventionist to consider might include: "To what extent does the proposed case plan factor in Mrs. Davis's needs as it relates to her current position in life (i.e., a widowed, retired, African American female)?" The incorporation of practice models that are evidence-based is an important consideration, but intervening based on the cultural needs and interests of the Davises is just as significant.

at which children move through the system is often influenced by the court's competing responsibilities to protect them, make timely decisions about their futures, and protect parents' rights.

Observers of the child welfare court process have noted that some of the major impediments to effective work on behalf of children and families include a lack of cooperation and poor working relationships between the courts and child welfare agencies and the difficulty that the courts experience with personnel and information and data management (Badeau, 2004). Given these challenges and the fact that it is the court that makes several crucial legal determinations, including decisions to place a child in out-of-home care, reunify a child with his or her family, terminate a parent's rights, or allow an adoption to occur, any actions toward cultural adaptations to the system of child welfare on behalf of African American children must focus on the court.

Cultural adaptations to the court process may stem from some of the modern reform efforts currently taking place in many legal jurisdictions across the country. Broadly speaking, three major reform efforts have taken shape in child welfare courts since 1980: Model Courts, Court Improvement Programs, and the implementation of court performance standards. Model Courts were initiated through private foundation funding as pilot efforts to develop mechanisms that would allow courts to make "reasonable efforts" that were required in relation to federal law. "Model Courts serve as models of systems' change identifying impediments to the timeliness of court events and delivery of services for children in care, and then design and implement court- and agency-based changes to address these barriers" (National Council on Juvenile and Family Court Judges, 2008:1). As Model Courts evolved, they began to "engage in a number of innovative strategies to improve both court performance and outcomes for children" (Badeau, 2004:4). Innovative practices and reform efforts witnessed under Model Court efforts include redesigning courtrooms, improving court access, redesigning calendars to be more child and family accommodating, involving community leaders in court activities, and placing judges in leadership roles designed to make overall system improvements (Badeau).

The Court Improvement Program permits local courts to apply for federal grants in order to improve their court system. Some of the court improvements that have been made concern the quality and depth of court hearings, legal representation, the timeliness of decision making through the use of technology and better data management systems, court staff and quality, and levels and nature of collaboration among the court, community, and child welfare agencies (Badeau, 2004). Other, more general reforms and improvements that have been made to the family and juvenile court process include the implementation of court performance standards.

Building on the progress currently under way in family and juvenile courts, a critical role for the court system is that of gatekeeper. The courts have the opportunity to limit the involvement of African American children in the child welfare system, as children who experience the child welfare system do so largely as a result of allegations of child neglect, typically associated with poverty. Other factors that may contribute to the active experience of African American children in the child welfare system include inadequate service and support critical to minimizing risk and increasing safety; also, racial bias and limited cultural knowledge among child welfare workers are relevant (U.S. GAO, 2007).

It has been argued that child welfare systems too often remove children from their parents' care as a result of misreading expressions of poverty as neglect. The subsequent trauma that children face from being removed from their home is thought to have as much psychological effect as being left in resource-depleted environments, yet the condition is rarely addressed (Turcios, 2009).

The court system can apply the cultural adaptation perspective to its work by commissioning Model Court experiments and Court Improvement Program pilots to tackle the issue of differentiating child neglect and child poverty. Such adaptations can assist in targeting critical resources and interventions to mitigate the risks associated with poverty among African American families and others. Innovations and reforms could include the following:

1. Application by the court system of the cultural adaptation perspective by commissioning Model Court experiments and Court Improvement Program pilots that tackle the issue of differentiating child neglect and child poverty. It will then be instructive to determine if such delineations affect the number of children entering CPS systems with substantiated cases of neglect.

2. A court-led effort to oversee mandatory periodic review (the review panel should involve indigenous community representation) of all cases involving child removal when the child was returned to the care of a parent less than ninety-six hours after being removed. The short duration between child removal and return may suggest a case with a low level

Cultural Adaptations in Safety and Risk Assessment Processes

The practice approach with the Davis family began with the assigned worker convening a Child and Family Team (CFT) meeting with the family in tandem with the preliminary hearing. The lead caseworker empowered Mrs. Davis by positioning her to define the composition of the team, which included Mrs. Davis's son Samuel, her daughter Sandy, a longtime family friend who was also Linda's godmother, and their pastor. Also, the CFT meeting was held in an environment that felt safe to the family and affirmed them culturally. That meeting place was the Family Life Center run by their church. Mrs. Davis felt supported and was comforted by the presence of her family, friend, and pastor during the CFT meeting. During the meeting the worker led the group in a review of the conclusions that were reached as a result of the assessment that had been newly conducted. The family's needs and strengths were reviewed in a cultural context. For example, protective factors (e.g., Dwight's involvement in sports and his determination to achieve academically) were highlighted. Male involvement in the lives of the children through Samuel's presence and willingness to continue to be a resource for his mother in the care of the children were recognized. The adaptations made to the assessment process left Mrs. Davis encouraged and sensing that the agency and workers were invested in her success in the care of her grandchildren.

of risk that could have been better addressed through the provision of services as opposed to child removal.

3. Court leadership to prompt a review of state statutes to determine the extent to which definitions of neglect unfairly predispose investigators to render decisions that do not adequately account for willful maltreatment produced by poverty and a lack of adequate resources.

Child Placement and Care

Out-of-home care is typically used when children cannot be maintained safely in their home, when they are experiencing behavioral or emotional conditions that place them or others in jeopardy, or when there is a conflictual relationship between a child and a caregiver. There are multiple out-of-home care arrangements, including family foster care, kinship care, treatment foster care, residential/group care, emergency care, shared family care, another planned permanent living arrangement (APPLA), and long-term foster care (LTFC) (for a more complete description of each type of care, see the Child Welfare Information Gateway at www.childwelfare.gov.) Whatever the type of care that children experience, children and their families are helped and supported through a casework model that includes engagement, relationship building, assessment, case planning, service implementation, progress monitoring, and evaluation of outcomes.

Efforts to provide safe, responsive, and effective services to children who experience out-of-home care are adversely effected by multiple challenges that the child welfare system faces. Chipungu and Bent-Goodley (2004) note that among the many challenges experienced in the foster care system is its equity, given the disproportionate representation of African American children. Countless child welfare advocates have expressed concern about racial disproportionality in out-of-home care, and a myriad of approaches have been implemented to address the condition. Some of the most prominent attempts to address issues of equity as discussed in the Child Welfare Information Gateway (2011a) include the following:

- Cultural competency training of staff
- Recruiting and retaining culturally matched workers, foster parents, and other service providers
- Emphasis on the use of standardized safety and risk assessment tools
- Advancing the use of differential response
- Emphasis on the use of kinship care
- Colocation of services and collaborations with faith-based, ethnic, and other community organizations

CULTURAL ADAPTATIONS IN SUPPORT SERVICES FOR AFRICAN AMERICAN FAMILIES

Cultural adaptations to casework models to intervene with African American children and families begin with enhancing the philosophical underpinnings of casework efforts. An appreciation for cultural adaptation begins with three elements: cultural integrity, cultural affirmation, and cultural efficacy.

Cultural integrity is a professional orientation that acknowledges the harms and injustices that African American children have experienced in the child welfare system. For example, behaviorally, a practitioner who is governed by the principle of cultural integrity consciously acknowledges and differentiates child neglect from child poverty. A practice approach steeped in cultural integrity prompts practitioners to scrutinize legal proceedings, agency practices, assessment tools, and the very laws on which intervention is based. Cultural integrity is demonstrated by a professional stance that requires a critical review of case decisions when such a process can lead to improvement in outcomes for children and their families. Finally, casework that is governed by the notion of cultural integrity seeks the involvement, advice, and counsel of cultural informants who monitor service accountability.

A casework approach that is informed by cultural affirmation recognizes that cultural and environmental expressions can often be misinterpreted. For example, practitioners concerned with the importance of cultural affirmations communicate and acknowledge that myths about African American childrearing practices abound and that some of those myths lead to racial bias in decision making. For instance, corporal punishment is a style of discipline that is acceptable to some and not to

---

Cultural Adaptations in Support Services

The professionals assigned to work with the Davis family demonstrate *cultural integrity* by ensuring that Mrs. Davis is aware of the financial impact that various placement options might have on her family. These discussions occur early on during the placement phase. It is during the placement phase that workers engage Mrs. Davis in a critical and honest review of her financial and support options, including the state's nonneedy caretaker program, licensed foster care, special needs adoption subsidies, and the guardianship assistance program. *Cultural affirmations* are present throughout professional involvement with the Davis family. Caseworkers acknowledge Mrs. Davis's selfless nature and her commitment to take on the sacrifices that she is making to rear three young children. Supervisors and managers support Mrs. Davis's caseworker by acknowledging the extra effort she has shown to adapt agency processes and procedures to meet the needs of the children and their grandmother. *Cultural efficacy* is more likely to develop because the professionals assigned to work with Mrs. Davis are recognized and supported by their peers and superiors.

others. Many interventionists have a "zero tolerance" for corporal punishment. Their professional judgment of what constitutes abuse may culturally clash with a parent's style of discipline. Therefore, a concerted effort to pose alternatives to corporal punishment that are within a family's cultural bounds could be the focus of intervention instead of steps to seek removal of a child when harm was not the intent. Cultural affirmation leads practitioners to value the importance of the parent-child relationship and in doing so work to reduce unnecessary harm that is produced through premature child removal.

Cultural efficacy is produced when caseworkers feel effective in their work with African American children and families. Caseworkers must be assisted and supported to exercise the highest levels of competency and care when intervening with families. Caseworkers' performance is largely based on their concept of self and their sense of competence. Social Learning Theory (Bandura, 1977) suggests that adapting interventions and approaches so that they yield effective outcomes for African American children will assist caseworkers in developing expectations for their own performance and that of others.

SUMMARY AND CONCLUSION

An important feature of this chapter is the review of traditional and new models for investigating child maltreatment, the family, and juvenile court processes, and casework approaches to reducing racial disproportionality in child placement and out-of-home care. In exploring contemporary approaches to child maltreatment investigation and child protection, we assessed the suitability of these approaches with African American clients. We offered cultural adaptations to both the philosophy and approach to child welfare practice for each of the three major system components: protection and investigation, court process, and child placement.

DISCUSSION QUESTIONS

1. Take and defend a position about the extent to which you believe African American children suffer higher rates of maltreatment or are more likely to be reported and substantiated for maltreatment.

2. The child welfare system is charged with providing safety/protection, well-being, and permanency for the children in its care. It has been argued that the system has very little control of risk factors and safety issues that bring children to its attention. In other words, the disproportionality represented in maltreatment reporting is beyond the system's scope of responsibility. Once African American children are in care, service disparities resembling maltreatment disparities become apparent. What explains the service inequities that African American children experience? To what extent is there a relationship between the causes of maltreatment disparities and service disparities?

3. Discuss the advantages and disadvantages of using structured child maltreatment safety and risk assessment tools as they pertain to the issue of racial disproportionality.

4. Discuss the correlations between poverty and neglect. Discuss how child welfare professionals can avoid confusing neglect with poverty. Using a cultural adaptation perspective, consider how the system can balance the harms experienced as a result of child removal against protecting children from imminent risk of harm.

ACTIVITIES FOR ONGOING LEARNING

1. Using the National Incidence Studies of Child Abuse and Neglect, select a category of abuse and neglect and develop a trend analysis of its prevalence rates from NIS-1 through NIS-4. After mapping the data, provide a critical analysis of what factors might account for the shifts in rates and trends. Explanatory factors can include but are not limited to sociocultural shifts, policy changes, reporting practices, data-monitoring systems, or changes in practice or interventions.

2. Using the Child Welfare Outcomes Report Data custom report builder profiling your state, develop a report about any child abuse and neglect topic of interest to you. For example, the custom data builder can provide information about foster care, permanency, maltreatment by type, age, ethnicity, and so on.

3. This project will require you to conduct a Values Assessment. The assessment should occur at two levels:

   A. *Level one: social services client.* Conduct a brief assessment of an African American client. The client should represent the demographic profile (e.g., income, education, neighborhood region) most typically served by your local social service structure.

B. *Level two: child protective services.* Conduct a brief values assessment of your local child protection services department.

The objective of the assignment is for you to get a sense of your client's values, beliefs, morals, and worldview as well as a general feel for the core values that guide the work of your local CPS office. Any questions that you deem acceptable in meeting this objective are appropriate, but as a general guide, the following questions could be posed to the client:

1. What do you value, treasure, or hold dear?
2. What makes you unique?
3. What would your closest friend say is your core conviction or belief?
4. What frame of reference do you typically use to help you to make important decisions? (Suggested probe: During the toughest times of your life, what would you say you learned most about yourself?)
5. What is best for a child? (Note: Do not define "best" for the respondent. Leave it open to his or her interpretation.)

To generate a response about the local CPS department's core values, you should interview a CPS supervisor or worker. Alternatively, if you cannot get access to a CPS official for an interview, gather written material (pamphlets, Web site information, forms, agency brochures, posters displayed throughout the agency) that contains a statement of the agency's core values. Through either the interview or the content analysis of the agency's written material, derive answers to the following questions:

1. What does the agency value, treasure, or hold dear? (Suggested probe: What is the agency's primary value?)
2. What makes the agency unique?
3. What would collateral agencies in the community or other child welfare stakeholders say are CPS's primary values, beliefs, or guiding philosophies?
4. What frame of reference does the agency typically use to help make important decisions? (Suggested probes: To what extent are a family's views, wishes, and knowledge factored into important case decisions? In handling controversial matters or making tough decisions, what has the agency discovered about itself?)

5. What is best for a child? (Note: Do not define "best" for the respondent. Leave it ambiguous.)

Following the two interviews, record your impressions about the client's and the agency's values and beliefs. Note the similarities and differences, and the overall tone, conviction, or certainty of each person's responses.

REFERENCES

American Public Human Services Association. 2009. *A Framework for Safety in Child Welfare.* Washington, D.C.

Badeau, S. 2004. *Child Welfare and the Courts.* Washington, D.C.: Pew Charitable Trusts. http://www.pewtrusts.org/uploadedFiles/wwwpewtrustsorg/Reports/Foster_care_reform/BadeauPaper[1].pdf.

Bandura, A. 1977. Self-efficacy: "Toward a Unifying Theory of Behavioral Change." *Psychological Review* 84:191– 215.

Child Welfare Information Gateway (CWIG). 2008a. *What Is Child Abuse and Neglect?* Fact Sheet. http://www.childwelfare.gov/pubs/can_info_packet.pdf.

———. 2008b. *Differential Response to Reports of Child Abuse and Neglect.* Washington, D.C.: U.S. Department of Health and Human Services. http://www.childwelfare.gov/pubs/issue_briefs/differential_response/.

———. 2010. *Family Engagement.* http://www.childwelfare.gov/pubs/f_fam_engagement/f_fam_engagement.pdf.

———. 2011a. *Addressing Racial Disproportionality in Child Welfare.* Washington, D.C.: U.S. Department of Health and Human Services, Children's Bureau.

———. 2011b. *Assessment Terms and Definitions.* http://www.childwelfare.gov/systemwide/assessment/overview/terms.cfm.

Children's Defense Fund. 2007. *America's Cradle to Prison Pipeline.* Washington, D.C.

Chipungu, S. S., & T. B. Bent-Goodley. 2004. "Meeting the Challenges of Contemporary Foster Care." *The Future of Children* 14 (1): 75–93.

Courtney, M. E., R. P. Barth, J. D. Berrick, D. Brooks, B. Needell, & L. Park. 1996. "Race and Child Welfare Services: Past Research and Future Directions." *Child Welfare* 75:99–135.

Denby, R. W. 2011. "Kinship Liaisons: A Peer-to-Peer Approach to Supporting Kinship Caregivers." *Children and Youth Services Review* 33 (2): 217–25.

Drake, B., J. M. Jolley, P. Lanier, J. Fluke, R. P. Barth, & M. Jonson-Reid. 2011. "Racial Bias in Child Protection? A Comparison of Competing Explanations Using National Data." *Pediatrics* 127 (3): 471–78.

Hawkins, M. K. 2009. "Spotlight: Franklin County: Protecting Children by Strengthening Families." *Alternative Response Quarterly* 2 (1): 5.

Johnson, W. 2004. *Effectiveness of California's Child Welfare Structured Decision Making Model: A Prospective Study of the Validity of the California Family Risk Assessment.* Oakland: California Child Welfare Structured Decision Making Project, for the California Department of Social Services. http://www.nccd -crc.org/crc/crc/pubs//ca_sdm_model_feb04.pdf.

Kaplan, C., & A. Rohm. 2010. *Ohio Alternative Response Pilot Project: Final Report of the AIM Team.* http://law.capital.edu/uploadedFiles/Law_Multi_Site/ NCALP/2010_Executive_Summary_Final_AIM_Team.pdf.

Loman, L. A., & G. L. Siegel. 2004. *An Evaluation of the Minnesota SDM Family Risk Assessment: Final Report.* St. Louis: Institute of Applied Research.

Marts, E. J., E.-K. O. Lee, R. McRoy, & J. McCroskey. 2008. "Point of Engagement: Reducing Disproportionality and Improving Child and Family Outcomes." *Child Welfare* 87 (2): 335–58.

McRoy, R. G. 2004. "The Color of Child Welfare Policy." In *The Color of Social Policy.* Edited by K. Davis & T. Bent-Goodley, 37–64. Washington, D.C.: Council on Social Work Education.

———. 2008. "Acknowledging Disproportionate Outcomes and Changing Service Delivery." *Child Welfare* 87 (2): 205–10.

National Council on Juvenile and Family Court Judges. 2008. *Model Courts.* http://www.ncjfcj.org/images/stories/dept/ppcd/newmodel%20court%20 brochurefinal.pdf.

Roberts, D. E. 2002. *Racial Disproportionality in the U.S. Child Welfare System: Documentation, Research on Causes, and Promising Practices.* Report prepared for The Annie E. Casey Foundation. http://www.familyandchildwellbeing. com/images/Minority_Overrepresentation_in_Child_Welfare_-_Dorothy _Roberts_AECF_Paper.pdf.

Schene, P. 2001. "Meeting Each Family's Needs: Using Differential Response in Reports of Child Abuse and Neglect." *Best Practice, Next Practice* (Spring): 1–14. National Child Welfare Resource Center for Family-Centered Practice. http://www.hunter.cuny.edu/ socwork/nrcfcpp/downloads/newsletter/ BPNPSpring01.pdf.

Sedlak, A. J., J. Mettenburg, M. Basena, I. Petta, K. McPherson, A. Greene, & S. Li. 2010. *Fourth National Incidence Study of Child Abuse and Neglect (NIS–4): Report to Congress.* Washington, D.C.: U.S. Department of Health and Human Services, Administration for Children and Families.

Shusterman, G. R., D. Hollinshead, J. D. Fluke, & Y. T. Yuan. 2005. *Alternative Responses to Child Maltreatment: Findings from NCANDS.* Washington, D.C.: U.S. Department of Health and Human Services, Office of the Assistant Secretary for Planning and Evaluation. http://aspe.hhs.gov/hsp/05/child-maltreat -resp/index.htm.

Turcios, E. 2009. "Remaining vs. Removal: Preventing Premature Removal When Poverty Is Confused with Neglect." *Michigan Child Welfare Journal* 7 (4): 20–28.

U.S. Department of Commerce, U.S. Census Bureau. 2009. *Income, Poverty, and Health Insurance Coverage in the United States: 2008.* http://www.census.gov/prod/2009pubs/p60–236.pdf.

———. 2010. *Income, Poverty, and Health Insurance Coverage in the United States: 2010.* http://www.census.gov/prod/2011pubs/p60–239.pdf.

U.S. Department of Health and Human Services. 2009a. *Child Maltreatment 2009.* http://www.acf.hhs.gov/programs/cb/pubs/cm09/cm09.pdf.

———. 2009b. *Child Welfare Outcomes 2004–2007: Report to Congress.* http://www.acf.hhs.gov/programs/cb/pubs/cwo04–07/cwo04–07.pdf.

———. 2009c. *The AFCARS Report: Preliminary FY 2008 Estimates as of October 2009.* http://www.acf.hhs.gov/programs/cb/stats_research/afcars/tar/report16.htm.

———. Administration for Children and Families, Children's Bureau. 2010. *The AFCARS Report: Preliminary FY 2009 Estimates as of July 2010.* http://www.acf.hhs.gov/programs/cb/stats_research/afcars/tar/report17.htm.

———. Office of Planning, Research & Evaluation. 2011. *Who Are the Children in Foster Care?* http://www.acf.hhs.gov/programs/opre/abuse_neglect/nscaw/reports/children_fostercare/children_fostercare.pdf.

U.S. Government Accountability Office (GAO). 2007. *African American Children in Foster Care.* Report to the Chairman, Committee on Ways and Means, House of Representatives. Washington, D.C.

5

Permanence for Children

Reading the U.S. Constitution carefully and conducting a literal and analytical interpretation of its contents will not produce a statement of explicit guaranteed protections or rights for children in this country. Instead, the Constitution places responsibility for a child with the parent(s) or guardian. A state may intervene in the affairs of a family to protect the interests of children only as prescribed by law. The primary referent allowing states to intervene is known as *parens patriae*. As adapted and used in the United States, *parens patriae* refers to the power of the state. The state is sovereign and becomes the guardian of persons under legal disability and of minors. Adoption of this legal concept enables the government to intervene in the lives of children and their families when parents are unable or unwilling to assume the role of principal caregiver (Gifis, 1996).

Children are influenced by the society in which they live. The degree to which their needs are met reflects society's priorities, values, and political orientation. In the United States the custom is that a minor child's basic needs—for food, shelter, and clothing—are met by and within a family structure. It is also the custom in the United States that when families are, for a variety of reasons, incapable of meeting the basic needs of their children, support is available through informal (family members, friends, neighbors) and formal (for-profit and voluntary organizations, government) agencies and organizations. Support services may be provided through religious institutions, private human service agencies, or government agencies.

The government system of support services and interventions aimed at protecting children, justified by *parens patriae* with historical precedence and sound legal foundation, is generally referred to as child welfare. This public system exists with funding and regulatory directives from

Using Prevention to Achieve Permanence

Research confirms there is an overrepresentation of racial and ethnic groups, particularly African Americans and Native Americans, in the child welfare system when compared to their representation in the general population (McCoy, 2004; Casey-CSSP Alliance for Racial Equality, 2006; Overrepresentation of Minority Youth in Care, 2008). While the first three National Incidence Studies of Child Abuse and Neglect (NIS) found no relationship between race and the incidence of child maltreatment after controlling for poverty and other risk factors (Sedlak & Broadhurst, 1996), the most recent NIS (NIS-4) report showed African Americans experiencing higher rates of maltreatment in certain categories—primarily neglect. Analyses of the data suggest the slight increase in rates of maltreatment can be explained in part due to the income gap between African American and white children.

Prevention services can enhance child and family well-being across racial and ethnic groups (for a full discussion, see chapter 6). Funding reduction for child welfare services typically results in diminished allocations for prevention services (Lemon, D'Andrade, & Austin, 2005). Culturally appropriate targeted prevention services with African American families and other families of color can mitigate risk factors of poverty and parental incarceration that impact child placement decisions (Child Welfare Information Gateway [CWIG], 2011). The Helping Families Prevention Neglect initiative in Baltimore, Maryland, enhances permanence outcomes for families by strengthening families to reduce and prevent risk factors and enhance protection factors in families at risk for neglect. The target population of African American families (85 percent of those served) received culturally focused strengths-based home visits and community based services to include community outreach, support groups and concrete services. The home visitation component is based on a successful nurse home visiting program model (Olds et al., 2007). The program represents a collaboration between the University of Maryland School of Social Work and the University of Maryland College of Medicine, Pediatrics Division, and resulted in the: reduction of risk factors such as parental depression and stress; increase of protective factors including social support and parenting satisfaction; increase in child well-being and child safety (DePanfilis, 2002).

This project is important for a number of reasons; it effectively addressed permanence for families and child well-being. Strengthening families promotes effective parenting and may prevent out of home child placement; prevention services directed to children can screen for developmental, physical and emotional health problems. A comprehensive service plan may ensure healthy outcomes for children.

While prevention services may be targeted, the impact on the general child welfare population is also beneficial.

all levels of government. Federal laws aimed at protecting and supporting children and their families are implemented at the state and local
levels based on state laws. Major federal laws that created national child
welfare policies are outlined and discussed in chapter 3. State sovereignty
results in a variety of interpretations and applications of federal laws;
states often create laws based on specific local needs as well. An examination of all state-level initiatives is beyond the scope of this book. However, we can say that variation within states reinforces the importance
of an experienced workforce of social workers and other human service
providers who are knowledgeable about state and local child welfare
policies, as well as the federal laws from which many state laws emanate
and with which there must be congruence.

DEFINING PERMANENCE

The formal child welfare system aims to support children and their families to prevent problems and to promote family stability. When problems exist associated with permanent safe housing, poverty, chemical
dependency, or inadequate health care, the government-sanctioned child
welfare system (including public and private agencies) must intervene.
Investigations into life circumstances of families may result in the provision of services aimed at strengthening families or the temporary or
permanent removal of a child from the home to ensure safety.

Knowledge of child welfare history supports the notion that in the
1960s and 1970s, improvements in medical techniques used to validate
patterns of physical child abuse brought increased attention to that
growing phenomenon. Attention directed to child maltreatment along
with enhanced knowledge and improved information among the general public concerning expectations and the responsibility to report suspected cases of maltreatment contributed to increased numbers of children temporarily being removed from their homes and placed in foster
care. Concerns that some children were needlessly removed from their
homes and that once removed many remained in foster care too long
(foster care drift) led to calls for reform. As discussed in detail in chapter 2, in 1980 the Adoption Assistance and Child Welfare Act (AACWA)
(PL 96-272) was passed and amended the Social Security Act, establishing foster care maintenance payments for children in state-managed

protection programs; also established were adoption assistance payments made on behalf of children with special needs who were adopted from the foster care system.

The provision of federal support for foster care payments to states and the creation of adoption assistance payments on behalf of children with special needs created innovative policy directives aimed at encouraging permanency. However in addition to these provisions, the AACWA for the first time established federal standards for case planning and review requirements for children entering or in foster care. States were also required to make "reasonable efforts" (see glossary) to prevent the placement of a child in foster care; if placement was inevitable, states were expected to work toward reuniting the child with her or his parents as appropriate. Legislative history reflects the intent of lawmakers to create policies that would protect the integrity of the family unit while ensuring the safety of minor children (Curtis, 1996).

VALUES ASSOCIATED WITH PERMANENCE

There are standards or values typically associated with specific professions that work with families, and the idea of "best practices" suggests that standards of care may be attributed to approaches for providing services. In child welfare, planning for the permanent care and placement of a child is conceptualized within the context of a system of care. A system of care is a service delivery approach that builds partnerships with other service providers to create an integrated process for meeting families' multiple needs. Some of the core values associated with child welfare practice are a child-centered and family-focused approach to service delivery and the use of coordinated service delivery systems that provide culturally competent services that are also community based. The goal of all services should be to achieve permanence in the life of every child.

Based on the conceptual model of the Individuals with Disabilities Education Act of 1975 (PL 94-142)—meeting the needs of children with developmental disabilities within the least restrictive environment and through cooperative agreements with multiple child-serving agencies— a system of care for child welfare evolved. The child welfare system of care is characterized by interagency collaborations, individualized service plans, cultural competence, community-based services, accountability, and full participation of families and youth (Child Welfare Information Gateway [CWIG], 2008). Systems of care typically focus on improving access to and availability of services and reducing service and funding fragmentation. Attention has also been directed to improving the skills, knowledge, and attitudes of frontline service providers.

The Children's Bureau conducts a Child and Family Services Review (CFSR) to assess state child welfare agencies' performance on seven outcomes and seven system factors. Findings from these reviews have resulted in documentation of the need for a comprehensive strategy to support children and their families in the areas of safety, permanency, and child well-being (CWIG, 2008). Through the coordinated provision of behavioral health prevention and treatment services, primary health care, and special education services, it is conceivable that systems of care might prevent out-of-home care and reduce the number of placements. While a system of care is based on the availability of services within a given community, the expectation is created that a purposeful, individualized plan of services is based on the needs of each family.

The individualized nature of a system of care approach is consistent with a family-focused orientation in child welfare. In child welfare, while a child may come to the attention of child protection services, the family as a unit is considered in developing a plan to create the best option for permanence for the child. A family-focused orientation is particularly important when working with families who may have a negative perception of child welfare workers as those who investigate allegations of maltreatment and in doing so may question parenting skills or a parent's capacity to care for their child. Families who are poor and who may be racial or ethnic minorities have historically had challenging experiences with officials in public welfare agencies and other systems on which a family member is dependent for services, care, or treatment. Other systems of care include public schools, public health agencies, and the criminal justice system (Chapin Hall Center for Children, 2008; Chipungu & Bent-Goodley, 2003; Hill, 1972, 2006). When a family is the center of decision making in creating a plan of services and supports, there should be—at least in theory—less likelihood that stereotypical interpretations of family problems may result in poorly defined service plans or unresponsive services. If the family is truly the focus of the intervention, can the intervention be child centered? From a culturally adapted perspective of strengthening and supporting families, the family unit must be central to the service planning process. If optimal functioning is to be realized, the developmental, social and emotional needs of each family member must be considered within the context of a system of care. If a child comes to the attention of the child protection system and allegations of maltreatment are substantiated, the immediate needs of the child must be evaluated first and plans put in place to address those needs.

A system of care should be in place to prevent family disruption by providing supports aimed at strengthening families so that problems may be resolved—be it the need for safe housing or service intervention for domestic violence or behavioral health problems. In the event disruption occurs, reunification may also occur. For African American families it is questionable whether culturally appropriate services are in place to create an appropriate system of care, given the disproportional placement of children in the out-of-home care system and correspondingly higher rates of reporting, substantiation, and child placements out of the home. Family income is a factor that must be considered relative to the number of children removed from their homes because of neglect.

Systems of care that serve poor families do not typically have community-based services that are planned for and by indigenous residents. Racial bias in decision making that limits the consideration or use of certain intervention strategies limits the capacity of programs to strengthen families (Chapin Hall Center for Children, 2008; Close, 1983).

For example, African American women make up a relatively small percentage of women who use illicit drugs, yet they are more likely to have their children removed from their homes for prenatal exposure to drugs (Chipungu & Bent-Goodley, 2003). If mothers are incarcerated for illicit drug use, the likelihood of treatment is very limited; among women who are not incarcerated but seek effective drug treatment, opportunities remain limited. Treatment programs, when available, may not be culturally adapted and responsive to restrictions associated with income, personal availability owing to employment, and childcare obligations.

Social science researchers have demonstrated how disproportional placement of children in out-of-home care is affected by poverty and poverty-related issues such as unemployment (Chipungu & Bent-Goodley, 2003; Curtis & Alexander, 2010). Since African American and Latino children are more likely to live in poverty, they are more likely to enter the child welfare system as a result of inadequate housing, health care, nutrition, or other circumstances that may be categorized as neglect. An adequate income is a critically important element for creating a system of care aimed at strengthening families.

Family-focused child welfare begins with the goal that each child may grow and be nurtured in a safe, loving home. To protect children from maltreatment within the framework of family-centered child welfare when families are challenged and need support related to employment, job training, or transportation, behavioral health prevention and treatment, respite care for children with special needs, or childcare, a culturally responsive community-based system of care with requisite services should be available.

THE CONTINUUM OF PERMANENCE OPTIONS

Passage of the Adoption and Safe Families Act of 1997 (ASFA) (PL 105-89) rejuvenated the permanency mission in child welfare by providing a series of changes designed to expedite the process of securing permanent homes for children who have been removed from their homes and placed in foster care. Most of the provisions of ASFA amended Title IV-B or IV-E of the Social Security Act, thus continuing to authorize grants to states for child welfare activities, including foster care and adoption assistance. The law created spending provisions to give states financial incentive payments for increasing the number of adoptions among children in foster care.

Among child advocates there is concern that judges and a number of states too broadly interpreted the federal provision associated with the AACWA requiring states to make "reasonable efforts" on behalf of abused and neglected children or children at risk for placement out of the home, so that they might remain in the home or return if removed. It has been argued that family preservation and reunification were pursued at any costs, including cases where a child's safety or health might be in jeopardy (Whitelaw-Downs, Moore, & McFadden, 2009). ASFA seeks to clarify concerns about reasonable efforts by prioritizing safety through several procedural provisions.

States continue to be required to make reasonable efforts to avoid the need to place children in foster care and to return a child home if removed, but ASFA established exceptions to this provision or requirement. States need not make efforts to preserve or reunify a family if a court finds that a parent has killed one of the children, lost parental rights of another child, or committed felony assault against the child or sibling. The federal law also enables states to withhold services to preserve or reunify a child with the family if a court finds that a parent has subjected the child to "aggravated circumstances." Each state has the option of defining aggravated circumstances, but federal guidelines cite torture, chronic abuse, abandonment, and sexual abuse as possible circumstances for this category.

The Adoption and Safe Families Act establishes permanency goals or options. The options exist on a continuum that begins with in-home support and ends with the permanent removal of a child from the home with adoption as the goal. A continuum of permanence options includes the following:

1. The family is in need of support receives services.
2. Reunification with the child's family occurs after temporary removal from the home.
3. Guardianship by a relative or foster parent becomes the goal when neither reunification nor adoption is feasible.
4. Adoption becomes the goal when reunification with the family is not possible.

PERMANENCY OPTIONS

A major challenge for child welfare practitioners—particularly since passage of ASFA—is the need to balance two competing goals: respecting family autonomy and ensuring child safety. The legislative intent of ASFA identifies the primacy of child safety as a policy goal. The social history leading to this targeted policy focus included a number of factors. During the 1970s and 1980s increased numbers of children were included in the foster care census; foster care drift seemed to be the norm for many children in placement. President Clinton expressed concern about the trend and challenged the executive branch and Congress to develop legislation aimed at reducing the number of children in foster care by 2002.

To better ensure permanency and healthy outcomes for children, ASFA specifies that efforts to preserve or reunify a family can be made concurrently with efforts to place the child for adoption or guardianship. Referred to as "concurrent planning," this practice model aims to address multiple problems within a family (e.g., substance abuse, domestic violence) by combining the use of focused family outreach, expedited timelines for permanency hearings, and potentially permanent family foster care placements (Katz, 1999). While concurrent planning has been analyzed and challenged, particularly given the complexity of family conditions and large caseloads of child welfare workers nationwide, the goal of melding child safety with family autonomy is difficult for even the most experienced worker, particularly with limited resources for services and family supports.

Parents and other caregivers, including adoptive and foster parents, may require a host of services to strengthen the family unit. Respite care for parents and other caregivers, early developmental screening of children to assess their needs and then assistance in meeting needs, mentoring, tutoring, and health education are some of the types of services families may require to strengthen and sustain their unit. Parent support group activities would also be included in this category of service, as well as counseling and home visitation services. All these services would be allowable as family support services under the Stephanie Tubbs Jones Child Welfare Services provisions of the Social Security Act, Title IV-B.

When support services are not enough to stabilize a family and promote optimal functioning, it may be necessary to temporarily remove a child from his or her home. There are numerous reasons that temporary placement in foster care may occur. Issues of neglect due to limited financial resources within a family may occur when medical care is not provided or emergency medical services are required; legal action involving a parent or parents and emergency shelter needs may also result in temporary out-of-home placement. Services aimed at enabling the family to function in a healthy and nurturing manner are then required and take the form of reunification or preservation services.

In most states there is no defined field in the administrative database for "intact" families' case opening and closing data—such data must be inferred from case placement data. Payment voucher databases often lack key identifying information, such as names, so it is not possible to link service provision to specific families. There are protocols within protective service systems aimed at determining the "risk of placement" based on familial conditions and characteristics of family members. The incidence of risk can be a major indicator of the likelihood for opening a case for an intact family. When a case is open for an intact family, the services that may be indicated are generally referred to as family preservation services. Once an open case results in the temporary removal of a child and placement out of the home, services aimed at strengthening the families so the family may be unified again are referred to as reunification services.

Prior to the passage of ASFA, the most desirable permanent placement for children was with their family—thus preserving the family was the explicit goal of the Adoption Assistance and Child Welfare Act, the prevailing federal policy governing child welfare service systems. The key phrase within the ACCWA that related directly to family preservation is "reasonable efforts," referring to the expectation that states provide necessary supports aimed at preventing unnecessary placement of children in out-of-home care. The enabling legislation did not define "reasonable efforts," and the level and degree of state involvement and commitment to preserving families varied, from providing intensive home-based family services and counseling to limited transportation and child daycare support for working parents. Evaluations of family preservation programs have not definitively demonstrated that placement prevention limits or eliminates the future likelihood of allegations of maltreatment and placement out of the home. Prevention services are often the target of critics for this very reason.

Reasonable efforts to prevent an out-of-home placement or reunify children may be provided for as long as they are needed, and herein lies the problem in the thinking of many child welfare administrators. The intensity of services provided should increase during times of crisis, when removal is imminent, and after a child has been removed from the home. However, limited resources are typically targeted to services for which outcomes are measurable and quantifiable. Parents who may require long-term training or retraining to compete in the paid labor force or those in need of intensive behavioral health care intervention so they might function better as a parent are not likely to be supported with services requiring lengthy ongoing intervention.

Research has identified bias among workers in the types of services workers are more likely to arrange or provide, as well as bias among the children and families workers are most likely to refer for service (Close, 1983; Denby & Curtis, 2003). Child welfare workers have expressed bias against providing medical and income maintenance support to African

American families; a national study of child welfare administrators confirmed worker preference against targeting family preservation services to these children and families. Instead, workers identified a preference for supporting "sick" children or families with very young children (Denby & Curtis, 2003).

Similar to the medical care system in this country, many child welfare administrators in the position to direct resources to children and families at risk of family disruption are more likely to serve families only after a critical problem or condition (analogous to a physical illness) has been identified (Chipungu & Bent-Goodley, 2003; Karger & Stoesz, 2009; Katz, 1999). Family supports that are culturally adapted to the needs of family members should target respite care to families with special needs children or those experiencing crises resulting from a child's behavior; likewise, family-centered values among professionals and as a characteristic of programs require consideration of general stress and a parent's inability to nurture as the basis for services to prevent the unnecessary removal of children from their homes. This is particularly important for families living in poverty.

When it is necessary to remove a child from the home and it is not in the child's best interest to be returned home, another permanency option that may be appropriate is adoption. The foster care system nationwide has thousands of children eligible for adoption, but the foster care system must compete with private and foreign adoption programs and initiatives. The need for adoption placements and the limited options available to potential adoptive parents have resulted in the creation of innovative programs aimed at recruiting and training foster and adoptive parents for whom states may use Title IV-B child welfare services funds available for recruitment and training. For example, some states have put in place an intensive family resource system that uses foster parents to facilitate the concurrent planning goal of identifying individuals who might provide foster parent support and also serve as a potential permanent adoptive parent. This network of trained families provides a vital family resource aimed at supporting children and families in the out-of-home care system by committing to the children in their care, whether reunification becomes the permanent plan for a child or the child may be considered for permanent placement in the family's home (Casey Family Programs, 1997). These programs depend on a strong passion for children among resource families and require extensive training to ensure foster families are prepared to meet the counseling and support needs of the child's family through the use of objective, family-focused, goal-oriented services.

Adoption is a cornerstone of permanency planning. With passage of the AACWA in 1980, special emphasis was placed on promoting the adoption of children in foster care, and a federally sponsored subsidy became available to families who adopted a child with special needs. The "special needs" category, according to the law, may include children with special medical conditions, sibling groups, older children, and African American children—racial and ethnic minorities who were and continue to be a disproportionately large segment of children in foster care and eligible for adoption. ASFA continued the provision for subsidized adoptions for children with special needs but also created fiscal incentive payments to states to increase the number of foster care adoptions.

Children eligible for adoption must have their parental rights terminated. The ASFA provisions require states to initiate proceedings to terminate parental rights (TPR) under certain conditions: for children who have been in foster care for fifteen of the past twenty-two months, for infants who are determined by state law to be abandoned, or in any case where the court has found that a parent killed another child or committed felony assault against the child or a sibling. If the child under any of these conditions is living with a relative, the state may—according to federal law—determine that it is not in the child's best interest to terminate parental rights.

Relative guardianship, kinship care, and adoption by relatives have grown in preference and use as state options to achieve permanency. The Department of Health and Human Services (DHHS) authorized waivers to states from Title IV-B and IV-E to conduct demonstration projects with the following purposes: (1) to identify and address barriers to adoption for foster children; (2) to identify and address parental substance abuse problems that result in foster care placement for children, including placement of children together with their parents in appropriate residential treatment facilities; and (3) to address kinship care. ASFA required DHHS to submit a report to Congress on the issue of kinship care, including recommendations for policy.

The Fostering Connections to Success and Increasing Adoptions Act of 2008 (PL 110-351) has been lauded by many for creating funding to support initiatives some states had initiated previously through waivers only. The policy confirmed federal subsidy support for any eligible child who leaves foster care for placement with a grandparent or other relative who agrees to become the child's legal guardian. Eligibility for the Title IV-E kinship guardianship assistance is tied to the child's prior eligibility for Title IV-E foster care maintenance payments and thus linked with prior law AFDC eligibility rules.

There is a paucity of research aimed at evaluating the effect of ASFA provisions. One provision in conflict with a family-centered goal of family reunification is the legal weight attached to enabling states' ability to terminate parental rights, thus making a child eligible for adoption. When parental rights are terminated more readily than permanent placement opportunities are validated, the end result will likely continue and multiply the experience of foster care drift for many children. The increased incidence of foster care drift will certainly have the greatest effect on those in greatest need of a permanent home—African American children. Critical analyses of parent narratives from judicial hearings for those whose parental rights are being adjudicated reveal strong concern by parents that, contrary to expecting that terminating parental rights will result in an adoptive family replacing the biological parent, the overburdened child welfare system will become their replacement (Wilhelmus, 1998).

According to the Congressional Research Service (Spar, 2002), the ASFA provision intended to promote adoption through incentive payments to states that increase the number of foster child adoptions has resulted in marked increases in these adoptions. Congressional appropriations have been increased over the original authorized spending of $20 million per year because of state pull-downs. This incentive payment initiative is similar to one in place after passage of the Child Abuse Prevention and Treatment Act of 1974 (PL 93-247), which rewarded states for heightened attention to reducing child maltreatment by increasing Title IV-E foster care payments. The foster care incentive payments were eventually changed as the number of children removed from their homes and placed in foster care increased dramatically. When increased numbers of children are being placed in adoptive homes, it is a good policy outcome if placements are indeed permanent and do not result in adoption disruption. Ensuring that children are in culturally compatible placements—particularly for children older than 3 years—is essential to effectively planning for permanence.

Policy analysts and program advocates must consider why a policy that results in increased foster child adoptions does not significantly affect the number of African American children in foster care. TPR practices within the judicial system should also be evaluated more closely to determine child placement outcomes and the role of family members and relatives in placement decisions.

In arguing for the cultural adaptation of policies and programs to meet the unique needs of African American children in the out-of-home care system, it is critical to note that formal guardianship by relatives in child welfare is an adaptation of practices long associated with the African American community. In the late 1960s and the 1970s, as the number of African American children placed in foster care rose dramatically, child welfare administrators and advocates criticized the African American community for not formally adopting children. Hill (1972) conducted research for the National Urban League in which he surveyed African American families and documented their practices of giving childcare and household demographics. African Americans during the time of the research informally "adopted" children of family members when parents were unable to care for their children. The arrangements were temporary, but some informal adoptions did result in a permanent arrangement.

Segregation and de facto segregation necessitated the creation of systems of support within the confines of the African American community—services others could access through both voluntary and public human service agencies. African Americans who sought support through the public child welfare system experienced indifference from social workers; families experiencing home studies for preplacement consideration or home visits for foster care approval rarely received favorable dispositions (Curtis, 1996; Hill, 1972, 2006). Bias in decision making associated with many aspects of the child welfare system has been a long-standing quality (Curtis, 1996; Denby & Curtis, 2003; Hill, 1972, 2006).

The implementation of a kinship guardianship policy that supports and does not penalize family members for stepping up to help care for child relatives is culturally adaptive and should be retained. The legislation creating this policy is authorized only for a limited time. If Congress is to support this practice, it will require the reauthorization of legislation, and it will be important that child welfare advocates monitor closely the actions of Congress.

Preparing Children and Caregivers for Permanence

THE DAVIS FAMILY

Mrs. Davis's caseworker engaged the family in the process of permanency planning guided by two primary premises. First, she assured that Mrs. Davis was aware of the range or permanency options available to her so that she could make a pressure-free decision about what would be both in her interest and in the interest of the children. Second, the worker set a course of action that would prepare Mrs. Davis and the children to be successful no matter the permanency option selected. Recognizing that African American kinship caregivers may have very limited financial resources and the wherewithal to care for their relatives' children, the caseworker conducted a thorough permanency assessment with the family. The permanency assessment was a process that evolved over the course of a series of Child and Family Team meetings in which there was a critical analysis of the children's socio-emotional needs as well as Mrs. Davis's. Throughout the assessment process the caseworker was reminded of the following question: From a cultural vantage point, what are Mrs. Davis's views, beliefs, and feelings about adoption? This was an important consideration because of the agency's orientation toward achieving permanency through adoption. The caseworker rejected the pressure of her organizational culture. Also, Mrs. Davis's parenting capacity, stress and strain, and her caregiving experiences were normalized during the course of her engagement with the caseworker. Differences between her childrearing beliefs and the recommendations made by the agency were viewed from a cultural lens, not as pathology. Finally, advocacy with the court on the family's behalf was conducted and resulted in a decision to support Mrs. Davis and the children in a subsidized guardianship arrangement while she and the children underwent recommended services and therapeutic interventions.

SUMMARY AND CONCLUSION

Children are dependent on adults to care for them and to provide for all their basic needs. Family-centered child welfare practice recognizes the primacy of the family in the life of a child and asserts the importance of every child having the opportunity to be raised in a safe and caring environment. The concept of permanency in the life of a child refers to the opportunity for continuity in caregiving throughout childhood and adolescence. When permanency in a child's own home is not possible for whatever reason, it may be necessary to temporarily remove the child from the home. Should this occur there are programs and services in place designed to strengthen the family unit so that it might function optimally—experiencing reunification.

When reunification is not possible, other options for permanency exist to include adoption and kinship guardianship. While there are challenges associated with each option, the ultimate objectives are to protect normalcy in childhood and ensure that children are safe and nurtured.

DISCUSSION QUESTIONS

1. Why is there resistance to considering the income gap between African American and white children as a causal factor for increased maltreatment among African American families, particularly as it relates to neglect?

2. Why did the goal of permanence for children evolve from making reasonable efforts to reunify children with their parents to seeking termination of parental rights and emphasizing adoption?

3. Does the federal government overstep its bounds in establishing a time frame within which parental rights should be terminated for children who have been in the out-of-home care system so that they may be considered for adoption?

4. Should states be required to make adoption assistance payments available to relative caregivers who adopt and make foster care payments available to all relative foster parents?

ACTIVITIES FOR ONGOING LEARNING

Prepare a paper that addresses the following questions:

1. Is the time frame for terminating parental rights contained within ASFA adequate to treat a parent who may be struggling with behavioral health care concerns? Provide a rationale for your position. What recommendations would you propose for this time-sensitive provision?

2. When resources are limited, how do administrators decide which services to emphasize on behalf of children and families? Identify an administrator of a child-serving agency within your community. Request an interview and ask for points of consideration that can and should be used in making hard decisions or choices relative to service priorities.

3. Based on your understanding of concurrent planning in child welfare, identify five strengths associated with this practice model and five limitations. Critically assess your response and prepare a one-page position statement assuming a position either supporting or not supporting the dually focused policy goal.

4. Identify five agencies you would include in a child- and family-focused system of care in your community. Are these services readily accessible for those requiring services? Are the provided services culturally competent in your opinion? Provide a rationale for your position.

REFERENCES

Casey Family Programs. 1997. *Implementing Change in Child Welfare: Lessons from Family to Family*. Baltimore: Casey Family Programs.

Chapin Hall Center for Children. 2008. *Understanding Racial and Ethnic Disparity in Child Welfare and Juvenile Justice*. Chicago: Chapin Hall Center for Children at the University of Chicago.

Child Welfare Information Gateway (CWIG). 2008. *Systems of Care*. Washington, D.C.: U.S. Department of Health and Human Services, Administration for Children and Families, Children's Bureau.

Chipungu, S. S., & T. B. Bent-Goodley. 2003. "Meeting the Challenges of Contemporary Foster Care." *The Future of Children* 14 (1): 75–93.

Close, M. 1983. "Child Welfare and People of Color: Denial of Equal Access." *Social Work Research and Abstracts* 19 (4): 13–20.

Curtis, C. M. 1996. "The Adoption of African American Children by Whites: A Renewed Conflict." *Families in Society: Journal of Contemporary Human Services* 77 (3): 156–65.

Curtis, C. M., & R. Alexander. 2010. "Correlates of African American Children In and Out of Their Families." *Families in Society: Journal of Contemporary Social Services* 91 (1): 85–90.

Denby, R., & C. M. Curtis. 2003. "Why Children of Color Are Not the Target of Family Preservation Services: A Case for Program Reform." *Journal of Sociology and Social Welfare* 30 (2): 149–73.

Depanfilis, D. 2002. *Helping Families Prevent Neglect: Final Report*. Study funded by the U.S. Department of Health and Human Services, Children's Bureau

1996–2002 (Grant Number 90 CA 1580). Baltimore: University of Maryland School of Social Work. http://www.family.umaryland.edu/ryc_research_and _evaluation/publication_product_files/selected_presentations/presentation _files/pdfs/final_report.pdf

Gifis, S. 1996. *Baron's Law Dictionary.* Hauppauge, N.Y.: Baron's Educational Series.

Hill, R. B. 1972. *Strengths of Black Families.* Lanham, Md.: University Press of America.

———. 2006. *A Synthesis of Research on Disproportionality in Child Welfare: An Update.* Washington, D.C.: Center for Study of Social Policy & Casey Family Programs.

Karger, H., & D. Stoesz. 2009. *American Social Welfare Policy: A Pluralist Approach.* 6th ed. Boston: Pearson Education.

Katz, L. 1999. "Concurrent Planning: Benefits and Pitfalls." *Child Welfare* 158 (1): 71–87.

Lemon, K., A. D'Andrade, M. J. & Austin. 2005. "Understanding and Addressing Disproportionality in the Front End of the Child Welfare System." Berkeley: Bay Area Social Services Consortium. http://cssr.berkeley.edu/basic/public/ Edvidence For Practice3_Dispro_Full Report.pdf.

McRoy, R. 2004. "African American Adoptions in Child Welfare." In *Child Welfare Revisited: An Africentric Perspective.* Edited by J. E. Everett, S. P. Chipunga, & B. R. Leashore, 256–74. New Brunswick, N.J.: Rutgers University Press.

Olds, D. L., et al. 2007. "Effects of Nurse Home Visiting on Maternal and Child Functioning: Age-9 Follow-up of Randomized Trial." *Pediatrics* 120 (4): e832. http://pediatrics.aapublications.org/content/120/4/e832.full.

Sedlak, A.J., & D. D. Broadhurst. 1996. *Executive Summary of the Third National Incidences Study of Child Abuse and Neglect.* http://www.chldwelfare.gov/pubs/ statsinfo/nis3.cfm.

Spar, K. 2002. *Child Welfare: Implementation of the Adoption and Safe Families Act.* Congressional Research Service Report for Congress. Washington, D.C.: Library of Congress.

Whitelaw-Downs, S., E. Moore, & E. J. McFadden. 2009. *Child Welfare and Family Services: Policies and Practice.* 8th ed. Boston: Pearson Education.

Wilhelmus, M. 1998. "A Content Analysis of Parent Narratives in Termination of Parental Rights Trials: Emerging Themes on the Legal Loss of Children." Ph.D. diss., Ohio State University.

6

Child and Parent Well-Being

In child welfare the phrase "child well-being" refers to the combined effect of major indicators associated with optimal development for physical, emotional, and social growth among children. Indicators of child well-being are compiled and evaluated nationwide across income and socioeconomic differences. A majority of children in out-of-home care come from economically disadvantaged families, meaning that they are likely to live in neighborhoods that pose challenges for safety and well-being because of crime and poor housing quality, and they typically experience limitations when it comes to receiving services and benefits. General indicators of child well-being include family income, housing, transportation, education, marital status of parents, physical and dental health, behavioral health, and the absence of involvement with the juvenile justice system. Once a child comes into contact with the out-of-home care system, there are services and systems of support in place that the child and family may need to strengthen and sustain the family unit. Children may require a variety of services aimed at enhancing their chances for healthy and emotionally stable outcomes.

In this chapter we will not address all indicators of child well-being for children. Instead we provide an overview of several primary indicators of well-being relative to African American children in the child protective service system, based on available data. The indicators of income, health, mental health, education, and contact with the juvenile justice system will be addressed relative to the effect on well-being among these children. Parental well-being is a primary determinant of child well-being and will be discussed in this chapter as well. African American children in child protective service systems generally experience poorer outcomes compared with other children; the indicators discussed here are important in ensuring sustainable, long-term well-being for all children, but

EXISTING TRENDS

Principles and Programs That Support Children's Well-Being

THE HARLEM CHILDREN'S ZONE

Child well-being is influenced by a myriad of individual, interpersonal, organizational, community/neighborhood, and policy factors. Some of the threats to well-being for African American children begin at birth: African American infants are twice as likely as European American infants to be born with low birth weight (U.S. Department of Health and Human Services [USDHHS], National Center for Health Statistics, 2009). Moreover, children's well-being is influenced by parental and family well-being. For example, 13 percent of African American children have mothers who did not complete high school, compared with only 5 percent of European American children (Aud, Fox, & Kewal Ramani, 2010). Highly disadvantaged neighborhoods are characterized as having high rates of unemployment, poverty, single-parent households, segregation, and density of children. Sharkey (2009) found that more than three-fourths of African American children born between 1985 and 2000 were born and reared in "high disadvantaged" neighborhoods. Neighborhood mapping shows high correlations between child welfare system involvement and residential life in high disadvantaged communities and neighborhoods.

In response to the factors that threaten African American child well-being, innovative programs that build on the inherent strengths and protective factors found in African American communities are showing promise of success. One such program is the Harlem Children's Zone (HCZ). The HCZ operates from two principles: (1) start early in the lives of children to help them in a sustained way; and (2) develop adults who will surround children and help them to succeed. The HCZ recognizes the important interplay among individual, family, and community well-being. It works to strengthen and empower families because it recognizes that children do well when their families do well and families do well when their communities are well (Harlem Children's Zone, 2012). The HCZ offers early childhood, elementary school, middle school, high school, and college educational programming. Also, family, community, and health programs are provided, including mental health services, nutrition and obesity education, and drug and alcohol counseling, to name just a few. The evidence of the program's effectiveness can be seen in its students who attend the Promise Academy. Eighty-nine percent of these children score at or above grade level on multiple proficiency tests. School readiness scores for the preschoolers who participate in the HCZ's Harlem Gems program increase remarkably. The program's success prompted President Obama to launch Promise Neighborhood grants across the country to help local communities improve educational outcomes for children by working holistically across child- and family-serving systems.

particularly for the vulnerable children in out-of-home care. The chapter concludes with a discussion of practice considerations and strategies that increase both child and parent well-being. It also provides a cultural adaptation of existing efforts and intervention approaches.

HEALTH AND MENTAL HEALTH DISPARITIES AFFECTING AFRICAN AMERICAN CHILDREN

In 2007 the U.S. Health Resources and Services Administration's Maternal and Child Health Bureau supported and developed a child health and well-being survey that was administered by the Centers for Disease Control and Prevention's National Center for Health Statistics. This National Survey of Children's Health (NSCH) represents a comprehensive assessment of multiple indicators of children's health and well-being that include physical and mental or behavioral health, health care, and social well-being. Social well-being includes aspects of family life and neighborhood characteristics that can affect children's health (USDHHS, 2009).

When survey results indicate that 84 percent of children in the United States, according to their parents, are in excellent or very good health and approximately 89 percent of children receive annual preventive health care checkups and sick child care as needed, the concerned child advocate must ask, "What about the other 16 percent of children who are not in excellent health?" Similarly, while 78 percent of children aged 1 to 17 years old receive annual preventive dental visits and 70 percent of children have good oral health, 30 percent of children do not have adequate dental care and good oral health. Of children living in families with incomes below the federal poverty level (FPL), less than 50 percent experience excellent or very good oral health. Income-poor children are less likely to receive their health care through a "medical home," defined as being a regular source of medical care meeting the criteria for accessibility, continuity, comprehensiveness, coordination, compassion, and cultural sensitivity.

Race and ethnicity also affect the likelihood of having a medical home: 68 percent of white children but only 44 percent of African American children receive health care through such an integrated coordinated system of care. Also, poor children with developmental, behavioral, or emotional problems are less likely to receive behavioral health-care services, according to their parents (USDHHS, 2009).

Health insurance is a major indicator of the availability of health care in the United States. Approximately 10 percent of children lacked health insurance, and 15 percent lived in households in which there was a gap in coverage during the year prior to the NSCH. Children from low-income families were more likely to experience at least one period in the year prior to the NSCH in which there was a gap in health-care coverage. Over 24 percent of children in households whose income is less than 200 percent of the FPL lacked consistent health insurance coverage. According to the survey results, children with limited or no health insurance are more likely than those with insurance to go without preventive health and dental care and are less likely to received needed mental health service than children with health insurance.

Many low-income children and adolescents depend on Medicaid for health care. This joint federal-state program finances health care for low-income individuals, including children. The Supplemental State Children's Health Insurance Program (SCHIP) is a state-regulated supplemental insurance program for children that may involve either Medicaid-funded expansions or private (state-initiated) alternatives. Access to health care through public health insurance programs like Medicaid has been linked to improved physical health and behavioral health outcomes (Karger & Stoesz, 2009; Phillips et al., 1998). However, children in foster care, compared with children from similar socioeconomic backgrounds, have significantly higher rates of chronic physical disabilities, serious emotional and behavioral problems, developmental delays, and poor school achievement (Rosenfeld et al., 1997; Simms & Halfon, 1994). Youths who live at home but who have been referred to the child welfare system have a higher risk for emotional disorders and developmental problems (Burns et al., 2004; James et al., 2004).

Medicaid and SCHIP are important for ensuring that children served by the child welfare system receive both medical and behavioral health care. However, only children who are in Title IV-E foster care placement are definitely eligible for Medicaid. Children who remain in their homes may apply for the program, but eligibility is based on family income or disability status. Social workers and other professionals may work with families to ensure that a range of needed services are provided in the system of care options in each community. If a child is not provided with a service care coordinator who facilitates all health care and other service needs, special needs and medical conditions may go undiagnosed and untreated for periods of time. States that have not put in place those

The Assessment Process: What Cultural Adaptations Are Required?

A *culturally adapted model* of assessment begins with the collection of information in the absence of any preconceived thoughts as to the needs of the client system or the approach for intervention. The social worker began by collecting information from Mrs. Davis and other significant family members such as Samuel, Jr., her son; the worker met and interacted with each child. The caseworker's assessment of Dwight noted that he appeared to be of appropriate chronological stature. Jackson was also of age-appropriate stature, but Michel was delayed in his development. His motor skills appeared consistent with a 9- or 10-month-old. He would pull up on the furniture but was not yet walking. Linda was using drugs during her pregnancy with Michel, which is the likely basis for his developmental delay, but final diagnoses will come only after a complete medical evaluation is completed. Current medical records for the three boys are incomplete.

Prior to moving in with their grandmother, Dwight, Jackson, and Michel were not totally up on their immunizations, according to records from the public health clinic Linda used for health care intervention. Jackson also presented dental concerns; he has been known not to brush his teeth as instructed by his mother or grandmother unless Dwight was with him and insisted that he brush as they prepared for school in the morning.

The school Dwight and Jackson attend noted that the boys were behind in their immunizations. They have not been seen by a physician since before Michel was born. While Linda was knowledgeable of the medical and dental needs of her children, addiction affects cognitive processing and often limits appropriate parental intervention. When children appear to be developmentally sound and behave in an age-appropriate manner, physical evaluations may be overlooked. Again, without making assumptions, a culturally adept caseworker will complete all social, medical, and behavioral assessments prior to drawing conclusions or making recommendations for intervention or service referral.

Each boy will receive a complete medical physical evaluation. Dental and vision assessments must also be completed. Michel's initial diagnosis resulted in his placement in a program on the other side of town to which he was transported on a school bus. Prior to her death Linda expressed dissatisfaction with the program and staff affiliated with Michel's program. Her mother encouraged Linda to engage the caseworker in a dialogue about Michel's progress, but to Mrs. Davis's knowledge Linda did not follow through. Once the boys were placed with Mrs. Davis, she requested through the social worker a neurological developmental assessment of Michel. When an evaluation has been completed and documented, a plan of age-appropriate intervention services can be outlined and initiated. It is imperative that the primary caregiver be fully appraised of Michel's diagnosis and prognosis for future developmental functioning. For Mrs. Davis to be an effective advocate for the intervention services her grandson needs, she must work closely with the assigned social worker and treatment specialists to receive the information and technical support to fully understand Michel's developmental strengths and limitations and what she can realistically expect of him at each developmental milestone—with proper long-term intervention services.

options to expand health-care coverage to families above 150 percent of poverty may deny necessary support to children in need of medical care and behavioral or mental health care.

BEHAVIORAL HEALTH CARE AND THE FOSTER CARE SYSTEM

As the number of children entering and remaining in the out-of-home care system increases, the incidence of emotional, behavioral, and developmental problems also increases. The American Academy of Pediatricians has stated that approximately 30 percent of children in foster care experience severe emotional, behavioral, or developmental problems (Barbell & Freundlich, 2002). A number of factors contribute to this increase in behavioral health problems among children and youths. The effects of persistent poverty, the use of alcohol and other drugs, physical health challenges and disorders that are difficult to manage, and juvenile behavior that results in adjudication through the courts all contribute to the increase in problem behaviors. Family disruption and the effects of racism in decision making around child placement options, as well as the diversion of children from other systems of care to foster care, also contribute to this phenomenon. The child welfare system is increasingly being used to care for children who might otherwise be placed in residential mental health care—where it exists—or the juvenile justice system (Barbell & Freundlich, 2002). The challenges children pose for competent comprehensive care and family intervention are complex.

Findings of the U.S. Surgeon General's Report (2001) show that disparities and inconsistencies exist in the use of mental health services.

Children in the child welfare system use behavioral health care services up to fifteen times more than other children receiving Medicaid support. Children in foster care are more likely to receive behavioral health service than other children served by the child welfare system. Children with a history of sexual abuse are three times more likely to receive mental health services, while children with a history of neglect are least likely to receive treatment. African American and Hispanic children are least likely to receive services, and they must display more pathology to be referred to mental health services. Developmental services and supports are accessed significantly less than would be expected given the rate of developmental problems assessed in the population.

Of great concern is the fact that children are not being diagnosed and referred for treatment or interventions at a rate consistent with the incidence of both behavioral and developmental problems associated with the population (Children's Bureau, 2003). If the majority of children who come to the attention of child protective service systems nationally suffer from neglect and this is the subpopulation least likely to receive services, a majority of children are not being served. The disparate response to children of color once again demonstrates the bias that exists and/or the lack of training and skill required to make appropriate assessments within culturally diverse populations.

Discussed below are five of the conditions that are most pervasive among children in the out-of-home care system and that make African American children's state of well-being more precarious than ever: (1) severe emotional disturbances (SED) in general; (2) reactive attachment disorder (RAD); (3) the vulnerability of children's mental health to posttraumatic stress; (4) attention deficit and hyperactivity disorder (ADHD); and (5) depression. The latter condition is often associated with adults, but there is growing recognition of its prevalence among children engaged in the out-of-home care system. Following exploration of these five mental health conditions, we analyze the vulnerabilities that African American children face, including the lack of care.

Severe Emotional Disturbances

Increasingly the child welfare and children's mental health fields are focusing on children's mental health needs. There is a growing recognition that although they express them differently, young children, youths, and adolescents are almost as likely to suffer mental health difficulties as are adults. Although there is some variance in how children express such difficulties, some of the typical indications include disturbances in sleep patterns, difficulty eating, inability to regulate behavior and mood, inappropriate boundaries (e.g., expressing affection and seeking it from strangers), disruptive behavior in school and preschool settings, and problematic behaviors in home and community settings. These types of mental health difficulties are believed to be especially pervasive among children involved in the child welfare system, and they may continue over time (Burns et al., 2004; Kortenkamp & Ehrle, 2002; USDHHS, Office of Planning, Research & Evaluation, 2011). The overall classification of severe emotional disturbance is typically used to describe DSM-diagnosable mental, behavioral, or emotional disorders that children experience. Severe emotional disturbances are definable under the DSM when they are pervasive (exhibited in multiple contexts, including school, home, social, or community), are persistent (occurring frequently over a period of two to four weeks), and have a significant effect on the child's daily functioning or affect the child's activities of daily living.

Children with emotional problems present unique challenges to child welfare staff. Increased service needs among children coupled with large caseloads, gaps in services, disparities in access, and limited knowledge of mental health problems in children make it difficult for workers to meet their behavioral health needs. Foster parents, relatives, and birth parents require time and support to meet the challenges of parenting troubled children and youth. Behavioral health problems do not disappear once children are adopted or reunified with their families. Children and parents—adoptive, foster, and birth parents—need postadoptive or postreunification services to work through and live with the lifelong effects of child maltreatment and family disruption (Kortenkamp & Ehrle, 2002).

Untreated mental health disorders in children can threaten their emotional well-being, social well-being, language development, cognitive abilities, motor skills, and physical growth. Young children are especially dependent on parents and caregivers and the environments in which they live to reduce the developmental harm that can occur when mental health disorders go unrecognized and untreated.

Reactive Attachment Disorder

Reactive attachment disorder (RAD) is a disorder found in children, particularly those who have suffered abuse or neglect or a significant separation from a primary caregiver during early childhood. Approximately 1 percent of U.S. children suffer from RAD (Encyclopedia of Mental Disorders, 2011). In a sample of toddlers who experienced maltreatment and were currently in the foster care system, researchers discovered the prevalence of RAD to be as high as 38 to 40 percent (Zeanah et al., 2004). The condition emanates from a failure to experience an attachment to a caregiver during infancy and early childhood. RAD is mostly exhibited in social interactions when a child may engage others inappropriately. It typically has two forms: inhibited (inability to respond in a developmentally appropriate manner to social situations) or disinhibited (excessive regard, interaction, or displays of familiarity or affection with strangers). Reactive attachment disorder is referred to as deprivation/maltreatment disorder in the *Diagnostic Classification of Mental Health and Developmental Disorders of Infancy and Early Childhood* (*DC: 0–3*) (Zero to Three, 2011).The *DC: 0–3R* was developed in 1994 to provide guidelines useful in the diagnosis of mental health and developmental disorders experienced in the first four years of life. It is used as a complement to the *Diagnostic and Statistical Manual of Mental Disorders* (DSM-III-R).

To fully understand RAD, a brief review of attachment theory is helpful. Attachment begins developing at birth and is solidified by about age 4 or 5. Attachment is typically thought of as a bond, connection, or emotional identification with a familiar caregiver. Broadly there are four categories of attachment: secure, avoidant, anxious, and disorganized. A *securely attached* child has experienced a caregiving relationship that he or she feels good about and is characterized as predictable, responsive, and consistent. The child has developed a trust of a caregiver because his or her needs have been met in a satisfactory and appropriate manner. An *avoidant* child perceives his or her caregiver to be inconsistent. The child's needs may have not been met. Characteristically, children who are believed to be avoidant may exhibit a lack of empathy toward others and may tend to seek isolation. Children who function in the category of *anxious attachment* may be clingy toward parents, be excessively tearful in the presence of their caregivers, show hoarding behavior, and experience difficulty following directions. *Anxious* children do not trust that their caregivers will return after an absence because the type of care they have received has been unpredictable. *Disorganized* children become easily frustrated, lack affection toward parents, and may even be self-injurious. This category is most typically seen in children where severe maternal depression is of concern or among children who have suffered extreme abuse or deprivation.

The issue of attachment is of special concern for children who experience the child welfare system early in their development. A primary and consistent caregiver provides a child with an opportunity to receive and give affection, form trust, and grow emotionally, socially, cognitively, and behaviorally. Child welfare system youths typically experience several placements and multiple caregivers. Inconsistency in caregiving threatens attachment in young children and is associated with a host of negative outcomes (e.g., poor peer relationships, inability to self-regulate, diminished coping skills). The two hallmarks of early development (the need to trust and to feel secure) are in jeopardy for young children in the child welfare system who experience separation from their parents.

Trauma: Posttraumatic Stress Disorders and Complex Trauma

According to the *Report of the Surgeon General's Conference on Children's Mental Health* (2001), children are increasingly victimized by systems intended to support them. The emotional, behavioral, and developmental needs of children are not being met by child welfare institutions and others charged with their care. The report states that poverty, social environments characterized by instability, parents or caregivers whose psychological well-being may be questionable, along with the traumatic experience of abuse, neglect, and separation from home can lead to a variety of emotional problems for children and a greater likelihood of poor outcomes. Children in foster care are at high risk for mental health problems, and approximately half the children in foster care have adaptive functioning scores in the problematic range. Among children from birth to age 6 years, 50 to 65 percent are in the problematic range in terms of developmental status, and up to 60 percent of 2- to 20-year-olds present behavior problems. Among 6- to 17-year-olds, about 40 percent meet the criteria for any diagnosis with moderate impairment (Children's Bureau, 2003).

Posttraumatic stress disorder (PTSD) is a type of anxiety disorder whose symptoms can begin in childhood. It is recognized as a disabling condition because for those who have the condition, anxiety is no longer used as a healthy coping mechanism but is instead a disabling condition. In general, anxiety disorders are thought to exist in about 8 percent of U.S. children between the ages of 13 and 18, and the symptoms typically emerge around age 6 (National Institute of Mental Health, 2011a).

Trauma can be sudden, repeated, or sustained events that include actual or threatened death or serious injury that has a significant effect on children psychologically. Not all traumatic events lead to PTSD in children. There are two types of trauma diagnoses: posttraumatic stress disorders and complex trauma. Symptoms of PTSD in children can include recurrent bad dreams, flashbacks, startle reaction, intense emotional responses to trauma reminders or triggers, difficulty with sleep, numbing affect, and reliving trauma through play (Center for Early Childhood Mental Health Consultation, 2011). Complex trauma, also referred to as complex PTSD, "describes how children's exposure to multiple or prolonged traumatic events impacts their ongoing development. Typically, complex trauma exposure involves the simultaneous or sequential occurrence of child maltreatment and may include psychological maltreatment, neglect, physical and sexual abuse, and witnessing domestic violence" (Center for Early Childhood Mental Health Consultation, 2011:6).

The types of traumatic incidents that child welfare system–involved children experience can include sexual abuse or assault, physical abuse or assault, emotional abuse/psychological maltreatment, neglect, serious accident or illness/medical procedure, being a witness of domestic violence, being a victim or witness of community violence, school violence, interpersonal violence, traumatic grief/separation, and system-induced trauma (National Child Traumatic Stress Network, 2008a). Children in the child welfare system have high rates of PTSD. For example, Dubner and Motta (1999) found that 60 percent of sexually abused children have PTSD, 42 percent of physically abused children have the condition, and 18 percent of children in foster care who experienced neither sexual nor physical abuse still have PTSD. They may have developed the condition as a result of being exposed to domestic and neighborhood violence (Marsenich, 2002). The prevalence of PTSD among foster care alumni is 30 percent (Pecora, 2008; Pecora et al., 2005).

For children in the child welfare system, traumatic stress threatens their safety in many ways. For example, a child may not be able to protect himself or herself from abuse that can occur because of the inability to regulate moods and behavior, and the child may develop self-destructive behaviors (National Child Trauma Stress Network, 2008a). Likewise, the ability of the child to achieve permanency is at risk when there is traumatic stress because, again, the child may not be able to regulate his or her moods, and thus behavior, placements, reunification, and adoption may be adversely affected. The child's lack of trust of others and impaired attachment can reduce others' lack of empathy toward him or her and thus negatively influence the development of positive interpersonal relationships (National Child Trauma Stress Network, 2008a). Finally, the type of traumatic stress experienced by child welfare system–involved children threatens their overall well-being because of the negative cognitive and emotional experiences that the condition produces. Untreated PTSD is highly detrimental and has been shown to produce adverse conditions later in life. For example, PTSD typically exists with other mental health and emotional disorders as well as substance-abuse conditions (Hamblen & Barnett, 1999; Harney, 2000). Children with PTSD experience problems with school performance (Goodman, 2002) and interpersonal relationships (Hamblen & Barnett, 1999; NIMH, 2001; Solomon, 2005). As adults, children who experienced PTSD are at increased risk for physical health problems and financial difficulties (Solomon, 2005).

Attention Deficit and Hyperactivity Disorder

Attention deficit hyperactivity disorder is considered "one of the most common mental disorders in children and adolescents. Symptoms include difficulty staying focused and paying attention, difficulty controlling behavior, and very high levels of activity" (NIMH, 2011b:1). Other symptoms believed to be associated with the disorder should be considered in the context of cultural determinants, but they include the desire to have constant contact with people or objects, impulsivity, and high-intensity sensory stimulation. It is believed that onset of ADHD may occur at birth. However, especially important in the context of child welfare system–involved children, environmental stressors are also believed to be associated with ADHD. ADHD is believed to be an anxiety response that children exhibit as a result of living among environmental stressors.

According to the American Psychiatric Association (2000), 3 to 7 percent of American school-aged children have ADHD. Its occurrence is more common among foster children; it is believed that 10 to 20 percent of these children meet the diagnostic criteria (Garland et al., 2001; Mc-Millen et al., 2005; Simmel et al., 2001; Steele & Buchi, 2008). Linares et al. (2010) believe that ADHD in foster care youth may be reflective of the placement experience. They studied 252 maltreated children in 95 families for four years and found that parenting quality and placement stability are factors in reducing symptoms of ADHD.

Although little is known about the long-term effects of ADHD, some believe that the condition lingers into adolescence and adulthood. Schweitzer (2001) and the American Psychiatric Association (2000) report that 60 percent of children who experience ADHD continue to have symptoms in adulthood. The long-term effects of untreated ADHD in children involve a host of negative outcomes, including peer rejection (NIH, 2011b) poor self-esteem (Barkley, Anastopoulos, & Buevremont, 1991; Greenhill, 1998); and substance abuse (Elia, Ambrosini, & Rapoport, 1999). Likewise, ADHD has been associated with personal stress, parental frustration, and marital strain (Kilcarr & Quinn, 1997; New York University Child Study Center, 2011; NIH Consensus Statement, 1998). As the condition persists into adulthood, individuals are met with another set of challenging conditions, including increased likelihood of adult criminal involvement (Fletcher & Wolfe, 2009), lower-status jobs, minimal progression of schooling, and higher rates of antisocial personalities (Murphy & Schachar, 2000).

Depression

The long-standing belief that children do not experience depression has been countered by several empirical studies. For example, according to the National Comorbidity Survey-Adolescent Supplement (NCS-A), about 11 percent of U.S. adolescents experience a depressive episode by age 18 (NIMH, 2011c). The Midwest Evaluation of the Adult Functioning of Former Foster Youth found major depression to be one of the most prevalent mental health conditions experienced by former foster care youth (Courtney et al., 2005). As noted by the Northwest Alumni Study, which examined 479 alumni of foster care, the prevalence of major depression among foster care alumni (41.1 percent) is double the rate of the general population (21 percent) (Pecora, 2008; Pecora et al., 2005;

Pecora et al., 2009). The signs of depression in children can include complaints of feeling physically ill, school refusal, excessive worry, clinginess, negativity, grouchiness, and trouble in school (NIMH, 2011c).

Intrapsychic, environmental, and biological determinants are the three conditions typically thought to influence major depression, and, when left untreated, depression in children is thought to lead to more serious illnesses during adulthood (Weissman et al., 1999). Also, depression in children and adolescents generally coexists with such other conditions as substance abuse, anxiety, or disruptive behavior and can lead to poor academic performance, interpersonal conflicts, and risk of suicide.

VULNERABILITIES FACED BY AFRICAN AMERICAN CHILDREN

While poverty is not a causal factor for child maltreatment, there is a correlation between children living in poverty and children living in the out-of-home care system. This dynamic poses specific problems. Children from persistently poor families have lower levels of performance on standard tests of language and school readiness and are thought to have more externalizing and internalizing behavior problems, such as anxiety and depressive disorders or maladaptive behaviors such as bullying (NICH, 2005). Additionally, children who live in poverty are less likely to have medical health insurance and therefore have limited access to third party–paid behavioral health care.

African American children, older children, sibling groups, and children who may be eligible for adoption subsidies because of medical or emotional special needs may require comprehensive specialized services. Such care, including behavioral health care, is dependent on comprehensive medical coverage. For children in foster care, the Medicaid system is the primary source of funding for behavioral health care in states that use these funds for such care. States have begun to use different benefit designs to ensure mental health and alcohol and other drug treatment for Medicaid-eligible consumers. Two service delivery designs have been used by states specifically for providing behavioral health: managed care and carve-out programs. Snowden, Cuellar, and Libby (2003) determined that the use of different benefit types influenced the availability of mental health care and also influenced contact with other systems of care, such as juvenile justice. For example, a carve-out program model

Dwight assumed a protective role with his brothers. He would at times attempt to discipline Jackson. Michel was fussy and did not sleep through the night. Dwight would often get up to comfort him, but once the boys were living with Mrs. Davis, she attempted to prevent this "intervention." She thought it was important that Dwight get adequate rest so that he would be able to perform well in school. A thorough assessment of each child by the social worker should provide notation of their physical stature relative to their chronological age, but also indicate recognition of their emotional and social developmental strengths and tendencies—which is also *culturally relevant.*

Dwight is recognized in school to be helpful to his classmates and teachers alike. He is displaying caregiver tendencies toward his brothers, most likely recognizing and addressing his mother's limitations in providing such care and support when she was using drugs. While his caregiving tendencies represent personal strength, he is a young child who also displays the outward behaviors associated with grief; he is grieving the loss of his mother. He cries openly in school and, when asked, expresses sadness and despair over her death.

It will be critically important to carefully monitor Dwight's progress in school and his grieving process. While grief is a normal emotional response and each person manages grief differently, Dwight's age—10 years—places him at risk for outcomes that may reflect a resilient response to this mother's death or may result in deeper despair. A child's expression of loss should not be dismissed as something he or she will grow out of. Children who are placed in foster care or in a guardianship relationships are more likely than children in the general population to be involved in the criminal justice system, and they are at higher risk for teen pregnancy and parenting (Massinga & Pecora, 2004). Attending to the needs of children to prevent the onset of problems, particularly among those who may be at risk for a behavioral health challenge, is consistent with best practice intervention strategies and also with cultural adaptive approaches to service.

That Mrs. Davis is a concerned and committed, caring grandmother and caregiver does not mitigate the importance of monitoring the progress of Dwight and his brothers relative to managing the significant life-altering experience of their mother's premature, accidental death. It is important for the primary caseworker to be cognizant of Mrs. Davis's grief process and support services she may require as the primary caregiver.

may tend to reduce the amount of time required to make initial contact with the juvenile justice system (Scott, Snowden, & Libby, 2002).

In summary, there is research support (Garland et al., 2000) for the observations that African American foster children do not receive the mental health services they need and that their receipt of services is far less than that of their European American counterparts. Research also reveals that when African American children access mental health services, it typically occurs in the context of emergency settings (Christodulu et al., 2002; National Center for Health Statistics, 2006), and even then their conditions and needs go undiagnosed and unmet (Kunen et al., 2005). Moreover, African American children are more likely to access mental health services in connection with their involvement in the juvenile justice system (Neeley-Bertrand, 2001). Mental health services to African Americans are often incomplete and of low quality (Alegria et al., 2002; Chow, Jaffee, & Snowden, 2003). Service discontinuation is a problem because some African American mental health clients feel misunderstood by providers (Northwest Federation of Community Organizations, 2005; Van Ryn & Fu, 2003).

EDUCATION

Children in the out-of-home care system are disproportionately poor and therefore are more likely to experience a wide range of negative outcomes that can affect their future. Education is one of the major factors associated with child well-being, but education is also a critical indicator of future-oriented outcomes or adult well-being. Poor children are more likely to experience negative academic outcomes—particularly during early childhood (Brooks-Gunn & Duncan, 1997; Gershoff, Aber, & Raver, 2003). Poverty has also been linked to a greater likelihood of adolescent high school dropout rates, low academic achievement, and behavioral and emotional problems. The foundation for educational success begins in early childhood. This section discusses the importance of cognitive, social, and emotional development of children. We also address the importance of responsive service delivery to maltreated infants and toddlers, and we discuss the educational attainment and the developmental needs of children and adolescents as they prepare to disengage the child welfare system. Finally, we review the educational conditions of African American youth engaged in the child welfare system.

Early Childhood Physical, Cognitive, Social, and Emotional Development

Child welfare practitioners work on behalf of children guided by the knowledge that child development is complex and occurs interactively across multiple domains, including physical, social, emotional, language, and cognitive and motor development. Although development is shaped by environmental, genetic, and cultural factors, a child's positive development is largely influenced by nurturing and responsive relationships with caregivers and other significant individuals. Other moderating variables that influence a child's growth and development include temperament and environmental deficiencies. What a child experiences during his or her early years is directly connected to later adult experiences, including success and adversity.

The National Survey of Child and Adolescent Well-Being (NSCAW), which studied children living in foster care, reported that about 27 percent experience lasting or recurrent health problems, with the most common problem being asthma. Additionally, about 4 percent have difficulty that began at or before birth (e.g., fetal alcohol syndrome). The good news is that most foster children receive the health care that they need and are up-to-date on immunizations; over three quarters receive dental care. In terms of cognitive and social development, the NSCAW reports that when comparing foster children with their national peers, foster children are lower on almost every measure of positive and normal development. For example, foster children are thought to be at risk because of their low levels in social and life skills, neurodevelopment, verbal and nonverbal intelligence, reading and math scores, and behavior reports. Many of the adverse well-being conditions noted by the NSCAW have their origins in maltreatment and the conditions that children face during infancy and as toddlers (USDHHS, Office of Planning, Research & Evaluation, 2011). Next we explore the importance of increasing child well-being by directing attention to the need to intervene in maltreatment during the early years of life.

Maltreated Infants and Toddlers

Although early childhood is one of the most vulnerable time periods of human development, more and more infants and toddlers are being placed in the foster care system (Chipungu & Bent-Goodley, 2004). Annually approximately 200,000 children age 3 or younger become involved with the child welfare system, and more than 76,000 of them are removed from their parents' care (USDHHS, 2008). Infants and toddlers are the largest child welfare demographic. In 2009, 31 percent of the children who entered foster care were 3 or younger (USDHHS, 2010b). Child welfare experts debate the wisdom of placing very young children in the foster care system. Some say that given the fact that early childhood is a fragile developmental phase, children should be safeguarded and removed from parents who are unable to provide for their care. Others argue that removal of a child from his or her primary caregiver during such a crucial developmental phase of life can result in irreparable harm. However, there seems to be a bit more consensus concerning brain development and the role of risks and resilience during childhood. Scientists agree that early childhood is a critical stage and have discovered that the origins of mental illness are rooted in brain development (NIMH, 2011d). Given the importance of brain development during the early phases of life, efforts must be made to alter risks and increase resilience in child welfare system–involved children by positively affecting a child's mental health. To promote positive infant mental health (i.e., an infant's intellectual, physical, and emotional growth and development), children must be provided with a "good enough" environment (Winnicott, 1964). Safe, nurturing, and positive connections with parents must be developed and supported so that infants and young children can develop properly and achieve good mental health.

The remarkable effects of maltreatment on young children can even include chemical changes to the brain and developmental impairments (Cohen, Cole, & Szrom, 2011). The importance of intervention and services for very young maltreated children has been recognized through federal legislative action. The Keeping Children and Families Safe Act of 2003 amended the Child Abuse and Prevention Treatment Act, and in doing so it required states to deliver early intervention services for children 3 or younger. Also, the Adoption and Safe Families Act of 1997 gives judges the responsibility of ensuring that young abuse and neglect victims receive early intervention services. Other policy and state-level programming approaches are being initiated to respond to the unique needs of maltreatment infants and toddlers (for a more complete review, see Cohen, Cole, & Szrom, 2011).

Educational Attainment in Foster Care Youth

The research examining the longitudinal effects of foster care on child well-being is limited. One of the more frequently referenced studies, conducted by Fanshel and Shinn (1978), examined a number of factors related to child well-being among children in both residential and foster home settings over a five-year period. The children in foster care who served as the study sample resided in New York, which at the time had a foster care population that was 50 percent African American; approximately 25 percent were Puerto Rican, and the remainder were white. Puerto Ricans were overrepresented in the sample, with white and African American children slightly underrepresented compared with all foster children in the state.

The IQ of children remained stable while in foster care, although some children experienced slight gains while others experienced losses. Slightly higher IQ scores were associated with older children and children whose parents visited while they were in foster care. In this study differences in race and ethnicity were slightly significant (Fanshel & Shinn, 1978). White children experienced losses in IQ by the end of the study, while African American children experienced no significant gains; Puerto Rican children enjoyed overall gains in IQ. Among children who were placed in a residential facility after being placed in a foster care home, increases in IQ were associated with attending an on-site school. The improved IQ measure and overall school performance associated with children in an on-site school are believed to be associated with a structured educational program as opposed to variations among foster parents in the supports they provided to both preschool and school age children. Foster parents often do not have the supports required to meet the educational and developmental needs of children and therefore have more difficulty creating positive experiences than children in institutional care settings may have (Weiner & Weiner, 1990). Resources available to foster care families today are minimal; residential facilities struggle to meet fundamental program costs, with very limited resources available to meet the special educational and support needs of children in care.

When it comes to overall school performance, white students outperformed all other children, and girls performed better than boys (Fanshel & Shinn, 1978). After the initial placement of a child out of the home, academic performance declined. This decline, however, was followed by overall academic improvement. Anecdotal information concerning the removal of a child from the home typically identifies a preference among children to be home with their families, notwithstanding the existence of maltreatment. For most people the circumstance of our living situation—that which we know—is typically preferred to that which is unknown. Expectations that a child sleep in a different bed, be fed by unknown adults, and be told what is permissible and what is not by an unfamiliar person are intimidating and frightening, especially for young children. This degree of extreme change in living circumstances is likely to result in changed if not uncertain behavior, particularly in a

Managing Disruptive Behavior in a Supportive Manner

Jackson, age 7, is described as displaying acting-out behavior. He was performing well in preschool prior to his mother's death. Since her death he is often sent to the principal's office for fighting, which has not yet resulted in suspension, though the principal is threatening suspension or transfer to a school for children with problem behavior. The principal is aware that Jackson's mother was recently killed in an automobile accident but does not believe this is necessarily the reason for his behavior.

As a young school-age child, Jackson must be referred to a social worker or other practitioner experienced in working with children. Prior to designing the intervention for him, the social worker should attempt to gather all available information to get a sense of the circumstances of his young life. The worker will speak with Mrs. Davis and with Jackson—individually and as a family unit. The social worker will determine if it might be appropriate to include Dwight in the information-gathering stage.

It will be important to establish a relationship with Jackson such that an environment of safety is created so he might be relaxed and not feel that he will be punished for any of the information he may share. However, he must understand the consequences of his behavior should another fight at school occur.

Mrs. Davis must grant full permission to engage Jackson in scheduled communication. Jackson must understand the expectations of him in the helping relationship and what together he and the social worker may be able to accomplish—putting a name to what may be troubling him and identifying alternative approaches for him to express his frustration, anger, and disappointment.

classroom or group setting. Once a routine is reestablished or stability affirmed, children and adolescents are more likely to improve or at least retain prior levels of academic performance.

What is known about IQ, educational attainment, and good behavior among children in foster care suggests that, when possible, parents should remain an integral part of the support system for children. Children whose parents remain engaged in their care, even through informal visits, will perform better academically. Structured activities or opportunities to create positive learning environments for children are important. If long-term academic success is to be realized for children who are at risk for negative outcomes, resources aimed at strengthening opportunities for educational success must be available to caregivers.

Transitioning into Adulthood: Conditions African American Youths Face

Through federally supported initiatives like the Title IV-E Independent Living Program, John H. Chafee Foster Care Independence Program, Education and Training Voucher Program, Transitional Living Program, and Medicaid health-care services, most states offer foster care youths who are aging out of the system supportive services designed to prepare them for adult living. Services and supports can include basic life-skills training, interpersonal skill building, educational and vocational opportunities, job preparation and career training, mental health treatment, and medical insurance to cover physical health care. Despite these provisions, African American youths formerly in the foster care system are faced with a host of life challenges (e.g., higher rates of teen pregnancy, incomplete educational attainment) that catapult them into a vulnerable adulthood. Very little research is available concerning the quality and adequacy of transitional living services and whether they have a positive effect on preparing foster care youth for adulthood.

The Joint Center for Political and Economic Studies Health Policy Institute (2007) conducted a study to understand the needs of youths who exit the foster care system. Although the study involved youths of various demographic backgrounds, a concerted effort was made to capture the experience of African American youths. According to the center, African American youths report the following: the perception that they have no advocates to guide them; no support for career decision making;

receiving support for transitioning into adulthood only after age 17; being inappropriately placed in special education courses; being placed in overcrowded foster homes; being placed in foster homes with no African American males (being reared by single women); inadequate life skills training; needing enrichment (e.g., Boy Scouts) or cultural activities but not receiving them; and premature departure from the system because of placement instability that forced many youths to forfeit their eligibility for independent living services.

CRIME AND JUVENILE JUSTICE INVOLVEMENT

Child Welfare and Juvenile Justice System Crossover

It is not uncommon to find that adolescents in the care of the child welfare system are simultaneously involved with the juvenile justice system. Several research studies have noted a correlation between child maltreatment and delinquency (Herrera & McCloskey, 2001, 2003; Mersky & Reynolds, 2007; Shaffer & Ruback, 2002; Siegel & Williams, 2003; Smith & Thornberry, 1995; Widom, 1989; Widom & Maxfield, 2001; Williams & Herrera, 2007; Zingraff, Leiter, Myers, & Johnsen, 1993). The justice system involvement trajectory for foster care youths continues into adulthood. Widom and Maxfield (2001) discovered that abused and neglected children's likelihood of being arrested as juveniles increases by 59 percent and their likelihood of being arrested as adults increases by 28 percent. Widom and Maxfield also noted that former child welfare system–involved individuals' likelihood for being arrested for a violent crime increases by 30 percent. The Administration for Children and Families (2008) noted that the adult arrest rate for former foster children is more than four times the national rate.

Youths involved in the juvenile justice system face a set of vulnerabilities, including mental health and substance-abuse disorders, that often complicate and sustain their contact with the juvenile and adult justice systems. Abram et al. (2003) found that most of the juvenile offenders in their study met the diagnostic criteria for both a substance-use disorder and a mental health condition, and Hussey, Drinkard, and Flannery (2007) found that 65 percent of the juvenile detainees they studied suffered co-occurring conditions, such as mental and substance-abuse disorders.

Risk Factors and African American Children's Justice System Involvement

Individual, family, peer, school, and community risk factors (Wasserman et al., 2003) place child welfare system–involved youths at increased vulnerability for justice system involvement. Among the individual factors, many of the emotional and behavioral health conditions previously discussed, including early antisocial behavior, poor cognitive development, low intelligence, and hyperactivity, have a profound link to delinquency. In addition to maltreatment, other family risk factors for delinquency include poor parenting, family violence, divorce, parental mental illness, and teenage parenting. Peer risk factors include association with deviant peers and rejection by peers. Finally, the school and community risk factors for delinquency and justice system involvement are many but include poor academic/school performance, poverty, and disadvantaged and disorganized neighborhoods.

Cahn (2006:4) states that "because of the complex interaction of socioeconomic disadvantage, institutional racism, and discriminatory sentencing policies, minority youth are more likely to be incarcerated than white youth." A sobering statistic is that African American youths make up 58 percent of the youths admitted to state prison (Poe-Yamagata & Jones, 2000). Cahn proposes a five-point plan for reforming the justice system that evidence shows delivers unequal justice and does not apply the leniency found in the notion of "developmental mistakes" to minority youths. Cahn's reform plan calls for increased use of diversion programs, providing alternatives to institutional placements that build family capacity, providing youths with effective legal counsel, providing youths with educational and rehabilitative services as prescribed by law, and stopping the trend of treating youth offenders as adults.

Given the "system crossover" phenomenon wherein child welfare system youths become juvenile justice system youths, there must be more emphasis placed on integrated system delivery. Howell et al. (2004) note that youths are often simultaneously involved in multiple service systems and that these systems must network, share information, and deliver services in an integrated manner. Additionally, given the set of risk factors that African American youths experience, education, mental health, child welfare, and juvenile justice systems must work cooperatively to increase youths' abilities to exit these systems successfully while building individual and family capacity.

THE WELL-BEING OF PARENTS AND CAREGIVERS

Many factors can make a child vulnerable to the negative effects of maltreatment. Some children grow up with seemingly very little and still survive against what appears to be insurmountable odds. Other children who seem to "have it all" may be troubled and unable to function. The cumulative effect of risks and opportunities in a child's life are created by their family and influenced by the neighborhood where they live, school experiences, and individual characteristics. The influence of family on the way children develop cannot be overemphasized; obviously, parental well-being is important if parents are to optimally meet the needs of their children. As with children, there are a number of indicators of well-being among adults—specifically African American adults who, like their children, are at risk in the United States for positive healthy outcomes. We review here a few of the major indicators, including finances/family income, health, mental health and substance abuse, housing/neighborhood, crime, and domestic violence.

Finances/Family Income

Family income is probably the one factor most directly related to child well-being and findings of child neglect. Income dictates the neighborhoods we live in and the housing we can afford, and in most communities housing is directly related to the schools children attend. Rural and urban city schools that serve children from lower-income families often experience insufficient funding from tax-based, marginalized resources. For children in these schools who require services aimed at addressing developmental and adaptive functioning limitations as well as behavior problems, the availability of services is limited. Health-care services for families in low-income neighborhoods may be limited because of inadequate health-care coverage or insurance, as opposed to inadequate facilities. Access to behavioral health care is for many families a factor of insurance coverage and Medicaid policy in state budgets. Some states do not provide behavioral health care to Medicaid-eligible consumers; states that have provided such services are cutting them during these times of growing state budget deficits and reduced tax revenues.

Family income affects not only our social environment and the circumstances of living; research suggests there is a relationship between family income and the experiences of children and their families once they are referred to the child welfare system. Researchers have studied the relationship between family reunification services and family income (Harris & Courtney, 2003; Wells & Guo, 2004; Whitaker & Maluccio, 2002). One study showed the length of time for reunification before and after the passage of the Personal Responsibility and Work Opportunity Reconciliation Act of 1996, which created the Temporary Assistance for Needy Families Act (TANF). Lower income was associated with slower reunification. Income is also associated with limited job skills and limited access to critical job-related supports, such as transportation and child care (Curtis & Alexander, 2010). Wells and Guo (2004) also found that income levels among African American women after the passage of TANF was a significant variable in the length of time it took families to experience reunification.

If family income affects the likelihood that reunification may occur or when it will occur, the types of supports available to families are critical. The child welfare worker becomes an essential partner in helping families mitigate the negative effects of low income by providing the types of supports—child care, transportation, job skills training, or health-care assessments required for work— required to participate in the paid labor force. Not only is caseworker judgment important, but state policies that dictate the support and services that will be provided must actually address income-related problems. The level of income a person achieves is directly correlated with the person's type of employment, level of education, and marital status.

Health, Mental Health, and Substance Abuse

Added to the types of stressors that parents in the child welfare system face are health, mental health, and substance-abuse problems. For example, substance abuse and child abuse and neglect go hand in hand. It is estimated that 11 percent of U.S. children live with at least one parent who is alcohol dependent or abuses drugs. Fifty-eight percent of the 1.88 million people who are treated for substance abuse in this country annually are parents, 27 percent of them have had their children removed from their care, and 37 percent have had their rights terminated. Likewise, mental health disorders tend to plague parents who are involved in the child welfare system. Although there is not conclusive research in this area, it has been estimated that 25 percent of the mothers involved in the child welfare system suffer significant psychiatric conditions. Many of these parents suffer the residual effects of early childhood trauma and abuse that they themselves experienced. Thus the cross-generational nature of abuse and neglect is profound. For others, poverty and other environmental conditions produce stress that impairs their ability to parent (National Child Traumatic Stress Network, 2008b).

The practice approach to working with parents who struggle with mental health and substance-abuse disorders involves intensive engagement, screening, and assessment techniques. Child welfare professionals must understand the link between maltreatment and mental health and substance-abuse disorders. For some parents, drug use may be an attempt to self-medicate their mental health struggles or to camouflage depression, anger, or life disappointments. Given the safety risks imposed by a parent who is impaired or who suffers from a mental health condition, child welfare intervention must involve screening referrals and an assessment of any harm that the child may have suffered as a result of parental drug/alcohol use. Given the fact that chronic and untreated mental illnesses, substance abuse, or co-occurring disorders account for a substantial number of failed reunification efforts, specialized attention must be devoted to securing this particular area of parental well-being.

Neighborhood/Housing Conditions

Curtis and Alexander (2010) examined census track data from 263 neighborhoods in Ohio to determine if variables related to the social environment can be correlated to the placement of African American children out of their homes and in foster care. The authors identified eleven of nineteen variables correlated with African American children and youths who do not live in their homes and who are typically attached to the out-of-home care system. The data suggest that if children are poor and live in neighborhoods in which there are large numbers of African American families, they are likely to live outside of their homes in foster care. This was particularly likely when large numbers of African American males in neighborhoods were living below the poverty level and had less than a high school education. Also correlated with children living out of their homes was the presence of both single male and single female heads of household.

It is important to remember, however, that negative correlations may be analyzed in two ways: high scores on one variable are associated with low scores on the second variable, but the reverse is also true. Unemployment among residents is associated with children living out of their homes; however, gainful employment and low numbers of African American males living in poverty are associated with children living with their families. Gainful employment for residents will have a positive effect on families living in that neighborhood. In the current economic environment in which many states are experiencing high unemployment, education and job training are essential for creating opportunities for marginalized workers to meet the demands of a changing global economy. Whether unemployment is due to structural unemployment or the loss of manufacturing and service-related jobs, economic recovery must also be directed to low-skilled and nonskilled workers (Curtis & Alexander, 2010). Structural factors that may be associated with negative outcomes for African American children are critically important and no less significant than personal attributes and behaviors among parents associated with the incidences of child abuse and neglect.

Income and employment status influence the housing options available to families. Children in the out-of-home system are most typically referred to child protective service agencies because of neglect—typically because of inadequate housing or the denial of needed health-care intervention. Poverty and low income are often associated with homelessness. Women and children are among the fastest growing group of those who live in poverty and constitute a new wave of homeless persons today (Anooshian, 2005; Battle, 1990). Families living without a permanent home can be people who have worked their entire life, such as employees of manufacturing plants that shut immediately and offer no alternative employment or compensatory package. For those who are afforded health-care benefits through employment, the termination of employment typically means the end of such benefits, particularly for low- and moderate-wage workers. When someone is forced out of a home and community, there is a loss of identity and a resultant sense of isolation experienced among family members. Feelings of guilt, anger, and helplessness often follow.

The negative effects of poverty for a child's development have been researched and documented (Moore et al., 2009). Children who live in poverty are at greater risk for negative outcomes in health, social, and emotional development and negative economic outcomes as adults. When compared with children from affluent or middle-income families, children from poor families are more likely to have low academic achievement, drop out of school, and have behavioral and emotional problems. There seem to be more detrimental effects of poverty for children whose families experience long-term poverty and children who are poor during early childhood (NICH, 2005).

Recent census data indicate that the number of children living in poverty increased between 2008 and 2009; children made up 35.5 percent of all people living in poverty in 2009. The number and percentage of children living in "deep poverty"—or in families with income below 50 percent of the federal poverty level—increased as well (U.S. Department of Commerce, 2010). The percentage of children living in deep poverty had been declining at the start of the twenty-first century but is now on the rise.

The poverty increase among the population of children is significant for a number of reasons. First, the federally funded child welfare system that provides resources to states for foster care uses Title IV-E of the Social Security Act, a funding stream that uses family income to determine eligibility. Family support services and reunification services are funded by Title IV-B and do not have income eligibility limitations based on federal law. However, when funds are limited, most local governments are likely to target resources to families with the greatest income-based need. In effect children and families come into contact with the child protective service system; Title IV-E will provide funding for children in licensed foster care but will not provide services to prevent families from coming into care. Federal funding should be available for services that get at the root causes of various forms of child maltreatment, including neglect, which is typically an income-related problem.

Poor and low-income families are also directly affected by economic downturns during which public services are cut. Personnel responsible for services aimed at ensuring health and safety become critical players who may also affect child well-being. Whether considering the placement of housing inspectors whose job it is to inspect broken elevator doors or monitor stockpiles of garbage in alleyways and public buildings, or health inspectors responsible for rodent exterminations, public personnel are important allies in keeping children safe and healthy. In many low-income neighborhoods today, auxiliary personnel in public schools such as nurse practitioners, social workers, guidance counselors, and special education teachers are almost nonexistent. When personnel are available in many public school settings, one specialist spends time between multiple schools and devotes time traveling between sites as opposed to providing specialty care.

These conditions exist as local governments struggle with the realities of diminished tax bases that cannot generate the revenue required for public safety—police, fire, sanitation—and education, transportation, recreation, and in communities where such services are paid for with tax revenues, behavioral health-care prevention and treatment. The limitations of personal income are magnified by the restrictions of local governments in providing critical services aimed at ensuring the health and safety of children and family members.

Because of the despair that is often associated with the loss of home, parents—single parents and those who are married—may present symptoms of depression and difficulty in managing everyday stress. In one study homeless mothers had higher levels of stress and depression than housed mothers who lived in poverty, and depression was associated with higher levels of avoidant behavior (Banyard & Graham-Scales, 1998). Another study identified homeless mothers who self-described their role of parent as being associated with frustration and difficulties associated with taking care of their children, surely in part because of the overwhelming responsibility of parenting when homeless (Hicks-Coolick, Burnside-Eaton, & Peters, 2003; Hicks-Coolick, Peters, & Zimmerman, 2007). In addition to the despair associated with homelessness, the majority of women who are homeless have experienced severe physical abuse or sexual assault at some time in their lives (Reif & Krisher, 2000).

Domestic Violence, Crime, and Parental Incarceration

It is estimated that as many as 10 to 15 million children are exposed to domestic violence each year, and up to 7 million children live in homes where they observe severe partner violence (Anderson, Danis, & Havig, 2010). There is a co-occurrence between domestic violence and child maltreatment (Bragg, 2003). One study found that in 41 to 43 percent of cases involving a serious child injury or death, there is evidence of domestic violence (Spears, 2000). Children raised in the presence of such violence have been associated with poor adaptive abilities, emotional well-being, social functioning, and physical health (Anderson, Danis, & Havig, 2010; Graham-Bermann & Edleson, 2001; Mullender et al., 2002). Children who are exposed to domestic violence grow up with a sense of powerlessness and subjugation, which if not acknowledged and addressed will stifle adult identity development essential to effective decision making and managing life's circumstances (Anderson, Danis, & Havig, 2010).

The U.S. Census (2009) reports that 2.8 million children do not live with either parent. According to estimates more than half (1.7 million) of these children do not live with their parents as a result of their primary caregiver's incarceration. There has been an increase in parental incarceration rates from 1991 to the present, with a 77 percent increase in father incarceration and a 131 percent increase in the number of mothers incarcerated (Christian, 2009). Incarcerated parents are disproportionately persons of color (African American, Hispanic), and the average sentence for the parent is 7.5 years (the average time served is 5 years) (Hairston, 2009).

In terms of age groups, 22 percent of the children whose parents are incarcerated are under the age of 5, and 28 percent are 5 to 10 years of age; 34 percent are 10 to 14; and 16 percent are 15 to 18 (Hairston, 2009). The effect of parental incarceration on children is profound and may differ by a child's age and developmental level. For example, it has been noted that parental incarceration can disrupt positive nurturing, produce instability for children, and provide tremendous financial strain on a family (Christian, 2009). Specifically, infants and toddlers risk attachment disruptions and disorganization, school-aged children suffer academic difficulties, and adolescents can experience delinquency, risky behaviors, and poor mental health outcomes (Dallaire, 2007; Dannerbeck, 2005; Gabel & Johnston, 1995; Hanlon, Carswell & Rose, 2007; Johnston, 1995; Phillips et al., 2002; Widom, 1995, 2000).

The incarceration of many parents seems to be linked to such conditions as substance abuse, poverty, mental illness, and family violence (Bouchet, 2008). Many parents' incarceration extends throughout their children's entire childhood (Hairston, 2009). Such lengthy prison stays impair reunification, thus making the separation that children experience permanent (Bouchet, 2008).

PRACTICE CONSIDERATIONS AND CULTURAL ADAPTATIONS FOR INCREASING CHILD AND FAMILY WELL-BEING

Child protective services workers cannot address all the problems that families present today—need for safe housing, employment and job skills training for parents, physical and behavioral health care, child behavior management, and the need to address the emotional trauma associated with domestic violence. Training and experience enable social workers to target limited resources to the multiple needs of families and assume the daunting task of assessing and prioritizing problems for appropriate intervention. This chapter would not be a comprehensive overview of the factors that affect the well-being of families if the reader were left with the idea that families coming to the attention of child protective service agencies—poor families, families who are challenged with health or behavioral health conditions, and families who may need to be strengthened through family support and prevention services—are weak, pathological, and at the brink of disruption.

While social researchers have researched variables or factors believed to impede stable family reunification, less attention has been directed to research that examines strengths among families in the child protective service system. The human spirit is amazingly strong and resilient. Traumatic experiences may limit the capacity of some individuals to cope and protect themselves from harm, using measures aimed at surviving physically and psychologically, while others display the resilience and capacity for perseverance and survival (Anderson, Danis, & Havig, 2010). Lietz and Strength (2010) conducted research aimed at identifying strengths associated with narratives of successful family reunification. The construct of resilience was applied to the family as a system by examining how families managed difficulties and grew stronger as collective units (Allison et al., 2003; Lietz, 2006, 2007; Walsh, 2002). "Resilience is more than simply managing or withstanding negative conditions. It encompasses survival as well as the emergence of positive change, growth, and resourcefulness in response to highly stressful events or experiences" (Lietz & Strength, 2010:203).

While different strengths were important to families at different times, ten strengths were associated with successful family functioning and resulted in positive reunification outcomes among the study families. The strengths identified include appraisal, boundary setting, communication, commitment, creativity/flexibility, humor, insight, initiative, spirituality, and social support (Lietz & Strength, 2010:205). The strengths were consistent among families who felt responsible for their condition or troubles and those who did not feel responsible. The strengths or behaviors and attributes associated with family reunification are similar to the qualities every family will probably need or make use of at some time. Every mother desires and values the support of her peers to make decisions. Whether it is a mother in the resilience study who faced suicidal thoughts (Lietz & Strength, 2010) or a mother whose child is diagnosed with a difficult-to-treat cancer, spirituality may be important and relevant for getting through everyday challenges for many families. Boundary setting may include the ability to separate oneself from unhealthy influences, including substances such as alcohol or other drugs. Determination to get through the difficult times as an intact family unit reflects commitment and insight to the dynamics of life that are unpredictable.

Finally, another family strength is parents' relationship quality, which is consistently and positively associated with a range of child and family outcomes. Child behavior problems, child social competence, school engagement, child depression, parent child interaction/communication, and parental aggravation are typically associated with parental relationship quality (NSCH, 2007). Unfortunately, the assumption about most low-income families is that they are headed by single females, particularly among minority racial and ethnic groups. Another assumption is that among married or cohabiting couples the quality of relationships is fraught with violence. Data from the National Survey of Children's Health (2007) challenge these stereotypes. The research confirms that parents in high-quality relationships, regardless of income status, have better-adjusted children with positive attitudes about marriage across social, economic, and racial and ethnic subgroups.

There are several inherent strengths embodied in the African American culture and possessed by individual children, families, and communities. These strengths can serve as the basis for making cultural adaptations to services so that they are more closely aligned with these families' needs. For example, in a study of African American males residing in foster care, Alford (2003:3) discovered that they embraced the following values: (a) "the importance of learning and giving back what you have learned and the will to strive for your best; (b) family solidarity and cultural interconnectedness; (c) condemnation of violence and unproductive behavior; and (d) reverence for the Creator." Likewise, the child welfare service system has advanced tremendously in recent years, and several initiatives are in place that demonstrate promising results in increasing child and family well-being. Table 6.1 presents a set of general principles that are intended to enhance child and parental well-being. These principles include guidelines for what can be done by practitioners who work with individuals and communities and for those who work at a system level.

TABLE 6.1
Cultural Adaptation Components That Enhance Child and Family Well-Being

Principles for Promoting Children's Well-Being in the Area of Health

- Put in place advocacy efforts that promote health equity.
- Work to allay clients' fears, mistrust, and negative sentiments about health professionals.
- Emphasize companion professional roles that focus on ecological restoration and environmental safety, including "clean community campaigns."

Principles for Promoting Children's Well-Being in the Area of Mental Health

- Financially incentivize integrated and coordinated mental health care between child welfare, mental health, juvenile justice, and education systems.
- Emphasize service equity and inclusiveness.
- Training of practitioners must emphasize the importance of preserving relationships and facilitating attachment.
- Consider incorporating nontraditional or healing arts (e.g., poetry, music) into interventions.

Principles for Promoting Children's Well-Being in the Area of Education

- Couple formal services with indigenous or voluntary helpers (e.g., African American philanthropic or Greek organizations). Indigenous helpers can be used to promote ethnic development, racial pride, and identification and to stress an achievement orientation.
- Allow shared ownership of the problems that are encountered by the community. Communities can be empowered to own both problems and solutions.

Principles for Promoting Parental Well-Being

- Place priority on promoting economic development and financial support.
- Adopt a professional orientation that behaviorally suggests that protecting children requires protecting families.
- Work to help parents strengthen their social networks, facilitate relationships, and maintain connections with those individuals who can serve as a resource or support.
- Consider incorporating religious or spiritual outlets into interventions and services.
- Community advocacy must run concurrent with individual-level intervention. The community intervention should address population risk factors.
- Help organize and validate such nontraditional social services as neighborhood co-ops (e.g., child care co-ops, food co-ops) with the purpose of providing practice assistance while simultaneously building neighborhood cohesion.
- Campaign to reduce the stigma associated with mental health disorders and normalize the experience of seeking intervention.

SUMMARY AND CONCLUSION

Children who experience family disruption require supportive foster or adoptive families who can understand the multiple placements experienced by some children, and the uncertainty that comes with family disruption and broken relationships. Culturally competent professionals capable of assessing the individual needs of each child and family member—including birth and adoptive or foster family members associated with the child's placement—will play an essential role if successful outcomes are to be realized. Community-based, culturally competent behavioral health care services are also essential to enhance opportunities for optimal personal development and healthy outcomes.

One way to socially adapt existing systems of care for children in child welfare is to strengthen investments in community-based behavioral health. Many states today face increased demands for behavioral health care while funds for services have been targeted for cuts. Recent allocations to state governments for behavioral health care from federal stimulus dollars for FY 2009 and FY 2010 that enhanced the match for Medicaid services will be eliminated, thus resulting in even greater reductions in many states. The demand for culturally competent care must be made in state legislatures so that children and families are not placed at risk for increased acts of maltreatment or worse. It is not uncommon to read newspaper accounts across the country of a parent who in desperation takes the life of a child or children and then perhaps himself or herself in a final act of desperation.

In some states changing demographics resulting in new immigrants from oppressed, war-torn countries require a variety of supportive services for students in schools and for adults who must adjust to a different culture. Posttraumatic stress associated with war and human mutilation practices among people in the countries of origin require comprehensive, intense interventions to strengthen families and facilitate optimal productivity and independence. For others, unemployment or pressures associated with single parenting may pose challenges that require supportive intervention.

We know that behavioral health care may decrease costs associated with juvenile corrections. The percentage of youths within the juvenile correction system who need mental health services or drug treatment support has increased. When specialized services are provided, the cost of juvenile detention is more expensive. Community-based services provided to children and youths prior to adjudication and referral to juvenile detention centers will be less costly and may engage the parent or guardian in the plans for service. Past experiences and present adjustment requirements pose tremendous demands on the families with whom children may be placed and the professional staff who provide support to children and their foster families. Likewise, children who may be placed in adoptive homes will also require specialized professional support.

DISCUSSION QUESTIONS

1. An interesting phenomenon occurs with respect to foster children's physical and mental health conditions: it has been observed that children's physical health improves during their stay in out-of-home care, but their mental health does not. Discuss what might account for this phenomenon.

2. Discuss the importance of parental well-being for the developing child and how it increases children's vulnerability for involvement in the child welfare system.

3. Why is long-term poverty and poverty during early childhood especially detrimental to children?

ACTIVITIES FOR ONGOING LEARNING

1. Develop a series of reaction papers using these suggested topics:

A. What, if any, is the connection between poverty and child abuse and neglect?

B. What, if any, is the connection between domestic violence and child abuse and neglect?

C. Discuss reactive attachment disorder and how it affects children involved in the child welfare system.

D. Discuss posttraumatic stress disorder and how it affects children involved in the child welfare system.

2. Children involved in the child welfare system often experience grief, loss, and separation. Discuss these conditions and their effect on children.

3. Discuss the condition known as severe emotional disturbance and its connection with child welfare children and youth.

4. Develop a monthly budget for a family of five—a mother and four children, ages 2, 4, 6, and 9. Use the following parameters:

• Monthly income is $548 (the income is derived from employment). The mother works four days per week as a janitor at a fitness club. The job does not provide benefits, and overtime is not an option.

• The cost of utilities averages $178 to $235 per month. The landlord pays for water, sewage, and garbage service, but the family must cover the cost of electricity and gas. The family does not have a home phone. The mother is able to use her neighbor's cell phone for calls related to work or the children.

• The family lives in a government-subsidized, three-bedroom apartment for which they pay $109 per month in rent.

• The family uses public transportation for the mother to get to work and to get the children to various appointments. Weekly bus passes are $28. The children ride the bus free of charge.

• The bus stops running before the mother's shift ends; a co-worker gives her a ride home. She gives the co-worker $10 per week for gas.

• The grandmother of the youngest child babysits whenever the mother needs it, taking care of both the 2-year-old and the 4-year-old, typically arriving at the home about 1:45 P.M, when the mother must leave for work. Although the grandmother does not seek payment, the mother attempts to pay her $30 per week. The mother's shift at work is 3:00 P.M. to 11:30 P.M. The 6- and 9-year-olds get out of school at 3:15. The mother pays a neighbor's 14-year-old daughter to walk to the school to meet the children, do homework, prepare dinner, and then put the children to bed. In return, the mother braids the teenager's hair and also gives her $20 to $25 per week.

• The family receives $161 in food stamps each month, but household items (e.g., over-the-counter medications, hygiene items, clothes, cleaning supplies) average $70 per month and cannot be purchased with food stamps. The 6- and 9-year-olds receive free breakfast and lunch at school.

Decide what the family can do without so that they can live within their budget. Discuss what necessities this budget does not allow. Discuss how such a budget affects the developmental needs of the four children. Discuss the conditions that the family's financial situation makes them vulnerable to experience. Note: The children all receive Medicaid, but the mother currently does not have health insurance. The mother does not receive child support. The father of her youngest child is incarcerated, and the father of the other three children is deceased. The deceased father did not pay into the Social Security system. The mother is on a waiting list to receive subsidized childcare services. She has requested a day shift from her employer but has the least amount of seniority so must wait for something to open up.

REFERENCES

Abram, K. M., L. A. Teplin, G. M. McClelland, & M. K. Dulcan. 2003. "Comorbid Psychiatric Disorders in Youth in Juvenile Detention." *Archives of General Psychiatry* 60:1097–1108.

Administration for Children and Families. 2008. *Adolescents Involved with Child Welfare: A Transition to Adulthood.* Washington, D.C.: Administration for Children and Families.

Alegria, M., G. Canino, R. Rios, M. Vera, J. Calderon, D. Rusch, & A. N. Ortega. 2002. "Inequalities in Use of Specialty Mental Health Services Among Latinos, African Americans, and Non-Latino Whites." *Psychiatric Services* 53 (12): 1547–55.

Alford, K. A. 2003. "Cultural Themes in Rites of Passage: Voices of Young African American Males." *Journal of African American Studies* 7 (1): 3–26.

Allison, S., K. Stacy, V. Dadds, L. Roeger, A. Wood, & G. Martin. 2003. "What Family Brings: Gathering Evidence for Strengths-Based Work." *Journal of Family Therapy* 25:263–84.

American Psychiatric Association. 2000. *Diagnostic and Statistical Manual of Mental Disorders, DSM-IV-TR,* 85–93. Washington, D.C.: American Psychiatric Association.

Anderson, K. M., F. S. Danis, & K. Havig. 2010. "Adult Daughters of Battered Women: Recovery and Posttraumatic Growth Following Childhood Adversity." *Families in Society: The Journal of Contemporary Social Services* 92 (2): 154–60.

Anooshian, L. J. 2005. "Violence and Aggression in the Lives of Homeless Children." *Journal of Family Violence* 20 (6): 373–87.

Aud, S., M. A. Fox, & A. Kewal Ramani. 2010. *Status and Trends in the Education of Racial and Ethnic Groups.* U.S. Department of Education, National Center for Education Statistics. Washington, D.C.: U.S. Government Printing Office.

Banyard, V. L., & S. Graham-Scales. 1998. Surviving Poverty: Stress and Coping in the Lives of Housed and Homeless Children. *American Journal of Orthopsychiatry* 68:479–89.

Barbell, K., & M. Freundlich. 2002. *Foster Care Today.* Seattle: Casey Family Programs.

Barkley, R., A. Anastopoulos, & D. C. Buevremont. 1991. "Adolescents with ADHD: Patterns of Behavioral Adjustment, Academic Functioning, and Treatment Utilization." *Journal of the American Academy of Child and Adolescent Psychiatry* 30:752–61.

Battle, S. F. 1990. "Homeless Women and Children: The Question of Poverty." *Child and Youth Services* 14 (1): 111–27.

Bouchet, S. M. 2008. *Children and Families with Incarcerated Parents: Exploring Development in the Field and Opportunities for Growth.* Baltimore: Annie E. Casey Foundation.

Bragg, H. L. 2003. *Child Protection in Families Experiencing Domestic Violence.* Washington, D.C.: U.S. Department of Health and Human Services.

Brooks-Gunn, J., & G. Duncan. 1997. "Effects of Poverty on Children." *The Future of Children* 7 (2): 55–71.

Burns, B. J., S. D. Phillips, H. R. Wagner, R. Barth, D. Kolko, & Y. Campbell. 2004. "Mental Health Need and Access to Mental Health Services by Youth Involved with Child Welfare: A National Survey." *Journal of the American Academy of Child & Adolescent Psychiatry* 43 (8): 960–70.

Cahn, E. S. 2006. *How the Juvenile Justice System Reduces Life Options of Minority Youth.* Washington, D.C.: Joint Center for Political and Economic Studies Health Policy Institute.

Center for Early Childhood Mental Health Consultation. 2011. *Recognizing and Addressing Trauma in Infants, Young Children, and Their Families.* http://www.ecmhc.org/tutorials/trauma/mod1_2.html.

Children's Bureau. 2003. "Mental Health Issues in the Child Welfare System." *Best Practice/Next Practice, A Publication of the National Child Welfare Resource Center for Family Centered Practice.* Washington, D.C.: Children's Bureau.

Chipungu, S. S., & T. B. Bent-Goodley. 2004. "Meeting the Challenges of Contemporary Foster Care." *The Future of Children* 14 (1): 75–93.

Chow, J. C., K. Jaffee, & L. Snowden. 2003. "Racial/Ethnic Disparities in the Use of Mental Health Services in Poverty Areas." *American Journal of Public Health* 93 (5): 792–97.

Christian, S. 2009. *Children of Incarcerated Parents.* March. Washington, D.C.: National Conference of State Legislatures.

Christodulu, K. V., R. Lichenstein, M. Weist, M. E. Shafer, & M. Simone. 2002. "Psychiatric Emergencies in Children." *Pediatric Emergency Care* 18:268–70.

Cohen, J., P. Cole, & J. Szrom. 2011. *A Call to Action on Behalf of Maltreated Infants and Toddlers.* Washington, D.C.: American Humane Association.

Courtney, M., A. Dworsky, G. Ruth, T. Keller, J. Havlicek, & N. Bost. 2005. *Midwest Evaluation of the Adult Functioning of Former Foster Youth: Outcomes at Age 19.* Chicago: Chapin Hall Center for Children at the University of Chicago.

Curtis, C. M., & R. Alexander. 2010. "Correlates of African American Children In and Out of Their Families." *Families in Society: Journal of Contemporary Social Services* 91 (1): 85–90.

Dallaire, D. H. 2007. "Children with Incarcerated Mothers: Developmental Outcomes, Special Challenges and Recommendations." *Journal of Applied Developmental Psychology* 28:15–24.

Dannerbeck, A.M. 2005. "Differences in Parenting Attributes, Experiences, and Behaviors of Delinquent Youth With and Without a Parental History of Incarceration." *Youth Violence and Juvenile Justice* 3 (3): 199–213.

Dubner, A. E., & R. W. Motta. 1999. "Sexually and Physically Abused Foster Care Children and Posttraumatic Stress Disorder." *American Psychological Association* 7 (3): 367–73.

Elia, J., P. Ambrosini, & J. Rapoport. 1999. Treatment of Attention-Deficit Hyperactivity Disorder. *New England Journal of Medicine* 340 (10): 780–88.

Encyclopedia of Mental Disorders. 2011. *Reactive Attachment Disorder of Infancy or Early Childhood.* http://www.minddisorders.com/Py-Z/Reactive-attachment-disorder-of-infancy-or-early-childhood.html

Fanshel, D., & E. Shinn. 1978. *Children in Foster Care: A Longitudinal Investigation.* New York: Columbia University Press.

Fletcher, J., & B. Wolfe. 2009. "Long-term Consequences of Childhood ADHD on Criminal Activities." *Journal of Mental Health Policy and Economics* 12 (3): 119–38.

Gabel, K., & D. Johnston. 1995. *Children of Incarcerated Parents.* New York: Lexington Books.

Garland, A. F., R. L. Hough, J. A. Landsverk, K. M. McCabe, M. Yeh, W. C. Ganger, & B. J. Reynolds. 2000. "Racial and Ethnic Variations in Mental Healthcare Utilization Among Children in Foster Care." *Children's Services* 3 (3): 133–46.

Garland, A. F., R. L. Hough, K. M. McCabe, M. Yeh, P. A. Wood, & G. A. Aarons. 2001. "Prevalence of Psychiatric Disorders in Youths Across 5 Sectors of Care." *Journal of American Academy of Child and Adolescent Psychiatry* 40 (4): 409–18.

Gershoff, E., J. Aber, & C. Raver. 2003. "Child Poverty in the United States: An Evidence-Based Conceptual Framework for Programs and Policies." In *Handbook of Applied Developmental Science: Promoting Positive Child, Adolescent, and Family Development Through Research, Policies, and Programs.* Edited by F. Jacobs, D. Wertlieb, & R. M. Lerner, 2:81–136. Thousand Oaks, Calif.: Sage.

Goodman, R. F. 2002. *Caring for Kids After Trauma and Death: A Guide for Parents and Professionals.* New York: Institute for Trauma and Stress, NYU Child Study Center. http://www.aboutourkids.org/.

Graham-Bermann, S., & J. Edleson. 2001. *Domestic Violence in the Lives of Children: The Future of Research, Intervention, and Social Policy.* Washington, D.C.: American Psychological Association.

Greenhill, L. L. 1998. "Diagnosing Attention Deficit Hyperactivity Disorder in Children." *Journal of Clinical Psychiatry* 59:31–41.

Hairston, C. F. 2009. *Kinship Care When Parents Are Incarcerated: What We Know, What We Can Do.* Report prepared for the Annie E. Casey Foundation. Baltimore: Annie E. Casey Foundation.

Hamblen, J., & E. Barnett. 1999. *Fact Sheet: PTSD in Children and Adolescents.* National Center for PTSD. http://www.ptsd.va.gov/professional/pages/ptsd _in_children_and_adolescents_overview_for_professionals.asp.

Hanlon, T. E., S. B. Carswell, & M. Rose. 2007. "Research on the Caretaking of Children of Incarcerated Parents: Findings and Their Service Delivery Implications." *Child and Youth Services Review* 29 (3): 362–84.

Harlem Children's Zone. 2012. *About Harlem Children's Zone.* http://www.hcz .org/home/.

Harney, M. 2000. "Child Abuse May Trigger Health Problems Throughout Life." *DFC Online* 1 (1) (May).

Harris, M. S., & M. Courtney. 2003. "The Interaction of Race, Ethnicity, and Family Structure with Respect to the Timing of Family Reunification." *Children and Youth Services Review* 25 (5/6): 409–29.

Herrera, V. M., & L. A. McCloskey. 2001. "Gender Differences in the Risk for Delinquency Among Youth Exposed to Family Violence." *Child Abuse and Neglect* 25 (8): 1037–51.

———. 2003. "Sexual Abuse, Family Violence, and Female Delinquency: Findings from a Longitudinal Study." *Violence and Victims* 18 (3): 319–34.

Hicks-Coolick, A., P. Burnside-Eaton, & A. Peters. 2003. "Homeless Children: Needs and Services." *Child and Youth Care Forum* 32:197–210.

Hicks-Coolick, A., A. Peters, & V. Zimmerman. 2007. "How 'Deserving' Are the Most Vulnerable Homeless?" *Journal of Poverty* 11 (1): 135–41.

Howell, J. C., M. R. Kelly, J. Palemer, & R. L. Mangum. 2004. "Integrating Child Welfare, Juvenile Justice, and Other Agencies in a Continuum of Services." *Child Welfare* 83 (2): 143–56.

Hussey, D. L., A. M. Drinkard, & D. J. Flannery. 2007. "Comorbid Substance Use and Mental Disorders Among Offending Youth." *Journal of Social Work Practice in the Addictions* 7 (1/2): 117–38.

James, S., J. Landsverk, D. Slyman, & L. Leslie. 2004. "Predictors of Outpatient Mental Health Service Use: The Role of Foster Care Placement Change." *Mental Health Service Research* 6 (3): 127–41.

Johnston, D. (1995). "Effects of Parental Incarceration." In *Children of Incarcerated Parents.* Edited by K. Gabel & D. Johnston, 59–88. New York: Lexington Books.

Joint Center for Political and Economic Studies Health Policy Institute. 2007. *Aging Out of the Foster Care System to Adulthood.* Washington, D.C.: Joint Center for Political and Economic Studies Health Policy Institute.

Karger, H., & D. Stoesz. 2009. *American Social Welfare Policy: A Pluralist Approach.* Boston: Allyn & Bacon.

Kilcarr, P. J., & P. O. Quinn. 1997. *Voices from Fatherhood: Fathers, Sons, and ADHD*. Bristol, Pa.: Brunner/Mazel.

Kortenkamp, K., & J. Ehrle. 2002. *The Well-being of Children Involved with the Child Welfare System: A National Overview*. National Survey of America's Families Series B, No. B-43. Washington, D.C.: Urban Institute.

Kunen, S., R. Niederhauser, P. O. Smith, & J. A. Morris. 2005. "Race Disparities in Psychiatric Rates in Emergency Departments." *Journal of Counseling and Clinical Psychology* 73 (1): 116–26.

Lietz, C. A. 2006. "Uncovering Stories of Family Resilience: A Mixed Methods Study of Resilient Families, Part 1." *Families in Society: The Journal of Contemporary Social Services* 87 (4): 441–58.

———. 2007. "Uncovering Stories of Family Resilience: A Mixed Methods Study of Resilient Families, Part 2." *Families in Society: The Journal of Contemporary Social Services* 88 (1): 147–55.

Lietz, C.A., & M. Strength. 2010. "Stories of Successful Reunification: A Narrative Study of Family Resilience in Child Welfare." *Families in Society: The Journal of Contemporary Social Services* 92 (2): 203–10.

Linares, L. O, M. S. MinMin Li, P. E. Shrout, M. Ramirez-Gaite, S. Hope, A. Albert, & F. X. Castellanos. 2010. "The Course of Inattention and Hyperactivity/Impulsivity Symptoms After Foster Placement." *Pediatrics* 125 (3): e489–e498. Originally published online February 1, 2010. DOI:10.1542/peds.2009–1285.

Marsenich, L. 2002. *Evidence-Based Practices in Mental Health Services for Foster Youth*. Sacramento: California Institute for Mental Health. http://www.cimh .org/Services/Child-Family/Past-Projects/EBP-in-Mental-Health-Services-for -Foster-Youth.aspx

Massinga, R., & P. J. Pecora. 2004. "Providing Better Opportunities for Older Children in the Foster Care System." *The Future of Children* 14 (1): 151–73.

McMillen, J. C., B. T. Zima, L. D. Scott, et al. 2005. "Prevalence of Psychiatric Disorders Among Older Youths in the Foster Care System." *Journal of the American Academy of Child and Adolescent Psychiatry* 44 (1): 88–95.

Mersky, J. P., & A. J. Reynolds. 2007. "Child Maltreatment and Violent Delinquency: Disentangling Main Effects and Subgroup Effects." *Child Maltreatment* 12 (3): 246–58.

Moore, K. A., Z. Redd, M. Burkhauser, K. Mbwana, & A. Collins. 2009. *Children in Poverty: Trends, Consequences, and Policy Options*. Child Trends Research Brief. Washington, D.C.: Child Trends.

Mullender, A., G. Hague, U. Iman, L. Kelly, E. Malos, & L. Regan. 2002. *Children's Perspectives on Domestic Violence*. Newbury Park, Calif.: Sage.

Murphy, P., & R. Schachar. 2000. "Use of Self-Ratings in the Assessment of Symptoms of Attention Deficit Hyperactivity Disorders in Adults." *American Journal of Psychiatry* 157:1156–59.

National Center for Health Statistics. 2006. *Health, United States, 2006 with Chart Book on Trends on the Health of Americans.* Hyattsville, Md.: U.S. Government Printing Office.

National Child Traumatic Stress Network. 2008a. *Child Welfare Trauma Training Toolkit.* http://www.nctsn.org/trauma-types.

———. 2008b. *Child Welfare Trauma Training Toolkit: Trainer's Guide.* http://www.nctsn.org/.

National Institute of Child Health and Human Development Early Child Care Research Network. 2005. "Duration and Developmental Timing of Poverty and Children's Cognitive and Social Development from Birth Through Third Grade." *Child Development* 76 (4): 795–810.

National Institute of Mental Health (NIMH). 2001. *Helping Children and Adolescents Cope with Violence and Disasters* [NIH Pub. NO. 01–3518]. Bethesda, Md.: NIMH.

———. 2011a. *Anxiety Disorders in Children and Adolescents (Fact Sheet).* http://www.nimh.nih.gov/health/publications/anxiety-disorders-in-children-and-adolescents/index.shtml.

———. 2011b. *Attention Deficit Hyperactivity Disorder in Children and Adolescents (Fact Sheet).* http://www.nimh.nih.gov/health/publications/attention-deficit-hyperactivity-disorder-in-children-and-adolescents/index.shtml.

———. 2011c. *Depression in Children and Adolescents (Fact Sheet).* http://www.nimh.nih.gov/health/publications/depression-in-children-and-adolescents/index.shtml.

———. 2011d. *Brain Development During Childhood and Adolescence (Fact Sheet).* http://www.nimh.nih.gov/health/publications/brain-development-during-childhood-and-adolescence/index.shtml.

National Survey of Children's Health (NSCH). 2007. *National Survey of Children's Health Report.* Washington, D.C.: National Center for Health Statistics.

Neeley-Bertrand, D. 2001. "Mental Health and Child Welfare: Waiting for Care." *Children's Voice.* Washington, D.C.: Child Welfare League of America. http://www.cwla.org/articles/cv0105mentalhealth.htm.

New York University Child Study Center. 2011. *New Survey Reveals All-Day Impact of ADHD on Children and Their Parents: ADHD Not Just a School-Day Disorder. Investigating the Mindset of Parents About ADHD and Children Today (I.M.P.A.C.T) Study.* http://www.aboutourkids.org/files/news/press_room/assets/impact.pdf.

NIH Consensus Statement. 1998. Diagnosis and Treatment of Attention Deficit Hyperactivity Disorder. *NIH Consensus Statement Online 1998 Nov 16–18* 16 (2): 1–37. http://consensus.nih.gov/1998/1998AttentionDeficitHyperactivity Disorder110html.htm.

North Carolina Division of Social Services and the Family and Children's Resource Program. 2005. "PTSD and Children in the Child Welfare System." *Children's Services Practice Notes* 10 (3): 1–11.

Northwest Federation of Community Organizations. 2005. *Closing the Gap: Solutions to Race-Based Health Disparities.* Seattle: Northwest Federation of Community Organizations.

Pecora, P. J. 2008. "Mental Health Disorders of Youth in Foster Care and Foster Care Alumni in the United States." *Outcome Network.* http://www.outcome -network.org/paper/282:mental_health_disorders_of_youth_in_foster_care _and_foster_care_alumni_in_the_united_states.

Pecora, P. J., R. C. Kessler, J. Williams, J. O'Brien, A. C. Downs, D. English, J. White, E. Hiripi, C. R. White, T. Wiggins, & K. E. Holmes. 2005. *Improving Family Foster Care: Findings from the Northwest Foster Care Alumni Study.* Seattle: Casey Family Programs.

Pecora, P. J., C. Roller White, L. J. Jackson, & T. Wiggins. 2009. "Mental Health of Current and Former Recipients of Foster Care: A Review of Recent Studies in the USA." *Child and Family Social Work* 14:132–46.

Phillips, K. A., K. R. Morrison, R. Andersen, & L. A. Aday. 1998. "Understanding the Context of Healthcare Utilization: Assessing Environmental and Provider Related Variables in the Behavioral Model of Utilization." *Health Services Research* 33 (5): 575–95.

Phillips, S. D., B. J. Burns, H. R. Wagner, T. L. Kramer, & J. M. Robbins. 2002. "Parental Incarceration Among Adolescents Receiving Mental Health Services." *Journal of Child and Family Studies* 11 (4): 385–99.

Poe-Yamagata, E., & M. A. Jones. 2000. *And Justice for Some: Differential Treatment of Minority Youth in the Justice System.* Washington, D.C.: Building Blocks for Youth.

Reif, S. A., & L. J. Krisher. 2000. "Subsidized Housing and the Unique Needs of Domestic Violence Victims." *Clearing House Review: National Center on Poverty Law.* Chicago: National Center on Poverty Law.

Rosenfeld, A., D. Pilowsky, P. Fine, M. Thorpe, E. Fein, & M. D. Simm. 1997. "Foster Care: An Update." *Journal of the American Academy of Child and Adolescent Psychiatry* 36 (4): 448–57.

Schweitzer, J. B. 2001. "Attention-Deficit/Hyperactivity Disorder." *Medical Clinics of North America* 85 (3): 757–77.

Scott, M., L. Snowden, & A. Libby. 2002. "Effects of Capitated Mental Health Services on Youth Contact with the Juvenile Justice System." *Journal of the American Academy of Child and Adolescent Psychiatry* 41 (12): 1462–69.

Shaffer, J. N., & R. B. Ruback. 2002. "Violent Victimization as a Risk Factor for Violent Offending Among Juveniles." *OJJDP Juvenile Justice Bulletin* (December): 1–10.

Sharkey, P. 2009. *Neighborhoods and the Black-White Mobility Gap.* Pew Charitable Trusts.   http://www.pewtrusts.org/uploadedFiles/wwwpewtrustsorg/Reports/ Economic_Mobility/PEW_SHARKEY_v12.pdf.

Siegel, J. A., & L. M. Williams. 2003. "The Relationship Between Child Sexual Abuse and Female Delinquency and Crime: A Prospective Study." *Journal of Research in Crime Delinquency* 40 (1): 71–94.

Simmel, C., D. Brooks, R. P. Barth, & S. P. Hinshaw. 2001. "Externalizing Symptomatology Among Adoptive Youth: Prevalence and Preadoption Risk Factors." *Journal of Abnormal Child Psychology* 29 (1): 57– 69.

Simms, M., & N. Halfon. 1994. "The Healthcare Needs of Children in Foster Care: A Research Agenda." *Child Welfare* 73:505–24.

Smith, C., & T. P. Thornberry. 1995. "Childhood Maltreatment and Adolescent Involvement in Delinquency." *Criminology* 33 (4): 451–77.

Snowden, L., A. Cuellar, & A. Libby. 2003. "Minority Youth in Foster Care: Managed Care and Access to Mental Health Treatment." *Medical Care* 41 (2): 264–74.

Solomon, S. D. 2005. "Traumatic Stress: Prevalence and Consequences." Paper presented at the National Institutes of Health Behavioral and Social Sciences Seminar Series. January. http://obssr.od.nih.gov/pdf/solomon.pdf.

Spears, L. 2000. "Building Bridges Between Domestic Violence Organizations and Child Protective Services." *The Building Comprehensive Solutions to Domestic Violence Policy, Practice and Vision Paper Series.* National Resource Center on Domestic Violence. http://www.vaw.umn.edu/documents/dvcps/dvcps .html.

Steele, J. S., & K. F. Buchi. 2008. "Medical and Mental Health of Children Entering the Utah Foster Care System." *Pediatrics* 122 (3): e703–e709. http:// pediatrics.aappublications.org/content/122/3/e703.full.

U.S. Department of Commerce, U.S. Census Bureau. 2009. *Family Structure and Children's Living Arrangements.* http://74.125.95.132/search?q=cache:jh6HSs 5YrxMJ:www.childstats.gov/americaschildren/famsoc1.asp+U.+S.+Census+20 08+children+living+with+relatives&cd=3&hl=en&ct=clnk&gl=us.

———. 2010. *Current Population Survey.* Washington, D.C.: Census Bureau.

U.S. Department of Health and Human Services, Administration for Children and Families, Administration on Children, Youth and Families, Children's Bureau. 2008. *Child Maltreatment.* http://www.acf.hhs.gov/programs/cb/pubs/ cm08/cm08.pdf.

———. 2010a. *Child Maltreatment 2008.* http://www.acf.hhs.gov/programs/cb/ pubs/cm08.

———. 2010b. *The AFCARS Report: Preliminary FY 2009 Estimates as of July 2010 (17).* http://www.acf.hhs.gov/programs/cb/stats_research/afcars/tar/report17.htm.

———, Health Resources and Services Administration, Maternal and Child Health Bureau. 2009. *The National Survey of Children's Health 2007.* Rockville, Md.: U.S. Department of Health and Human Services.

———, National Center for Health Statistics. 2009. *National Vital Statistics Reports: Births—Final Data for 2006* 57 (7) (January). http://www.cdc.gov/nchs/ data/nvsr/nvsr57/nvsr57_07.pdf.

―――, Office of Planning, Research & Evaluation. 2011. *Who Are The Children in Foster Care?* http://www.acf.hhs.gov/programs/opre/abuse_neglect/nscaw/reports/children_fostercare/children_fostercare.pdf.

U.S. Surgeon General. 2001. *Report of the Surgeon General Conference on Children's Mental Health: A National Action Agenda.* Washington, D.C.: Department of Health and Human Services.

Van Ryn, M., & S. S. Fu. 2003. "Paved with Good Intentions: Do Public Health and Human Service Providers Contribute to Racial/Ethnic Disparities in Health?" *American Journal of Public Health* 93 (2): 248–55.

Walsh, F. 2002. "A Family Resilience Framework: Innovative Practice Applications." *Family Relations* 51:130–37.

Wasserman, G. A., K. Keenan, R. E. Tremblay, J. D. Coie, T. I. Herrenkohl, R. Loeber, & D. Petechuk. 2003. "Risk and Protective Factors of Child Delinquency." *Child Delinquency Bulletin Series.* Washington, D.C.: U.S. Department of Justice Office of Justice Programs.

Weiner, A., & E. Weiner. 1990. *Expanding the Options in Child Placement: Israel's Dependent Children in Care from Infancy to Adulthood.* Lanham, Md.: University Press of America.

Weissman, M. M., S. Wolk, R. B. Goldstein, D. Moreau, P. Adams, S. Greenwald, C. M. Klier, N. D. Ryan, R. E. Dahl, & P. Wichramaratne. 1999. "Depressed Adolescents Grown Up." *Journal of the American Medical Association* 281 (18): 1701–13.

Wells, K., & S. Guo. 2004. "Reunification of Foster Children Before and After Welfare Reform." *Social Service Review* 78 (1): 74–95.

Whitaker, J. K., & A. N. Maluccio. 2002. "Rethinking 'Child Placement': A Reflective Essay." *Social Service Review* 76 (1): 108–34.

Widom, C. S. 1989. "Child Abuse, Neglect, and Violent Criminal Behavior." *Criminology* 27 (2): 251–71.

―――. 1995. *Victims of Childhood Sexual Abuse—Later Criminal Consequences,* Report No. 151525. Washington, D.C.: U.S. Department of Justice.

―――. 2000. "Child Abuse and Later Effects." *National Institute of Justice Journal* (January): 1–9.

Widom, C. S., & M. G. Maxfield. 2001. *An Update on the "Cycle of Violence."* NIJ Research in Brief. Washington, D.C.: U.S. Department of Justice, Office of Justice Programs, National Institute of Justice.

Williams, L. M., & V. M. Herrera. 2007. "Child Maltreatment and Adolescent Violence: Understanding Complex Connections." *Child Maltreatment* 12 (3): 203–7.

Winnicott, D. W. 1964. *The Child, the Family, and the Outside World.* Middlesex, England: Penguin.

Zeanah, C. H., M. Scheeringa, N. W. Boris, S. S. Heller, A. T. Smyke, & J. Trapani. 2004. "Reactive Attachment Disorder in Maltreated Toddlers." *Child Abuse and Neglect* 28 (8): 877–88.

Zero to Three. 2011. *DC: 0–3.* at http://www.zerotothree.org/child-development/
early-childhood-mental-health/diagnostic-classification-of-mental-health
-and-developmental-disorders-of-infancy-and-early-childhood-revised.html.

Zingraff, M. T., J. Leiter, K. A. Myers, & M. C. Johnson. 1993. "Child Maltreatment and Youthful Problem Behavior." *Criminology* 31 (2): 173–202.

A CASE STUDY: CULTURAL ADAPTATIONS AND RESEARCH INITIATIVES—FROM KINSHIP RESEARCH TO KINSHIP PROGRAMMING

A case study of the Clark County, Nevada, Kinship Support Program illustrates an approach to research translation. Following the case study, chapter 7 includes a discussion of how research findings related to the outcomes experienced by African American children and families can be used to frame advocacy efforts. The goal of the analysis is to demonstrate how research results can be used to effectively guide child welfare policy and program development that respond to the specific needs of African American children.

The Original Condition and the Need for Change

The Clark County Kinship Support Program was developed as a result of the Caring Communities Demonstration Project, a study that began as a collaborative effort between the Clark County Department of Family Services, the University of Nevada, Las Vegas, and several community-based partners. Clark County was awarded one of nine federal demonstration projects administered by the United States Department of Health and Human Services, Administration for Children and Youth, Children's Bureau, under Grant 90-CA-1717, Priority Area: 2003B2: Improving Child Welfare Outcomes Through Systems of Care. The purpose of the demonstration projects was to improve services to abused and neglected children. Clark County developed its demonstration project around the issue of kinship care. The need for services, supports, and permanent homes for children in Clark County increased dramatically over the two-year period preceding the research initiative. Child abuse/neglect investigations and children in need of placements increased by 30 percent and 56 percent, respectively, between 2000 and 2002. African American children constituted a significant portion of the children in care. About 8 percent of the Nevada child population was African American, yet during the period preceding the research initiative African American children made up 21 to 25 percent of the children placed in foster care. Despite what is known about the protective benefits of kinship care, Clark County lacked the infrastructure, policies, guidelines, and support structure that would facilitate the placement of children with relatives. Those children who did reside in kinship care received fewer services and their safety, well-being, and permanency outcomes were negatively affected (Denby, 2011).

The Initiative

The Caring Communities demonstration project's goal was to increase the safety, permanency, and well-being of children requiring out-of-home placement by increasing the number of children placed with relatives, and providing supportive services to children and relative caregivers. Seven objectives were identified for the initiative:

- Increase placements of children with kin when they must be removed from their homes.
- Increase the safety of children living with kin.
- Improve the physical and mental health of children living with kin.
- Increase the stability of placements with kin.
- Increase timely permanency for children living with kin.
- Increase the capacity of kin caregivers to care for the children living with them.
- Align child welfare infrastructure with System of Care (SOC) principles.

The initiative was designed around three major components: (1) system of care (SOC) infrastructure building, (2) child welfare service and program realignment, and (3) kinship infrastructure and capacity building. The SOC infrastructure building involved creating inter- and intra-agency partnerships through the use of planning and advisory councils. Additionally, SOC infrastructure building included the identification and implementation of agency improvement strategies such as development of emergency response units, alternative response tracks, and a 24/7 relative location and approval process.

The child welfare service and program realignment encompassed a total review of the agency's current practices. Several assessments were made to determine kinship care needs, cultural competency, and the array of services required and available. As a result, training programs were enhanced and tailored to the specific needs of workers and caregivers. Moreover, workgroups redesigned the agency's policies and procedures in ten service areas.

Finally, the aspect of the initiative that highlights many of the cultural adaptations that occurred to meet the needs of kinship children and families was the effort that led to kinship infrastructure and capacity building. Three conditions influenced the ability to build capacity: (1) the use of indigenous kinship liaisons (currently referred to as kinship specialists) to provide services and supports to families; (2) the expansion of the agency's diligent search unit; and (3) expanded community outreach efforts. Kinship liaisons (former and current relative caregivers themselves) provide information and support services, caregiver orientations, training, and support groups and focus on mentoring and educating caregivers (Denby, 2009). The diligent search (for relatives) unit was expanded to one full-time and two part-time positions. Finally, significant community outreach occurred by having kinship liaisons educate the internal staff, local community, and other stakeholder groups about kinship issues. The liaisons advocated for kinship needs and networked and communicated with various providers to obtain services and supports for kinship families.

The Research Outcomes

During the initiative the percentage of children placed with relative caregivers increased from a low of 16 percent in 2004 to 35 percent in 2007 and 32 percent in 2008. At the start of the demonstration project, about 15 percent of the intact sibling placements were composed of relative caregivers. By the end of the demonstration project, there was some growth (21 percent) in the number of intact sibling placements made to relative caregivers. During the initiative, the percentage of alleged reabuse cases of children placed with relative caregivers decreased from a high in 2005 of 13 percent to 4 percent in 2008. The occurrence of alleged reabuse was lowest in relative placements in 2008. The occurrence of reabuse was 9 percent for children placed with parents, 6 percent for children placed with nonrelatives, and 4 percent for children placed with relatives. The percentage of kinship care cases with children experiencing mental or physical health issues decreased over the five-year grant period from a 2004 high of 17 percent (behavioral disorders) and 13 percent (medical conditions) to a 2008 low of 10 percent (behavioral disorders) and 3 percent (medical conditions). Over the five-year period, the percentage of total licensed foster parents who were relative caregivers increased 10 percentage points, from 28 percent to 38 percent. The percentage of placement disruptions (e.g., change in relatives, regular foster care, hospitalization, therapeutic placement) for children in relative care varied, with a low of 9 percent in 2004 to a high of 15 percent in 2007, and then a drop in disruption rates again in 2008 to about 12 percent. The percentage of total kinship adoptions doubled from a low of 16 percent in 2004 to 32 percent in 2008.

In addition to the larger, system-level outcomes, a smaller, intensive intervention with seventy-four majority single African American female caregivers between the ages of 40 and 49 experienced equally impressive outcomes (Denby, 2011). After being assigned kinship liaisons for a 120-day period in which kinship caregivers received intensive services and support, kinship caregivers reported high rates of satisfaction. Kinship caregiver families consistently rated their kinship liaisons high on all five outcome measures: knowledge, trust/rapport, accountability, satisfaction, and support. Also, most caregivers (93 percent) indicated that they planned to care for the child or children on a permanent basis if they could not be returned home to their parents, and most caregivers (70 percent) were aware of the various permanency options they could pursue. Most (56 percent) indicated that they were not overwhelmed by the parenting responsibilities they had assumed, and most (81 percent) indicated that they were "not at all" depressed by the requirements to adequately care for the children. A large majority of the caregivers (89 percent) did not have any concerns about their ability to parent. Lastly, when caregivers were asked if they felt ill-prepared to deal with the emotional needs of the children in their care, nearly all (87 percent) reported that they did not. Caregiver capacity increased the longer they were involved with an assigned kinship liaison. The involvement of an indigenous kinship liaison influenced the type and quality of engagement that kinship families had with their assigned child welfare worker. Eighty percent of the caregivers indicated that their caseworker was respectful toward them; 79 percent reported that their culture, values, and beliefs have been respected with regard to caseworker interaction all of the time.

Denby, R. 2009. *Clark County Department of Family Services Kinship Liaison Program: A Small Program Making a Huge Difference* (Issue Brief–June). Las Vegas: University of Nevada, Las Vegas, School of Social Work.

———. 2011. "Kinship Liaisons: A Peer-to-Peer Approach to Supporting Kinship Caregivers." *Children and Youth Services Review* 33 (2): 217–25.

7

Cultural Adaptation and Research

Given the conditions faced by African American children and families who are involved in the child welfare system, cultural adaptations of research must consider three essential elements: evidence-based intervention, advocacy-based research, and performance-based research. The first part of this chapter begins with a description of various definitions and frameworks that have been used to describe evidence-based practice. Next the use of evidence-based practice (EBPs) in child welfare is discussed. We then present a framework for how EBPs can become culturally adapted so as to better address the needs of African American children. The second section pertains to advocacy-based research and illustrates how research results can be used to benefit African American children by influencing policy, funding, and programming. Three strategies are discussed: data convening/participation, data gathering, and data diffusion. Finally, the third section details how performance-based research can be used to promote more accountability for the outcomes experienced by African American children in the child welfare system.

EVIDENCE-BASED PRACTICE

Increasingly a call is being made for the use of evidence-based practices. Lawmakers, government/public funders, insurers, educators, and other stakeholders specify a preference for the use of EBPs or research-supported interventions. However, there is no universal definition or driving framework that captures evidence-based practices. What, then, are evidence-based practices? When defining them, consider the fact that they are generally thought about along a continuum of best practices. Researchers attempt to determine whether an approach, program,

EXISTING TRENDS

Promoting Effectiveness and Research Relevance

COURTS CATALYZING CHANGE: ACHIEVING EQUITY AND FAIRNESS IN FOSTER CARE

Much is known about the disproportionate rates of African American children in the child welfare system and the multiple adverse conditions they experience while navigating the system (Courtney et al., 1996; Curtis & Denby, 2011; Lu et al., 2004; and Yuan, Hedderson, Curtis, 2003). However, significantly less is known about effective interventions and approaches to addressing the problems and conditions that African American children and families face while engaged with the child welfare system. This chapter includes a discussion of how evidence-based interventions, advocacy-based research, and performance-based research can be used to address many of the problems that bring African American children into contact with the child welfare system. There are some emerging demonstration projects, evaluations, and research studies taking place in multiple states across the United States that have been designed to respond to the conditions that African American children and families face. One such project is the Courts Catalyzing Change: Achieving Equity and Fairness in Foster Care Initiatives (CCC), a project funded by Casey Family Programs and led by the National Council of Juvenile and Family Court Judges. One of the partners of the project is the U.S. Department of Justice, Office of Juvenile Justice and Delinquency Prevention. A goal of CCC is to coordinate the efforts of judicial experts in collaboration with other child- and family-serving system officials to articulate a national agenda aimed at implementing court-based training, research, and reform initiatives. The CCC disseminates research-based policy and practice guidelines to help child maltreatment court systems reduce disproportionality and disparities experienced by children and families of color. The initiative defines and develops relevant safety, permanency, and well-being measures and positions court leadership to use outcomes to strategize local plans to improve the experiences and conditions of children of color (Gatowski, Maze, & Miller, 2008). Using a measurement process referred to as "benchcard," one of the ways that the CCC developers assess the initiative's effectiveness is to have judges reflect on their decisions in an effort to mitigate the effect of system bias. CCC researchers have discovered reductions in foster care placement rates and increases in family placement rates (Krueger & Macgill, 2012). This chapter highlights the manner in which data participation, gathering, and diffusion as evidenced in the Courts Catalyzing Change initiative can be used to change the outcomes experienced by African American children and families when they are involved in the child welfare system.

or intervention works, and they use a three-tier classification: "promising practices," "evidence-based practices," and "science-based practices." A *promising practice* adheres to the following defining criteria:

1. It must include the characteristics used in other recognized interventions, programs, and approaches.
2. It possesses guidelines and protocols that produce effective outcomes.
3. It has a process for structuring continual quality improvement strategies.
4. It includes an evaluation plan.

Also, promising practices are at the beginning of the best-practices spectrum because they often lack sufficient outcome data necessary to substantiate a cause-effect relationship between the intervention and the outcomes.

The second point along the best-practice continuum, *evidence-based practice*, must meet two criteria:

1. There must be sufficient data demonstrating effective outcomes.
2. Expert review of the practice must have taken place concluding that there is sufficient evidence of the practice's effectiveness.

Many EBPs lack the specificity that is necessary for replication studies that would permit generalizability of the outcomes.

Science-based practices are distinguished from promising practices and evidence-based practices by the following characteristics (Association of Maternal and Child Health Programs, 2004):

1. The practice has been evaluated using a theory-based research methodology.
2. There is evidence of treatment fidelity, meaning the practice approach was implemented as intended; therefore, it can be reasonably concluded that, in fact, the observed outcomes are attributable to what is being studied and not to other extraneous factors.
3. They involve expert reviews guided by rigorous research standards that adhere to standardized scientific principles.
4. They ensure replicability.

The phrase "evidence-based practice" is often used interchangeably with other terminology. For example, another way of defining EBPs is the two-level approach used by the American Psychological Association in which interventions are either "well-established treatment" or "probably efficacious treatment." Well-established treatments have been shown to render results that are superior to a placebo or to another treatment or are equivalent to an established treatment across at least two between-group designs or ten or more single-case experiments. Well-established treatments are manualized approaches that have been replicated by two different researchers and have clearly defined samples. In contrast, probably efficacious treatments are categorized as such because two or more studies have documented the effects, there is at least one study that meets the criteria of a well-established treatment, or there are at least four studies that meet the criteria for a well-established treatment (Hogg Foundation for Mental Health, 2011). Although the definitions of evidence-based practice vary, what is behind the notion of evidence-based practice is recognition of a need to measure the effectiveness and

Evaluating What Works: Traditional Assessment of Outcomes and Interventions

1. Is the study replicable?
2. Is the study generalizable?
3. Was randomization used?
4. Was a control group used, or was there at least an appropriately matched comparison group (as well as other general questions concerning research rigor)?
5. Was evaluation/study of the intervention conducted by independent and qualified evaluators/researchers, and were the findings subject to peer and expert review?
6. What are the long-term effects of the intervention (has the program or intervention been studied longitudinally)?
7. Is the intervention/program cost-effective?
8. What are the fidelity and implementation outcomes?
9. Was the study conducted in a real-world versus model of efficacy setting?
10. How were research subjects targeted or matched for the intervention?
11. Does the intervention or program originate from a sound and identifiable theoretical basis?
12. Was the intervention/program based on a manualized approach?

effect of an intervention and document why observed outcomes were achieved, with the goal of replicability.

The accompanying box lists many of the decision points that are used to evaluate the evidence or outcomes observed in programs and interventions.

For the past decade there has been a significant push to articulate effective approaches to the treatment of child abuse and neglect. Several sources represent compendiums where the most efficacious treatments have been evaluated and categorized based on intervention type or the aspect of child maltreatment they purport to address (Chadwick Center for Children and Families, 2004; FRIENDS National Resource Center for Community-Based Child Abuse Prevention [CBCAP], 2009; Washington State Institute for Public Policy, 2008). In the field of child welfare, a prevailing definition of evidence-based practice originated in the field of medicine (Institute of Medicine, 2001) and is defined along three factors: (1) best research evidence; (2) best clinical evidence; and (3) consistency with family/client values (California Evidence-Based Clearinghouse for Child Welfare, 2011). This definition seems to improve on traditional notions of evidence because it accounts for the clinical perspective of the practitioner and recognizes the diversity in clients' values and family systems often seen in child welfare systems.

Despite the emphasis on evidence, in child welfare many of the prevailing interventions remain at the level of "promising" because their findings are inconclusive, or perhaps because the evidence- or science-based interventions have not been widely adapted.

DETERMINING EFFECTIVE INTERVENTIONS FOR AFRICAN AMERICAN CHILDREN AND FAMILIES

There is a push to close the gap that exists between research and policy and also to use evidence to inform child welfare practice and funding (Wulczyn et al., 2005; Yale University's Interdisciplinary Center for Bioethics, 2005). Likewise, as it concerns evidence-based practices, researchers are concerned about what is phrased as the gap between knowledge and the implementation of effective programs and interventions. In fact, Fixsen et al. (2005:2) write: "It has been well documented in many disciplines that major gaps exist between what is known as effective practices (i.e., theory and science) and what is actually done (i.e., policy and practice)."

There is challenge and debate concerning the relevance of science in addressing the human and social nature of child abuse and neglect. Also, others have observed that the difficulty with using EBPs in child welfare concern the issue of fidelity and implementation (Chaffin & Friedrich, 2004). Debate abounds about the extent to which programs should be implemented with strict fidelity versus the need for an individualized approach based on clients' particular needs and workers' styles and preferences. Such debates are relevant when one considers the use of evidence-based practices in child welfare interventions with the African American population.

Our argument concerning the use of evidence to inform policy and program implementation is that there is first a need to unpack the elements of evidence to be sure that "discoveries" are a true representation of African American children's experiences, values, and culture. Are "effective" practices truly effective with African American children and families?

Currently the debate about the use of EBPs in child welfare intervention is virtually silent on the issue of cultural fit or cultural context. Ironically, unlike child welfare, the mental health field has not shied away from engaging in discussion about how to make services more culturally appropriate and how to make evidence-based practices work in real-world settings (Holleran Steiker et al., 2008; Miranda et al., 2005; Martinez & Eddy, 2005; Whaley, 2003; Whaley & Davis, 2007). To ensure that research discoveries are culturally adapted to African American children, child welfare stakeholders should be concerned with several key elements that are not often addressed in discussions of what works and in evaluations of child welfare research and programs. The following key questions should be asked about efficacious programs and interventions and the research that undergirds them.

1. What percentage of the research subjects were heterogeneous groups of African Americans?

Few studies that evaluate the effectiveness of child welfare interventions consider ethnic composition, and even fewer include samples of African American research participants that represent diversity with respect to income, values, beliefs, and other cultural elements. Cultural adaptations to research recognize the heterogeneous nature of the African American culture and those African Americans engaged in the child welfare system.

2. To what extent were the interventions or models derived from cultural explorations of African American–identifiable values, characteristics, and features?

Child welfare interventions with African American families should strive to develop a flexible outcome approach. Definitions of service or treatment success should strive to go beyond measures of insight, introspection, and other catharsis-driven expressions. For example, neglect outcomes are often defined along the lines of the adequacy of concrete provisions: food, shelter, supervision, school attendance. Flexible outcomes would use these criteria and expand them by recognizing others as vitally important but culturally driven provisions. For example, reestablishing a previously estranged family tie, "joining church," attention to one's appearance, and successful racial socialization of children (Coard et al., 2007) are other ways of measuring service effect and outcome.

3. To what extent did indigenous groups or stakeholders share in the development of the intervention?

According to Holleran Steiker et al. (2008), the aim of cultural adaptations is to make interventions relevant and responsive to the needs of special populations and in doing so make the interventions work. One way of making interventions work is to include what Holleran Steiker et al. refer to as "culturally matched implementers." Indigenous stakeholders or culturally matched implementers can provide feedback about the approach by assessing its applicability to the needs of the targeted group.

4. Is the intervention delivered in context (i.e., matched with the economic and cultural group intended as the target)?

Evidence suggests that individuals conceptualize distress and need and seek help in different manners, and ethnic and racial patterns are observable (Hogg Foundation for Mental Health, 2011). The development of an intervention should be informed by a thoughtful exploration of the needs of the intended cultural group.

5. Do interpretations of the findings go beyond "black-white" comparisons to consider why observed differences and/or similarities might be present?

The enticement to use a one-size-fits-all approach to delivering services may have long existed because of the similarities shared across different American ethnic groups and cultures. Whaley and Davis (2007), Hall (2001), and Sue (1998) have observed that many ethnic minority groups in the United States share many of the cultural characteristics of mainstream groups, and therefore some culturally specific interventions may be effective across ethnic groups (Atkinson, Buí, & Mori, 2001; Lopez, Kopelowicz, & Canive, 2002). With this in mind, research results should provide information about how standard treatment protocols may be applicable to African American clients and conversely address why such treatments may not work for them as well.

6. What might be the relevant ethnographic or qualitative features of the findings?

Family dynamics such as social support, social context, and the acculturation process are thought to have an important effect on parents and children (Martinez, Eddy, & DeGarmo, 2003). Yet these and other variables may not always lend themselves to quantitative measurement. Researchers could consider the role of qualitative measurement studies in documenting the importance of child welfare outcomes.

7. Does the research take into account the credibility factor (i.e., to what extent did the research subjects place value in the intervention or respect the approach)?

Measures of client satisfaction are often included in research and evaluation studies. However, seldom are research participants asked to report about the extent to which they felt that the intervention or the intervener was culturally relevant or met their needs. Research that captures African American clients' opinions about the extent to which they were satisfied with services should involve questions about cultural relevance, fit, and context.

8. To what extent did therapeutic alliance play a role in observed outcomes? .

Culturally adapted research approaches take into consideration the importance of the *process* of treatment or services as much as they do the *outcome*. Care should be given to measure the extent to which the treatment or service professional appropriately engages a client. Too often clients can be categorized as "resistant" or "noncompliant" when the issue at hand might be the lack of a successful therapeutic engagement. In considering the evidence and what works, research should address effective engagement approaches that are used with African American clients.

9. Was the research conducted by culturally informed and qualified researchers?

Many of the studies that have been conducted to determine whether an intervention or service is scientific are conducted by highly skilled and qualified researchers. Issues of skills and qualifications should also consider the researcher's level of knowledge about the cultural groups within his or her study. The notion of researcher qualification should consider the extent to which the scientist is able to design or conceptualize a study that is culturally informed.

ADVOCACY RESEARCH

This section discusses the ways that research can be used to promote advocacy for culturally specific policy and service delivery aimed at improving the condition of African American children in the child welfare system. Advocacy research is conducted by individuals, groups, and organizations concerned about a social problem, issue, or condition and committed to effectuating change in policy, services, or laws. According to Marshall (2011), advocacy research can be considered a form of policy research when concerned parties strive to raise public awareness and shape policy that will ameliorate the particular social problem or condition that is of concern. We discuss a plan for using research for advocacy, consciousness raising, and coalition building. The plan involves data convening/participation, data gathering, and data diffusion, as illustrated in figure 7.1.

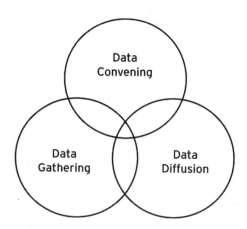

Figure 7.1 Components of advocacy research.

Data Convening/Participation

In child welfare, data convening should involve various professionals, general stakeholders, and the like, but the core of the coalition should be people and groups who are indigenous to the African American child welfare condition. A strategizing approach or method for organizing research advocates is that of *restorative justice practices*. *Restorative justice* is a broad term used in justice, education, and social service systems. It means that in the search for solutions, one engages those who have been harmed. Restorative justice can be about building partnerships, collaborations, and mutual responsibility between groups, people, or communities that might have varied interests but all share a central goal. Given the conditions that African American children in the child welfare system face, restorative justice should be central to the work of research advocates. During the data-convening phase of research advocacy, the following objectives are accomplished:

* Identifying partners and allies
* Developing statements of mutual interests/goals
* Incentivizing participation
* Developing strategies to handle inevitable conflicts
* Starting to instill a culture in which everyone's perspective is valued
* Identifying funding partnerships

Data Gathering

The second phase of research advocacy is data gathering. Data gathering is a process of collecting, organizing, and preparing information or data points. Data-gathering methods can include interviews, surveys, secondary analyses, meta-analysis of literature, synthesis of outcome reports, and original data collection through planned studies, experiments, or evaluations. Data gathering should focus on building credible and organized child welfare informatics systems that focus on culturally specific data frames. National child welfare data systems include the Adoptions and Foster Care Reporting and Analysis System (AFCARS), which is maintained by the U.S. Department of Health and Human Services, and the National Child Abuse and Neglect Data System (NCANDS). Although there are national child welfare database systems, African American child welfare research advocates should strive to develop informatics systems that are specific to localities, communities, and states; that are easily accessible for advocacy work; and that can be designed with specific utilization objectives in mind. For example, the child welfare informatics system might contain data specific to African American children's risk factors, service needs, service utilization patterns, and service outcomes and effectiveness. During the data-gathering phase of advocacy research, pertinent planning objectives should include the following:

- Identifying data needs and gaps
- Identifying relevant research questions and probes and the related research designs and approaches
- Securing culturally informed data interpreters
- Building cooperative data-sharing agreements
- Ensuring respectful engagement of research subjects or study participants

Data Diffusion

In its simplest form, data diffusion can be thought of as the dissemination of research results. However, as the issue concerns African American child welfare advocacy, data diffusion should be used with the purpose of raising awareness and promoting desired change. The data-diffusion aspect of research advocacy should include the following planning questions:

1. What are the appropriate data-dissemination venues?
2. Who needs to know the information that has been gathered?
3. Who are the appropriate "messengers"?
4. How can the data be used to influence policy and practice?

PERFORMANCE-BASED RESEARCH

In an effort to promote more accountability for the outcomes experienced by African American children in the child welfare system, adaptations to how research is currently used could include more performance-based authority. In using performance-based authority models, public and

Translating Research into Action: More Than a Presentation of Facts and Figures

The findings of the Caring Communities demonstration project were used to advocate for sustained investment in kinship programs, procedures, and policies. A systematic and data-informed advocacy-based approach to identifying child welfare clients' needs is critical in increasing awareness of the importance of organizational and system change. Likewise, data-driven approaches steeped in advocacy-based research are necessary for communicating to stakeholders the programs and approaches that have the highest likelihood of changing outcomes for African American children and families.

Prior to the end of the Caring Communities demonstration, the Clark County Board of Commissioners authorized permanent agency funding for three kinship liaison positions, thus ensuring program sustainability and recognizing the effectiveness of the kinship initiative. In assessing the case study, the elements (i.e., data convening/participation, data gathering, data diffusion) of our recommended advocacy research approach are easily transferable to multiple child welfare conditions affecting African American children. Starting with data convening/participation, the Caring Communities project convened and sustained a broad-based, caregiver-led advisory team that was representative of the large African American kinship population.

From this advisory structure, combined teams of researchers and caregivers planned for and engaged citizen advisory committees, judicial leadership, financial decision makers, and other community stakeholders (e.g., African American churches) by framing the problem, articulating its effect on vulnerable clients like African American children and families, and leading discussions about mutual interests and goals. The initiative was careful to use data-gathering techniques that would resonate with the target population and would be well received by professionals, paraprofessionals, and other groups. In addition to quantitative methods, kinship caregivers were engaged using group formats and in-depth case analyses. Also, at every stage of data collection representatives of the target populations were convened to assist in interpreting the data and providing explanations that were based in cultural narratives of the data.

It was important to analyze the data from a balanced perspective indicating both the negative and positive outcomes. In the Caring Communities project, data diffusion strategies were developed at the beginning of the project and then refined throughout. The initiative identified, trained, and supported African American kinship caregivers who augmented quantitative research results by providing qualitative testimonials and personal narratives of their experiences. Also, research translation ambassadors were found and engaged. For example, caseworkers provided written testimonials of how working alongside a kinship liaison positively affected their work with their kinship caregiver families.

Finally, one of the research advocacy approaches that helped to sustain and support the kinship program, its policies, and its procedures was aligning the data outcomes to stakeholders' existing improvement efforts. Buy-in for the initiative occurred because of unrelenting community engagement efforts. When it came time to make the case to decision-makers for program sustainability, it was community providers, clients, partners, and other invested groups (not researchers) who effectively translated the research outcomes and demonstrated how sustaining the project would lead to improvements for children and families. Decision makers were able to appreciate the business case that was being made given the fact that constituent groups demonstrated how using data outcomes improved kinship liaisons services, saved workers' time, and ultimately was a more efficient use of invested money and resources.

private child welfare service authorities would be monitored and their outcomes tracked at regular intervals, and those entities not adhering to community-defined benchmarks would surrender service authority to the agencies and organizations whose performance produces the best outcomes for children and families. Nationally child welfare performance monitoring is conducted by the U.S. Department of Health and Human Services Administration for Children and Families through the Child and Family Service Review (CFSR) process. The federal government is granted the authority to monitor and review state child welfare performance by 1994 amendments to the Social Security Act as a way to ensure state compliance with Title IV-B and Title IV-E. The purposes of the CFSR are to (1) assess state agencies' compliance with federal law; (2) document what children and families experience as they are engaged in the child welfare system; and (3) assist states in their work to serve children and families. The goal of federal monitoring, and thus the CFSR process, is to improve services and achieve the following outcomes:

Safety: (a) Children are, first and foremost, protected from abuse and neglect; and (b) Children are safely maintained in their homes whenever possible and appropriate. *Permanency:* (a) Children have permanency and stability in their living situations; and (b) The continuity of family relationships and connections is preserved for families. *Family and Child Well-being:* (a) Families have enhanced capacity to provide for their children's needs; (b) Children receive appropriate services to meet their educational needs; and (c) Children receive adequate services to meet their physical and mental health needs. (USDHHS, 2011:1)

When states are found not to be in compliance with CFSR-assessed areas, they are given an opportunity to develop what are referred to as Program Improvement Plans (PIPs). The PIPs detail the state's plan to set a corrective course of action to improve in areas of nonconformity. When states do not achieve required improvements, they are subject to federal penalties, which are largely connected to the rate of fiscal reimbursements that states receive from the federal government.

What we are proposing here concerning cultural adaptations to research approaches goes beyond the objectives of CFSRs. Through the research advocacy approaches described earlier in the chapter, stakeholder groups can move to reform child welfare services by installing alternative service authorities when current entities fail to achieve stated performance indicators. Fiscal penalties from the federal government to states run the risk of shifting resource burdens onto already overtaxed local governments. Alternative service providers, including private entities, indigenous organizations, and mandated public-private partnerships, should be considered when research shows poor performance on the part of the state authority. Table 7.1 contains examples of and suggested strategies for implementing performance-based authority models.

SUMMARY AND CONCLUSION

Research plays a significant role and has multiple utilities for effectuating change on behalf of the African American children and families who encounter the child welfare system. For example, the use of evidence-based practices is a strategy for ensuring quality in service delivery and accountability for the type of interventions that are used. However, evidence-based practices must be culturally relevant. Any considerations about the use of an evidence-based approach to tackle a child welfare problem must include a thorough exploration of the efficacy of the model in addressing the unique needs of African American children. Appropriate culturally adaptations to prevailing models should be made

TABLE 7.1
Performance-Based Child Welfare Service Authority Models

	Strategies and Suggestions	Challenges and Roadblocks	Methods for Overcoming Challenges
Macro-Level Research Advocacy	Establish state-level regulations that enable the operation of alternative service groups and organizations.	Opponents will argue that child welfare authority rests with state and/or counties and should not be shifted to private enterprises.	Statute could maintain state monitoring and regulatory authority with state authorizations, but service authority be given to the best performing organizations as determined by research outcomes.
Mezzo-Level Research Advocacy	Establish pilots and research demonstration sites that enable private and indigenous entities to show what they can achieve when given service authority.	Funding and allocation of resources will be needed to establish successful pilots.	Research advocacy involves influencing the research agenda and direction that is established by means of federal discretionary grant opportunities and private funding sources.
Micro-Level Research Advocacy	Evaluate the outcomes of programs that use performance-based approaches across all staff levels.	Hard-working child welfare staff who are already rarely affirmed and recognized for their efforts may feel imposed upon through the implementation of performance-based approaches.	Performance-based service authority models are not intended to be punitive but are designed to incentivize exemplary efforts. Child welfare staff should be engaged to co-develop the performance-based approach.

and then research conducted to test the effectiveness of the culturally adapted evidence-based model.

African American children stand to benefit from advocacy-based research. Research should go beyond "telling the story"; it should be used by organized coalitions to usher in necessary change. It is important that advocacy research include those individuals who are experiencing the child welfare system.

Finally, future research directions should look to testing the effects of performance-based service authority models. Policy practitioners and researchers run parallel courses in their efforts to make service systems more accountable for the outcomes that African American children experience in the child welfare system.

DISCUSSION QUESTIONS

1. Historically, have we assumed a one-size-fits-all perspective in child welfare with respect to the efficacy and effectiveness of child welfare programs, interventions, and services? If yes, why? Are there consequences to making assumptions about the fidelity of programs and service interventions across all racial and ethnic groups?

2. Discuss whether involving more racially and ethnically diverse subjects in studies of treatment efficacy and program effectiveness goes far enough in making cultural adaptations to research. If including more diverse subjects in studies is not enough, what else is needed to ensure that interventions will be culturally matched to specific client needs?

3. Debate the pros and cons of using performance-based child welfare service authority models.

ACTIVITIES FOR ONGOING LEARNING

1. Select a prevailing child maltreatment approach, program, or intervention that is used in your community or reported on in the professional literature. Evaluate the selected program against the criteria listed in this chapter. Develop a conclusion about the extent to which your selected program adheres to the standards of science, and then evaluate the extent to which the select program or intervention incorporates the recommended cultural adaptation elements concerning African American children and families engaged in the child welfare system.

2. Develop a research advocacy project in keeping with the three-phase approach discussed in this chapter. Select a topic of interest to you or a particular African American child welfare issue pertinent to your local community. In addition to developing and implementing the research advocacy project, maintain a personal journal that contains

daily/weekly reflections about your challenges, victories, setbacks, and accomplishments.

3. Develop a term paper that examines the federal Child and Family Service Review process. Emphasize your state's CFSR performance. Assess the adequacy of your state's Program Improvement Plan for addressing the conditions faced by African American children. What are the strengths and shortcomings of the CFSR process in improving African American child welfare outcomes?

REFERENCES

Association of Maternal and Child Health Programs Center for Best Practices. 2004. *Best Practices.* http://www.amchp.org/policy/bestpractice-definition .htm.

Atkinson, D. R., U. Bui, & S. Mori. 2001. "Multiculturally Sensitive Empirically Supported Treatments: An Oxymoron?" In *Handbook of Multicultural Counseling.* Edited by J. G. Ponterotto, J. M. Casas, L. A. Suzuki, & C. M. Alexander, 542–74. 2nd ed. Thousand Oaks, Calif.: Sage.

California Evidence-Based Clearinghouse for Child Welfare. 2011. *Importance of Evidence-based Practice.* http://www.cebc4cw.org/.

Chadwick Center for Children and Families. 2004. *Closing the Quality Chasm in Child Abuse Treatment: Identifying and Disseminating Best Practices: The Findings of the Kauffman Best Practices Project to Help Children Heal from Child Abuse.* http://www.chadwickcenter.org/Documents/Kaufman%20Report/Child Hosp-NCTAbrochure.pdf.

Chaffin, M., & B. Friedrich. 2004. "Evidence-based Treatments in Child Welfare Abuse and Neglect." *Children and Youth Services Review* 26:1097–1113.

Coard, S., S. Foy-Watson, C. Zimmer, & A. Wallace. 2007. "Considering Culturally Relevant Parenting Practices in Intervention Development and Adaptation: A Randomized Control Trial of the Black Parenting Strengths and Strategies (BPSS) Program." *Counseling Psychologist* 35:797–820.

Courtney, M. E., R. P. Barth, J. D. Berrick, D. Brooks, B. Needell, & L. Park. 1996. "Race and Child Welfare Services: Past Research and Future Directions." *Child Welfare* 75 (2): 99–135.

Curtis, C. M., & R. W. Denby. 2011. "African American Children in the Child Welfare System: Requiem or Reform." *Journal of Public Child Welfare* 5 (1): 111–37.

Fixsen, D. L., S. F. Naoom, K. A. Blasé, R. M. Friedman, & F. Wallace. 2005. *Implementation Research: A Synthesis of the Literature.* FMHI Publication No. 231. Tampa: University of South Florida, Louis de la Parte Florida Mental Health Institute, National Implementation Research Network.

FRIENDS National Resource Center for Community-Based Child Abuse Prevention (CBCAP). 2009. *Evidence-Based and Evidence-Informed Programs: Prevention Program Descriptions Classified by CBCAP Evidence-Based And Evidence-Informed Categories.* http://www.friendsnrc.org/joomdocs/eb_prog_direct.pdf.

Gatowski, S., C. L. Maze, & N. B. Miller. 2008. "Courts Catalyzing Change: Achieving Equity and Fairness in Foster Care—Transforming Examination into Action." *Juvenile and Family Justice Today* (Summer): 16–20. http://www.leg.state.nv.us/Interim/76th2011/Exhibits/ChildWelfare/E040412I.pdf.

Hall, G.C.N. 2001. "Psychotherapy Research with Ethnic Minorities: Empirical, Ethical, and Conceptual Issues." *Journal of Consulting and Clinical Psychology* 69:502–10.

Hogg Foundation for Mental Health. 2011. *Cultural Adaptation: Providing Evidence-Based Practices to Populations of Color.* http://www.hogg.utexas.edu/initiatives/cultural_adaptation.html.

Holleran Steiker, L. K., F. G. Castro, K. Kumpfer, F. F. Marsiglia, S. Coard, & L. M. Hopson. 2008. "A Dialogue Regarding Cultural Adaptation of Interventions." *Journal of Social Work Practice in the Addictions* 8 (1): 154–62.

Institute of Medicine. 2001. *Crossing the Quality Chasm: A New Health System for the 21st Century.* Washington, D.C.: National Academy Press.

Krueger, E., & S. Macgill. 2012. "Courts Catalyzing Change: Using an Equity Lens to Guide the Future." http://news.nasje.org/?p=367.

Lopez, S. R., A. Kopelowicz, & J. M. Canive. 2002. "Strategies in Developing Culturally Congruent Family Interventions for Schizophrenia: The Case of Hispanics." In *Family Interventions in Mental Illness: International Perspectives.* Edited by H. P. Lefley & D. L. Johnson, 61–90. Westport, Conn.: Praeger.

Lu, Y. E., J. Landsverk, E. Ellis-MacLeod, R. Newton, W. Ganger, & I. Johnson. 2004. "Race, Ethnicity and Case Outcomes in Child Protective Services." *Children and Youth Services Review* 26 (5): 447–61.

Marshall, G. 1998. "Advocacy Research." In *A Dictionary of Sociology.* http://www.encyclopedia.com/doc/1O88-advocacyresearch.html.

Martinez, C. R., Jr., & J. M. Eddy. 2005. "Effects of Culturally Adapted Parent Management Training on Latino Youth Behavioral Health Outcomes." *Journal of Consulting and Clinical Psychology* 73:841–51.

Martinez, C. R., Jr., J. M. Eddy, & D. S. DeGarmo. 2003. "Preventing Substance Use Among Latino Youth." In *Handbook of Drug Abuse Prevention: Theory, Science, and Practice.* Edited by W. J. Bukoski & Z. Sloboda, 365–80. New York: Kluwer Academic/Plenum Press.

Miranda, J., G. Bernal, A. Lau, L. Kohn, W. C. Hwang, & T. LaFromboise. 2005. "State of the Science on Psychosocial Interventions for Ethnic Minorities." *Annual Review of Clinical Psychology* 1:113–42.

Sue, S. 1998. "In Search of Cultural Competence in Psychotherapy and Counseling." *American Psychologist* 53:440–48.

U.S. Department of Health and Human Services (USDHHS). 2011. *Children's Bureau Child and Family Services Reviews Fact Sheet.* http://www.acf.hhs.gov/programs/cb/cwmonitoring/recruit/cfsrfactsheet.htm#.

Washington State Institute for Public Policy. 2008. *Evidence-based Programs to Prevent Children from Entering and Remaining in the Child Welfare System:Benefits and Costs for Washington.* at http://www.wsipp.wa.gov/rptfiles/08–07–3901.pdf.

Whaley, A. L. 2003. "Ethnicity/Race, Ethics, and Epidemiology." *Journal of the National Medical Association* 95 (8): 736–42.

Whaley, A. L., & K. E. Davis. 2007. "Cultural Competence and Evidence-Based Practice in Mental Health Services." *American Psychologist* 62 (6): 563–74.

Wulcyzn, F., R. P. Barth, Y. T. Yuan, B. J. Harden, & J. Landsverk. 2005. *Beyond Common Sense: Child Welfare, Child Well-Being, and the Evidence for Policy Reform.* Piscataway, N.J.: Aldine Transaction.

Yale University's Interdisciplinary Center for Bioethics and Casey Family Services. 2005. *Improving the Well-Being of Our Children: Closing the Gap Between Research and Policy.* A report from the symposium sponsored by Yale University's Interdisciplinary Center for Bioethics and Casey Family Services. New Haven: Interdisciplinary Center for Bioethics and Casey Family Services

Yuan, J., J. Hedderson, & P. Curtis. 2003. "Disproportionate Representation of Race and Ethnicity in Child Maltreatment: Investigation and Victimization." *Children and Youth Services Review* 25:359–73.

8

Meeting the Challenges to Bring About Change

This concluding chapter provides suggestions for the critical roles stake-holders in child welfare may assume in the crusade to improve the conditions for all children in the child welfare service system nationwide while improving the disparate condition of African American children.

THE IMPORTANCE OF A CULTURAL ADAPTATION PERSPECTIVE IN IMPROVING CHILD WELFARE CONDITIONS

To those who question our focused treatment of the condition of African American children in the child protection service system—notwithstanding the facts related to the disparate experiences among African American children relative to reports of suspected maltreatment, out-of-home placements, termination of parental rights, and success with achieving permanence—improvements made in the system of child protection will benefit all children and families. Individualizing the circumstances that contribute to child maltreatment allows for individualized responses to address the needs of children and their families. The diversity in communities across the United States makes it imperative that child protection systems broadly consider the cultural elements responsible for differences among the life experiences of children and families. In addition to African American, Hispanic/Latino, Native American, and Asian American families, in many communities across the country families of Somali, West African, Hmong, and Palestinian ethnic backgrounds—to list those whose numbers are increasing significantly—are being referred to child protection service systems in increasing numbers.

Social workers and other human service professionals need to be aware of cultural differences that may present as behaviors not known or completely understood among those oriented to Western European culture. For example, in the Somali culture those who display behaviors associated with mental health disorders may be locked in a room away from family members (Leban Bule, personal communication, October 12, 2011). There is major stigma associated with mental illness and developmental disabilities. If a school-age child is placed in a locked room because of behaviors that are not perceived as "normal," is this maltreatment? If a child welfare practitioner is confronted with these circumstances upon investigating allegations of maltreatment, what is the appropriate response? Should the child be removed from the home? Should the family be counseled by a cultural informant to acquire knowledge about mental illness, related symptomatology, and opportunities for treatment and recovery? When culturally diverse families—including those who are immigrants and who may experience significant challenges relative to embracing Western culture—are introduced to social service systems, family members require knowledge of local laws and parental expectations by the state. In the absence of information and understanding, social structures may "oppress, marginalize, alienate, or create or enhance privilege and power" (Council on Social Work Education [CSWE], 2008:3–7). With African American children and families, child welfare practitioners have historically viewed families as demonstrating pathological social behaviors and being resistant to change.

As social workers we are trained in professional programs of study based on educational standards generated and amended periodically by the Council on Social Work Education. The cultural differences among us require self-awareness to minimize the influence of personal bias and values in working with diverse populations (CSWE, 2008). Research literature demonstrating explicit, culturally influenced differences in child well-being prompted our pursuit of a conceptual model to better interpret the condition of African American children in the child welfare system (Hatcher et al., 2009; Martinez & Lau, 2011; Murray & Zvoch, 2010; Teti et al., 2009).

The term *cultural adaptation* builds on the construct of culture and the activity of adapting. Culture is a powerful construct that includes language, belief systems, family values, traditions, and approaches to relationships and childrearing. We provide a framework through which practitioners may evaluate the different conditions that bring children to the attention of the child welfare system; the appropriateness of intervention strategies may be considered based on knowledge and understanding of social values and conditions affecting family life and culturally informed consideration of outcomes for evaluating success associated with intervention strategies for child well-being and family stability.

THE CHALLENGE TO SOCIAL WORK EDUCATORS

Social workers are bound by the core value of social justice as a guiding framework during public policy advocacy. However, there is little disagreement among informed social workers, legal advocates, and child welfare practitioners that the single group most detrimentally affected by the current child welfare system is African American children (USDHHS, 2008; Hill, 2006; Roberts, 2002; U.S GAO, 2007).

As we consider the plight of African American children in the child welfare system, the overwhelming involvement of social workers in that service arena, and the fact that social work decrees combating injustice as its mission, we must ask: What is the effect of social work's presence in the system? To what extent is social work changing and challenging child welfare laws as they relate to African American children?

The Social Work Code of Ethics establishes the profession's values and standards and guides social workers' conduct. With respect to the social work value of *social justice*, social workers are charged to

> pursue social change, particularly with and on behalf of vulnerable and oppressed individuals and groups of people. Social workers' social change efforts are focused primarily on issues of poverty, unemployment, discrimination, and other forms of social injustice. These activities seek to promote sensitivity to and knowledge about oppression and cultural and ethnic diversity. (National Association of Social Workers, 2008)

Preparation for social work practice is guided by education standards articulated in the CSWE's Educational Policy and Accreditation Standards (EPAS). Student acquisition of core competencies is the desired outcome that social work education programs strive to obtain. With respect to preparing students to promote social justice and effectuate change, three of the ten competencies directly address this issue:

Educational Policy 2.1.4: Engage diversity and difference in practice. . . . Social workers appreciate that, as a consequence of difference, a person's life experiences my include oppression, poverty, marginalization, and alienation as well as privilege, power, and acclaim. Social workers: (a) recognize the extent to which a culture's structures and values may oppress, marginalize, alienate, or create or enhance privilege and power; (b) gain sufficient self-awareness to eliminate the influence of personal biases and values in working with diverse groups; (c) recognize and communicate their understanding of the importance of difference in shaping life experiences; and (d) view themselves as learners and engage those with whom they work as informants.

Educational Policy 2.1.5: Advance human rights and social and economic justice. . . . Social workers recognize the global interconnections of oppression and are knowledgeable about theories of justice and strategies to promote human and civil rights. Social work incorporates social justice practices in organizations, institutions, and society to ensure that these basic human rights are distributed equitably and without prejudice. Social workers: (a) understand the forms and mechanisms of oppression and discrimination; (b) advocate for human rights and social and economic justice; and (c) engage in practices that advance social and economic justice.

Educational Policy 2.1.8: Engage in policy practice to advance social and economic well-being and to deliver social work services. Social work practitioners understand that policy affects service delivery, and they actively engage in policy practice. Social workers know the history and current structures of social policies and services; the role of policy in service delivery; and the role of practice in policy development. Social workers: (a) analyze, formulate, and advocate for policies that advance social well-being; and (b) collaborate with colleagues and clients for effective policy action. (CSWE, 2008:3–7)

Considering the vulnerabilities of African American children in relation to the child welfare system, there is a clear need for social work educators to prepare students for a role in effectuating planned changed (i.e., social advocacy, human rights advocacy, reform, transformation, system change).

THE ROLE OF SOCIAL WORK EDUCATION IN IMPLEMENTING PLANNED CHANGE

The work of social activism even from the halls of academia has prevailed in the field of social work throughout its hundred-year history. Social justice advocates like Inabel Burns Lindsay (Crewe, Brown, & Gourdine, 2009) made remarkable inroads. Today, we must continue to ask ourselves: How do we as social work educators instruct students to think about those among us who are consistently marginalized? How do we encourage and promote the need for strong advocacy? For example, Comerford (2003) informs us that learning about diversity requires time and reflection. This sentiment, while certainly reasonable and representative of a pervasive school of thought in social work education, is short of what students need in order to carry out planned change (Dodd & Rivera, 2003). Could it be that many social work diversity, policy, and macro practice classes compel students to remain in the role of "hearers" or "observers," never fully equipping them with skills necessary to become "doers"? Public policy advocates and researchers admonish social workers and human service practitioners to speak up and out on behalf of people who are poor, disenfranchised, and underserved who seem not to have a voice in Congress, in state houses across the country, in social agencies, or in academe (Alvarez, 2001; Coakley, 2008; Curtis & Alexander, 2010; Dodd & Rivera, 2003; Freire, 1973; Lalas, 2007; Manalo, 2004). As social work educators is it reasonable for us to stop teaching students to change clients (particularly when client difficulties emanate from environmental forces) and instead instruct them to change or reform laws, systems, policies, and agency procedures?

Children in the out-of-home care system are recipients of services that are often administered through professional discretion. Put another way, it becomes a professional judgment call as to whether to remove a child from his or her home. Once the child is removed from the home, what supports are provided to the family unit? What services are needed by the child to make the child "whole" and adoptable? These critical points of opportunity to serve, support, treat, or advocate on a client's behalf may or may not be pursued owing to professional discretion. How are we preparing students for the difficult work of carrying out planned change?

Perhaps the lack of clarity about what should be taught and how it is to be taught is reflective of the larger debate concerning what about the child welfare system should be reformed. Cohen (2004) states that there are four traditions of planned change in child welfare reform efforts: (1) social reform, or large-scale change in macrogovernmental policy and allocation of new resources; (2) social mobilization, or organized confrontation (e.g., class action lawsuits) on behalf of the oppressed; (3) policy analysis, or the identification and replication through scientific analysis of programs that work; and (4) social learning, or the redesign and transformation of services and involvement of multiple stakeholder groups. We maintain that there is a role for each of these change strategies.

Creating Passion and Interest

The success of the child protective service system is directly related to the effectiveness and quality of the relationship between caseworkers and children and their family members. Caseworkers or social workers in child welfare are the primary point of contact and gatekeeper for child protective service systems. Social workers are critical change agents involved in decision making; they connect families with services and provide children in foster care with a sense of continuity and stability otherwise often missing in their lives.

Social workers in the child welfare arena are challenged, however, to play critical roles of system sustainer and child advocate in addition to policy enforcer, evaluator, and change agent. The reasons it is difficult for social workers to perform the critical tasks required to create necessary change and provide needed system reforms are numerous and include the complexity of child welfare cases, the growing number of children with special needs, an increase in families with drug- and alcohol-related problems, and the intricate paperwork demand that comes with heavy caseloads (U.S. GAO, 2003). As the Packard Foundation (2004:24) states, "increased emphasis on shortening time to permanency, compiling accurate data on children in care, and meeting accountability requirements have substantially increased paperwork and data entry demands and reduced the amount of time workers can spend with children and families."

Perhaps it is these work-setting issues that lead to high attrition rates within the child welfare workforce. Also, these system challenges may seem insurmountable to the social work student who is newly engaging this field of study. Still, passion and interest in planned change (particularly in the child welfare arena) begin with academic recruitment and admission of social work students who express a desire to work in public systems as reformers. We argue that social work educators can go only so far in creating interest among students so that they have a desire to study the implementation of planned change strategies. The passion and interest must already lie in the prospective student. Our job as educators, then, is to identify interested students and ensure that they will be exposed to a curriculum that provides instruction in planned change.

Imparting Knowledge About Planned Change Methods and Strategies

The successful delivery of planned change teaching content in social work programs will require at a minimum three things. First, we must teach teachers how to teach planned change content. We suggest that social work deans, directors, and others in curriculum leadership or administrative roles devise teaching forums, workshops, and summer institutes that prepare social work faculty to teach planned change content. Second, we must help social work educators define appropriate outcome measures for determining student mastery of planned change course material. Content concerning tracking student learning outcomes could be covered in teaching workshops. Third, we must reward and develop incentives for instructors who teach planned change. For example, social work administrators can support faculty in search of teaching grants or research grants that fund advocacy, system change, or state and community infrastructure building work. With respect to planned change in the child welfare arena, social work education administrators could support faculty applications for sabbatical or faculty development leave requests whereby faculty seek to develop partnerships for carrying out applied projects with local and state child welfare systems around advocacy work. Table 8.1 presents some possible teaching strategies.

THE CHALLENGE TO CHILD WELFARE ADVOCATES AND POLICY PRACTITIONERS

According to education policy standard 2.18 of the Council on Social Work Education's Educational Policy and Accreditation Standards, students of social work will "engage in policy practice to advance social

TABLE 8.1
Suggested Teaching Strategies

Strategies and Steps	Potential Roadblocks	Methods for Overcoming Roadblocks
Use an oppression framework as a conceptual basis for teaching. Use a legislative analysis to frame the problem. Require course readings pertaining to system transformation, reform, and activism. Structure class discussion/debates pertaining to reform challenges. Teach students the distinction between social change agents and social control agents. Design educational encounter experiences that force students out of their comfort zones. Invite community activists to class. Require mock legislation rewriting assignments. Require assignments that diagram the problems and devise related action plans.	Faculty malaise Uninformed student population with little appreciation for the power of social movements Student, university administration, and/or public perception that assignments and teaching strategies are too political University culture that is against human rights activism work	Cross-list child welfare courses with African American studies, political science, and law, and forge teaching partnerships/coalitions. Recognize faculty who teach reform with teaching innovation awards. Initiate public awareness campaigns on campus to get students interested in reform. Encourage students to examine the plight of African American children from all sides and to present evidence and outcome studies that support their analysis, rather than assigning or suggesting to students what their perspective ought to be. Suspend personal judgment of the issues and avoid disclosing political affiliation. Educate university officials about academic ethics, rights, freedoms, and responsibilities and the value of teaching activism.

and economic well-being and to deliver social work services." This standard reflects the core value of social justice and the expectation that social work practitioners must engage in policy practice to realize social change that can in effect promote social justice. Specifically, this policy practice–related standard states that social workers recognize that policy affects social service delivery, and therefore social workers (1) analyze, formulate, and advocate for policies that advance social well-being; and

(2) collaborate with colleagues and clients for effective policy action (CSWE, 2008:3–7).

The Council on Social Work Education identifies standards for the training of social work students because, as practitioners, we are expected to understand current structures and conditions that affect our practice. Social welfare history provides invaluable instruction as to the manner in which program and policy trends have informed service delivery approaches to child protection and permanence, as well as approaches to child well-being. Appreciation and understanding of child welfare history enable practitioners to determine which role within the policy practice realm—the role of policy advocate, analyst, developer, or researcher—is appropriate to achieve desired change.

Social work advocates and policy practitioners are expected to develop resolutions to social problems in ways that ensure that service injustice is not perpetuated. Individuals who do not experience equity in the delivery of social services—or those whose service outcomes are disparate when compared those of with others receiving similar services—must experience reformed child- and family-serving systems to reverse social inequities to social justice. If legislation reform is required to improve resource allocation, redirect or target services, or redefine program objectives, social workers engaged in the delivery of services are in the best position to interpret policy and program strengths and weaknesses. When amended, policy and program directives can contribute to enhanced program results or outcomes.

Over the years numerous reform initiatives aimed at improving the condition of children in the child welfare system have been put in place. Major federal laws are associated with reform efforts. For example, as discussed previously, the Adoption Assistance and Child Welfare Act of 1980 was implemented after years of advocacy and research by social workers and other child and family advocates who documented problems of children languishing in foster care for long periods of time; problems associated with family reunification once a child is removed from home were also identified as were problems associated with achieving permanency for older children and sibling groups, medically needy children, and children of color—specifically African American and Hispanic children. This legislation was touted as representing significant insight on limitations placed on workers, the frustrations of families, and promised improvements that would redeem the well-intentioned but failing system of out-of-home care in this country. Conceptually the AACWA was sound policy; at the time of its passage it lacked executive branch support, and weakened administrative rules limited the effectiveness of the enactment of the law.

The legislative history of the AACWA is one example of how a law intended to accomplish one goal can unintentionally affect racial groups. The law stipulated that permanency planning become a national priority, and it also created a national program to subsidize the permanent placement of children at risk for out-of-home placement. As stated in the statute, the at-risk population includes racial and ethnic minorities, sibling groups, older children, and children with "handicapping conditions" (U.S. Code Congressional, 1980).

Denby, Curtis, and Alford (1998) reported the findings of a national study of family preservation workers who indicated they do not believe that services should be prioritized to special populations, including minority children in the foster care system. Other researchers have documented similar preferences or the use of administrative discretion to limit or eliminate consideration of African American children from targeted services aimed at creating opportunities for permanency or reducing the risk of placement out of the home (Denby & Curtis, 2003; Hill, 2006; Roberts, 2002).

Many child welfare advocates and policy practitioners have a unique knowledge of policy goals and programmatic aims and are therefore in the best position to influence both the need for and the focus of evaluation efforts. Evaluation of policies, programs, and services becomes increasingly important when there is enhanced attention to service outcomes—such as today—and when demand for services is increasing without the requisite correlating change in fiscal appropriations to address need. Social workers must do more than "talk the talk."

Advocates and policy practitioners must engage in reform-creating behaviors and activities such as writing letters to legislators and administrative heads about program limitations and unjust outcomes for children. Workers must become expertly knowledgeable of regulatory change and administrative rules and begin to document their observations related to the strengths and weaknesses of program rules. Where targeting of services is required, workers must determine if the aim of a policy is realized. Are populations intended for outreach and support being served? Workers should seek opportunities to support agency decision making and evaluation. They might participate in agency committees or work groups aimed at program reviews or evaluations. Policy practitioners must become the voice for those who are not able to speak up for themselves or advocate for equitable and just service intervention; we must continue to challenge those practices that do not result in child well-being and family stability. Policy practitioners and advocates must remain vigilant and encouraged by the desire on the part of many to make necessary changes, at each point of contact and with each intervening strategy.

THE CHALLENGE TO SOCIAL WORK PRACTITIONERS

In addition to meeting the organizational challenges that limit professionals' ability to positively affect decision making and improve the experiences of all children and families in child protection service systems, training is paramount. Recruiting and retaining quality social workers are ongoing challenges in many communities. Most child welfare agencies do not require caseworkers to hold either a bachelor's or master's degree in social work, despite evidence that people with social work degrees have higher job performance and lower turnover rates (U.S. GAO, 2003).

Salaries are often a major factor in hiring practices, and salaries often vary significantly between public and privately affiliated workers. If agencies will openly recognize the critical role social workers can and must play as change agents for program reform, perhaps more social workers will be compelled to take on these challenging and demanding positions. People who earn a social work degree should be adequately compensated, and the benefit to individual agencies and the child welfare system that implement creative reforms aimed at improving the experiences of all children and minimizing the effects of disparate experiences and conditions for some will create social justice within a system that currently has none.

Thoughtful reform strategies are essential to address the disparate conditions experienced by African American children and other ethnic minorities within the foster care/child protective service system. Reform success is dependent on a well-trained and qualified staff. Agencies must create opportunities for professional social workers to engage in policy practice. Social work educators are required to prepare social work students for such roles and responsibilities. Social workers in direct contact with children and families—those who know the complexities of family circumstances and corrective actions, services, and supports necessary to strengthen, repair, or rebuild families—are encouraged to engage in advocacy, program and public policy research, and program and policy analysis and formulation aimed at addressing disparate conditions in the complex child welfare system serving the diverse needs of children and their families.

Assuming the role of policy practitioner and social reform agent is challenging work and typically does not provide immediate professional gratification. Institutional change, while essential and critically important, does not come quickly or easily, but practices that have created disparate experiences among children of color within the child welfare system must be reformed by social workers—those in position to understand the problems and trained to seek the change to correct such conditions. Table 8.2 addresses some possible advocacy strategies.

TABLE 8.2
Suggested Advocacy Strategies

Strategies and Steps	Potential Roadblocks	Methods for Overcoming Roadblocks
Identify partners and allies. What are the common goals/interests? What is everyone's incentive? Devise strategies for inevitable conflicts. Use everyone's perspective. Start activists clubs. Develop prepracticum and service-learning projects at community activists' sites. Develop reform strategies that use social networking and other communication technologies. Encourage student/worker use of media for public education campaigns.	Political exploitation Practitioner malaise Fragmented community-support base No active local social movements Difficulty motivating practitioners to go beyond "social service" perspective to advance a "social change" perspective in their prepracticum, volunteer, or professional roles	Dissuade practitioners from aligning the issue with any one political party/group; encourage bipartisan partnership building. Help practitioners to see themselves as "reformers." Help practitioners to see the connection between child welfare reform work and cultural competency. Work with field department/director to establish prepracticum sites specific to African American child welfare issues. Avoid the singular model of a self-help movement because it may become politicized; ownership of the problem needs to extend beyond those affected by the child welfare system.

THE CHALLENGE TO STUDENTS OF SOCIAL WORK

It may very well be the case that future cohorts of social work students, in collaboration with such disciplines as law, reject current inadequate answers to the challenges the field faces and insist on a more just and appropriate course of action. Students of child welfare can play a critical role in transforming practices by first rejecting the status quo. To do so, some students may find themselves in a situation in which they guide and direct their own educational pursuits. Table 8.3 highlights strategies that students can consider in their quest to become competent child welfare practitioners and their desire to effectuate change on behalf of African American children and families.

Many social work programs position students to engage in practice at a micro, mezzo, or macro level. Child welfare sequences (or child and family sequences, as they are termed in some schools of social work education) may have elements of all three levels of practice. Whatever the structure of the educational program, there are important considerations for child welfare students who desire to make a transformative change to the public child welfare system. First, students who are concerned with micro-level interventions can play an important role in transforming practice by leading the call for a critical examination of the appropriateness and validity of so-called evidence-based approaches. Students should assess the extent to which interventions and practice approaches take into account the specific needs of African American children. Interventions should be guided by principles of family engagement and family-centeredness and be based on strengths. The Child Welfare Information Gateway (2010) has cataloged some of the family engagement models thought to be most promising.

Mezzo-level students can play an important role in transforming child welfare practice by advocating for an accessible, effective, and appropriate service array that is responsive to the needs of children and families. Often child welfare professionals are limited in their work with children and families because their local communities lack adequate services and supports to which families can be referred. Many of the conditions (e.g., poverty, substance abuse, mental health difficulties) that are associated with child welfare system involvement are often difficult to eradicate because of the inadequate nature of local service infrastructures. Mezzo-level students may find a professional role that is beyond the child wel-

TABLE 8.3
Suggested Strategies for Self-Guided Learning

Strategies and Steps	Potential Roadblocks	Methods for Overcoming Roadblocks
Apply critical-thinking skills to all course-learning activities.	Bucking the system may not feel comfortable at times.	Your time as a student is the perfect opportunity to question, doubt, and seek the validity of standards of practice.
Select or create a practicum experience that will provide exposure to the most pressing child welfare issues facing your community.	The university may want you to select from a list of approved sites. Your choice of practicum site may not be among the approved or more traditional venues.	Thoroughly research your preferred practicum site. Gather detailed information about the agency's history and the background and qualifications of your potential agency field instructor. Be prepared to provide justification for how the practicum site can meet your educational objectives.
Use your research courses to acquire knowledge about applied research.	You may have to take additional coursework to supplement your research-learning objectives.	
Complete independent studies with professors who are actively engaged in research about African American children and families.	Research assistantships are often competitive, and professors' busy schedules can make them gravitate toward students who are more experienced.	Be creative in ensuring that your desire for additional knowledge keeps you on the right trajectory to graduate. Often applied research courses can be used to satisfy elective requirements or capstone experiences.
		Develop solid writing skills. Provide samples of your writing. Convince professors of the compatibility of your interests and their own.

fare agency itself. For example, they may find themselves advocating for and developing community-based workforce and economic development programs.

Professional practice in the area of early childhood development is another example of a professional role that students who are interested in child welfare may want to consider. Although such roles are not directly related to providing child welfare services, they are vital in minimizing the conditions that bring children and families to the attention of the child welfare system.

Finally, macro-inclined students certainly have a tremendous role in directing future child welfare laws. The Child and Family Services Improvement and Innovation Act of 2011 is the reauthorization of the Stephanie Tubbs Jones Child Welfare Services Program and the Promoting Safe and Stable Families (PSSF) Act. The law has many features, but it directs noticeable attention to improving child well-being through such courses of action as ensuring regular and frequent visitations to families by child welfare workers. Today's child welfare students (our future leaders) will seize the opportunities inherent in this and other types of federal law legislation. Macro-level students can design more effective visitation models. Also, they can push for the use of cultural adaptations to current practice models and advocate for legislative changes that require the use of approaches that have been shown to be effective with African American families. Macro-level students can help shape the future of the child welfare workforce. Family visitation as mandated by the Child and Family Services Improvement and Innovation Act has significant implications for child welfare workforce development. To achieve the goals of safety, permanency, and well-being, it is vital that child welfare systems have well-developed, competent, and supported workers (Denby, 2012). Macro-level students can lead the way in articulating the standards for what is required to achieve the necessary workforce. Paramount in the development of the workforce will be ensuring that workers are skilled in the delivery of services and programs that can lead to positive outcomes for African American children and families.

REFERENCES

Alvarez, A. R. 2001. "Enhancing Praxis Through PRACSIS: A Framework for Developing Critical Consciousness and Implications for Strategy." *Journal of Teaching in Social Work* 21 (1/2): 195–220.

Child Welfare Information Gateway. 2010. *Family Engagement*. http://www.childwelfare.gov/pubs/f_fam_engagement/f_fam_engagement.pdf.

Coakley, T. M. 2008. "Examining African American Fathers' Involvement in Permanency Planning: An Effort to Reduce Racial Disproportionality in the Child Welfare System." *Children and Youth Services Review* 30 (4): 407–17.

Cohen, B. J. 2004. "Reforming the Child Welfare System: Competing Paradigms of Change." *Children and Youth Services Review* 27 (6): 653–66.

Comerford, S. A. 2003. "Enriching Classroom Learning About Diversity: Supports and Strategies from a Qualitative Study." *Journal of Teaching in Social Work* 23 (3/4): 159–83.

Council on Social Work Education (CSWE). 2008. *Educational Policy and Accreditation Standards.* Alexandria, Va.: CSWE.

Crewe, S. E., A. W. Brown, & R. M. Gourdine. 2009. "Inabel Burns Lindsay: A Social Worker, Educator, and Administrator Uncompromising in the Pursuit of Social Justice for All." *Affilia: Journal of Women and Social Work* 23 (4): 363–77.

Curtis, C. M., & R. Alexander. 2010. "Correlates of African American Children In and Out of Their Families." *Families in Society: The Journal of Contemporary Social Services* 91 (1): 85–90.

Denby, R. W. 2012. "Child Maltreatment in Nevada." In *The Social Health of Nevada: Leading Indicators and Quality of Life in the Silver State.* Edited by D. N. Shalin, 1–25. Las Vegas: UNLV Center for Democratic Culture.

Denby, R. W., & C. Curtis. 2003. "Why Children of Color Are Not the Target of Family Preservation Services: A Case for Program Reform." *Journal of Sociology and Social Welfare* 30 (2): 149–73.

Denby, R. W., C. Curtis, & K. A. Alford. 1998. "Special Populations and Family Preservation Services: The Invisible Target." *Families and Society: The Journal of Contemporary Human Services* 79 (1): 3–11.

Dodd, S. J., & H. Rivera. 2003. "Addition and Subtraction: Cost Benefit Analysis as a Tool for Teaching Diversity Content in Social Policy." *Social Policy Journal* 2 (2/3): 107–21.

Freire, P. 1973. *Education for Critical Consciousness.* New York: Continuum.

Hatcher, S., T. Maschi, K. Morgen, & I. Toldson. 2009. "Exploring the Impact of Racial and Ethnic Differences in the Emotional and Behavioral Responses of Maltreated Youth: Implications for Culturally Competent Services." *Children and Youth Services Review* 31:1042–48.

Hill, R. B. 2006. *A Synthesis of Research on Disproportionality in Child Welfare: An Update.* Washington, D.C : Center for Study of Social Policy & Casey Family Programs.

Lalas, J. 2007. "Teaching for Social Justice in Multicultural Urban Schools: Conceptualization and Classroom Implication." *Multicultural Education* (Spring): 17–21.

Manalo, V. 2004. "Teaching Policy Advocacy Through State Legislative and Local Ballot-Based Advocacy Assignments." *Social Policy Journal* 3 (4): 53–67.

Martinez, J., & A. Lau. 2011. "Do Social Networks Push Families Toward or Away from Youth Mental Health Services? A National Study of Families in Child Welfare." *Journal of Emotional and Behavioral Disorders* 19 (3): 169–81.

Murray, C., & K. Zvoch. 2010. "Teacher-Student Relationships Among Behaviorally At-Risk African American Youth From Low-Income Backgrounds: Student Perceptions, Teacher Perceptions, and Socio Emotional Adjustment Correlates." *Journal of Emotional and Behavioral Disorders* 19 (1): 41–51.

National Association of Social Workers. 2008. *Code of Ethics for the National Association of Social Workers.* Washington, D.C: National Association of Social Workers.

Packard Foundation. 2004. *The Future of Children. Children, Families, and Foster Care: Issues and Ideas. A Guide for Policymakers and the Press.* Los Altos, Calif.: Packard Foundation.

Roberts, D. 2002. *Shattered Bonds: The Color of Child Welfare.* New York: Basic Civitas Books.

Teti, D., M. Black, R. Viscardi, P. Glass, M. O'Connell, L. Baker, R. Cusson, & C. Hess. 2009. "Intervention with African American Premature Infants: Four-Month Results of an Early Intervention Program." *Journal of Early Intervention* 31 (2): 146–66.

U.S. Code Congressional & Administrative News. 1980. *Legislative History, No.3, 96th Congress, 2nd Session 1980.* St. Paul: West Publishing.

U.S. Department of Health and Human Services, Administration for Children and Families, Administration on Children, Youth and Families, Children's Bureau (USDHHS). 2008. *Preliminary Estimates for FY 2006 as of January 2008.* http://www.acf.hhs.gov/programs/cb.

U.S. Government Accountability Office (GAO). 2007. *African American Children in Foster Care: Additional HHS Assistance Needed to Help States Reduce the Proportion in Care.* U.S. GAO-07–816. http://www.gao.gov/news.items/d07816.pdf.

Glossary

ADVOCACY RESEARCH A type of descriptive policy research done with the purpose of heightening public awareness of social problems so that action can be taken to ameliorate the problems.

AGGRAVATED CIRCUMSTANCES A phrase used in the Adoption and Safe Families Act to refer to conditions that will make the termination of parental rights automatic. The law provides examples of such circumstances as killing a child or severely and permanently physically harming a child; however, states must operationally define how the term will be applied or under what circumstances.

APPROPRIATION A separate piece of legislation required, once a law has been authorized and signed into law, by the budget process to designate the spending level for the law.

ASSESSMENT "The collection of information to inform decision-making about a child, youth, or family. It is always conducted as a means to an end—to identify issues the family is facing, design a plan, and provide services that will assist in resolving the issues identified" (Child Welfare Information Gateway, *Addressing Racial Disproportionality in Child Welfare* [Washington, D.C.: U.S. Department of Health and Human Services, Children's Bureau, 2011], 1).

ATTACHMENT A bond, connection, or emotional identification with a familiar caregiver that begins at birth. Broadly there are four categories of attachment: secure, avoidant, anxious, and disorganized.

ATTENTION DEFICIT AND HYPERACTIVITY DISORDER Considered "one of the most common mental disorders in children and adolescents. Symptoms include difficulty staying focused and paying attention, difficulty controlling behavior, and very high levels of activity" (National Institute of Mental Health, *Attention Deficit Hyperactivity Disorder in Children and Adolescents [Fact Sheet]* [2011], 1; http://www.nimh.nih.gov/health/publications/attention-deficit-hyperactivity-disorder-in-children-and-adolescents/index.shtml).

AUTHORIZATION Specific language that identifies special conditions or circumstances associated with a law passed by Congress, including the period of time the law will be in effect and the initial recommended funding.

BEST PRACTICES Approaches, programs or interventions that work, with varying levels of evidence, and are typically categorized along a continuum: promising practice, evidence-based practice, and science-based practice.

CARVE-OUT A type of medical services financing involving differentiating certain covered services and benefits and paying them under alternative arrangements and payment structures.

CATEGORIES OF CHILD MALTREATMENT A phrase that includes physical abuse, child neglect, sexual abuse, emotional abuse, and abandonment.

CHILD ABUSE AND NEGLECT "Any recent act or failure to act on the part of a parent or caretaker which results in death, serious physical or emotional harm, sexual abuse or exploitation; or an act or failure to act which presents an imminent risk of serious harm" (Child Welfare Information Gateway, *What Is Child Abuse and Neglect?* Fact Sheet [2008], 2; http://www.childwelfare.gov/pubs/can_info_packet.pdf).

CHILD PROTECTION A government-mandated action of safeguarding (i.e., protecting from or preventing harm) children who may be currently experiencing or are at risk of experiencing the effects of harmful conditions.

CHILD WELFARE HEARINGS Most states have some form of legal proceedings typically managed through a family, juvenile, or tribal court that involves seven types of hearings: (1) a protective hearing is where a determination is made about child removal and placement into an emergency shelter or temporary setting; (2) an adjudicatory hearing is a hearing to review factual data to make a determination or substantiation of child maltreatment; (3) a dispositional hearing (sometimes referred to as a placement hearing) is intended to legally determine who will care for the child and where the child will live; (4) periodic review hearings are six-month incremental hearings held so that the court can determine the progress that is being made on the case; (5) a permanency hearing solidifies the permanency plan; (6) termination of parental rights (TPR) hearings that are held to legally terminate a parent's rights; under the original Adoption and Safe Families Act of 1997, such hearings must take place for children who have been in care for fifteen of the past twenty-two months; and (7) an adoption and guardianship hearing, which is held to legally bind a child to another family by court approval of an adoption or guardianship (portions of these definitions from S. Badeau, *Child Welfare and the Courts* [Washington, D.C.: Pew Charitable Trusts, 2004]; http://www.pewtrusts.org/uploadedFiles/wwwpewtrustsorg/Reports/Foster_care_reform/BadeauPaper[1].pdf).

CHILD WELFARE OUTCOMES REPORT DATA A system that provides a custom report builder containing the most up-to-date data about child welfare outcomes. The annual data-reporting system provides state performance data in seven categories: (1) reduce recurrence of child abuse and/or neglect; (2) reduce the incidence of child abuse and/or neglect in foster care; (3) increase permanency for children in foster care; (4) reduce time in foster care to reunification without increasing reentry; (5) reduce time in foster care to adoption;

(6) increase placement stability; and (7) reduce placement of young children in group homes or institutions.

COMPLEX TRAUMA (ALSO REFERRED TO AS COMPLEX PTSD) "How children's exposure to multiple or prolonged traumatic events impacts their ongoing development. Typically, complex trauma exposure involves the simultaneous or sequential occurrence of child maltreatment and may include psychological maltreatment, neglect, physical and sexual abuse, and witnessing domestic violence" (Center for Early Childhood Mental Health Consultation, *Recognizing and Addressing Trauma in Infants, Young Children, and Their Families* [2011], 6; http://www.ecmhc.org/tutorials/trauma/mod1_2.html).

CONCURRENT PLANNING A practice model introduced in the Adoption and Safe Families Act and referring to the expectation that child welfare workers develop and follow a work plan that aims to preserve or reunify a family while simultaneously putting into place a plan for adoption or guardianship should reunification not work.

COURT IMPROVEMENT PROGRAMS A program that permits local courts to apply for federal grants to improve their court system.

DATA CONVENING An element of advocacy research when the efforts of various child welfare stakeholders (professionals and those indigenous to the problem) are organized into a coalition that aims to organize in a systematic manner a research agenda that brings about awareness and becomes a catalyst for change.

DATA DIFFUSION The dissemination of research results.

DATA GATHERING A process of collecting, organizing, and preparing information or data points.

DIFFERENTIAL RESPONSE "A CPS practice that allows for more than one method of initial response to reports of child abuse and neglect. Also called 'dual track,' 'multiple track,' or 'alternative response,' this approach recognizes variation in the nature of reports and the value of responding differently to different types of case" (Child Welfare Information Gateway, *Differential Response to Reports of Child Abuse and Neglect* [Washington, D.C.: U.S. Department of Health and Human Services, 2008], 3; http://www.childwelfare.gov/pubs/issue_briefs/differential_response/).

EVIDENCE-BASED PRACTICES A practice that meets the following criteria: (1) has data demonstrating positive outcomes; and (2) includes a review conducted by experts who have concluded that there is sufficient evidence of the interventions, program, or practice approach's effectiveness.

FAMILY FOSTER CARE A service provided by child welfare agencies whereby children under their care live with nonrelatives who have been specifically trained, certified, and monitored to provide such care.

FAMILY PRESERVATION SERVICES Services directed to families already in crisis or families deemed at risk for child maltreatment and subsequent family disruption. Once a case is established for an "intact family," services deemed appropriate to support the family unit are referred to as family preservation services.

FAMILY REUNIFICATION SERVICES Should an open case result in the temporary removal of a child from their home, services intended to strengthen the family unit so the family may be unified again are referred to as reunification services.

FOSTER CARE A temporary structured living arrangement or service that is planned and goal directed for children who cannot live with their birth family.

FOSTER CARE DRIFT The movement of children in and out of foster care placements without the benefit of a plan to ensure permanence for the child.

INFANT MENTAL HEALTH An infant's intellectual, physical, and emotional growth and development (for more details, see Center for Early Education and Development. http://www.cehd.umn.edu/ceed/publications/questionsaboutkids/imhenglish.pdf).

KINSHIP FOSTER CARE A formal arrangement whereby a relative (usually a grandparent, aunt, or uncle) provides day-to-day care for a relative's child who is under the supervision of the child welfare system.

LEAST RESTRICTIVE ENVIRONMENT A term associated with passage of the Adoption Assistance and Child Welfare Act. Borrowed from special needs education reform and suggests that, when possible, children should be cared for in their home or in a homelike environment that is least destructive to the life of the family unit.

MANAGED CARE A type of medical services financing used to reduce cost; improve quality of care; share the cost of care between the beneficiary and the insurance company; manage the necessity, frequency, and type of care received; and define a pool of healthcare providers via contract.

MEDICAL HOME A regular source of medical care meeting the criteria of accessibility, continuity, comprehensiveness, coordination, compassion, and cultural sensitivity.

MODEL COURTS "Model Courts serve as models of systems change identifying impediments to the timeliness of court events and delivery of services for children in care, and then design and implement court- and agency-based changes to address these barriers" (National Council on Juvenile and Family Court Judges, Model Courts [2008], 1; http://www.ncjfcj.org/images/stories/dept/ppcd/newmodel%20court%20brochurefinal.pdf).

NATIONAL CHILD ABUSE AND NEGLECT DATA SYSTEM (NCANDS) A national database created through federal legislation that provides child abuse statistics composed of case-level data for all children who are involved in the child protection system.

NATIONAL INCIDENCE STUDIES OF CHILD ABUSE AND NEGLECT (NIS) A data-reporting system that is congressionally mandated and provides abuse and neglect estimates and also measures change in incidences from the earlier time waves.

NATIONAL SURVEY OF CHILD AND ADOLESCENT WELL-BEING (NSCAW) A survey administratively coordinated by the Administration for Children and Families and developed through a research collaboration as a response to a congressional mandate that arose from the Personal Responsibility and Work Opportunities Reconciliation Act of 1996. The NSCAW is a national, longitudinal database spanning 1997 to 2010 and containing firsthand reports from children, parents, and caseworkers about child abuse and neglect and child and family well-being.

ORPHAN TRAINS A transportation network introduced by Reverend Charles Loring Brace and the New York Children's Aid Society that transported over 200,000 children from their families—primarily from the East Coast—to communities in the Midwest and Great Plains regions.

PARENS PATRIAE A term established through English common law and borrowed by colonists that refers to the role of government in assuming responsibility for the care of dependent children when parents do not or cannot assume such responsibility; it refers to the sovereign right of government to protect children.

PERFORMANCE-BASED CHILD WELFARE SERVICE AUTHORITY MODELS In using performance-based authority models, public and private child welfare service authorities would be monitored and their outcomes would be tracked at regular intervals. Those entities not adhering to community-defined benchmarks would surrender service authority to those agencies and organizations whose performance produces the best outcomes for children and families.

PERMANENCE A goal in child welfare that refers to the expectation that every minor child should have the opportunity to be nurtured in a safe and caring environment with a biological parent or parents, a relative, guardian or adoptive parents. Permanence may be achieved with a series of options on a continuum that begins with in-home support and ends with the permanent removal of a child from their home with adoption as the goal.

PERMANENCY PLANNING A term associated with passage of the Adoption Assistance and Child Welfare Act. Requires informed decision making relative to the needs of a child and his or her family that should be outlined in a plan that, when followed, will result in a permanent home for the child.

PLACING OUT Also referred to as binding out, a practice started during the early nineteenth century that involved removing children from their homes— particularly in urban, crime-ridden areas—and placing them in new homes in the frontier states of the Midwest and Great Plains regions.

POSTTRAUMATIC STRESS DISORDERS IN CHILDREN Symptoms associated with a traumatic event (e.g., car accident, witnessing violence), repeated events, or sustained events. PTSD develops when a person has been exposed to death, the threat of death, or injury that results in significant psychological harm (for a more thorough review of how trauma symptoms are used to diagnose this condition in children, see *The Diagnostic Classification of Mental Health and Developmental Disorders of Infancy and Early Childhood–Revised [DC: 0–3 R]* [Washington, D.C.: Zero to Three Press, 2005]).

PREVENTION A term associated with passage of the Adoption Assistance and Child Welfare Act. In the context of child welfare, refers to the application of a plan of the services that are available to a family to keep children from being unnecessarily removed from their homes and placed in foster care.

PROMISING PRACTICES A practice that includes the following defining criteria: (1) includes the values and characteristics inherent in other recognized interventions, programs, and approaches; (2) possesses guidelines and protocols that lead to effective outcomes; and (3) involves continual quality improvement strategies and contains an evaluation plan.

REACTIVE ATTACHMENT DISORDERS A disorder, thought to be uncommon, that is found in children, particularly those who have suffered abuse or neglect or a significant separation from a primary caregiver during early childhood. The condition emanates from a failure to experience an attachment to a caregiver during infancy and/or early childhood. RAD is mostly exhibited in social interactions when a child may engage others inappropriately. It typically has two forms: inhibited (inability to respond in a developmentally appropriate manner to social situations) or disinhibited (excessive regard, interaction, or displays of familiarity or affection with strangers).

REASONABLE EFFORTS A phrase included in the ACCWA to suggest the level or degree of effort agents of the state should make to prevent the removal of a child from the home. It is a nebulous term that has been often criticized as evoking great variability among state administrators and the courts.

RESTORATIVE JUSTICE A broad term used in justice, education, and social service systems. It means that in the search for solutions, one engages those who have been harmed. Restorative justice can be about building partnerships, collaborations, and mutual responsibility between groups, people, or communities that might have varied interests but all share a central goal.

REUNIFICATION A term associated with passage of the Adoption Assistance and Child Welfare Act. Refers to the practice of returning a child to his or her home who had been removed temporarily; it is an option for permanence when family supports can be put in place to ensure optimal family functioning.

SCIENCE-BASED PRACTICES A practice defined by the following elements: (1) an intervention, program, or practice has been evaluated with a theory-based research methodology; (2) there is evidence of fidelity where the intervention, program, or practice approach was implemented as intended so that there is a reasonable conclusion that, in fact, the observed outcomes are attributable to that which is under study as opposed to some other extraneous factors and include expert reviews where the research standards used are considered rigorous and adhere to the principles established by the scientific community; and (3) an assurance that outcomes are replicable and the observed results can be demonstrated in multiple settings.

SEVERE EMOTIONAL DISTURBANCES A classification typically used to describe DSM-diagnosable mental, behavioral, or emotional disorders that children experience. Severe emotional disturbances are definable under the DSM when they are pervasive (exhibited in multiple contexts including school, home, social, or community), persistent (occur frequently during a period of two to four weeks), and have a significant effect on the child's daily functioning or affect the child's activities of daily living.

TEMPORARY ASSISTANCE FOR NEEDY FAMILIES A federal block grant program providing cash assistance to families with young children in need of economic support. Enacted with passage of the Personal Responsibility and Work Opportunity Reconciliation Act of 1996, this program replaced AFDC and, like AFCD, requires states to operate a foster care and adoption assistance program under Title IV-E of the Social Security Act.

THERAPEUTIC/TREATMENT FOSTER CARE A form of care designed for placement of children who have specific types of medical or mental health needs. Therapeutic/treatment foster parents typically receive more training, more monitoring, and higher stipends than regular family foster care.

TRANSRACIAL PLACEMENT Placing children of one ethnic or racial background with an adoptive or a foster family of a different ethnicity or racial background.

Index